ANALYZING
Drama

"I think the ideas and premises of the author, James R. Russo, in the book *Analyzing Drama: A Student Casebook*, are sound. He is correct that there are not many books in the field that provide actual *examples* of essays in play analysis, and that there is a market for such a book, since nearly every student who takes an Introduction to Drama, Theater Appreciation, or Theater History course is obliged to write play analyses.

Russo's writing in this volume indicates a clear knowledge of context, and his prose style is lucid as well as engaging. The list of plays he writes about contains some old chestnuts, but the geographical and cultural diversity of the rest of the list is impressive. Also, his delivery of "jargon-free" essays is refreshing (and, as the author points out, a significant deviation from other such texts).

As indicated above, I see the market for this book as comprised primarily of undergraduates, who can use the essays as models for their own work. I do think the book could also attract a significant audience of theater enthusiasts who would appreciate alternative readings of some classic plays. The international scope of the play-list might well also attract a global, English-speaking audience. As for the book's pedagogical apparatus, Russo promises—and delivers—a lot, and I think that the volume's overall scope is quite impressive. *Analyzing Drama* thus represents the kind of book I could well use in my own classes."

DR. JOHN BASOURAKOS, Fu Jen Catholic University, Taiwan

"The essay-based approach in *Analyzing Drama: A Student Casebook* is what gives this text the most appeal. I know that, as an instructor, I could pair such a book with a dramatic anthology and assign specific essays to align with the plays we are studying in class. The competitors' books often reference multiple examples of dramatic texts throughout, but it is not practical (and often not necessary for understanding) to require students to read the full plays. With Russo's text, I could quickly skim the table of contents and, using the play titles and the key analytical questions, identify a clear structure for my coursework. I'm sold on *Analyzing Drama*, and I trust my students will be, too."

DR. ATILLA SILKÜ, Ege (Aegean) University, Turkey

"In my experience, theater and drama students come into college studies with three knowledge questions or gaps: How are plays structured? How can we analyze plays? And (especially at the advanced undergraduate and graduate levels) how does one write a scholarly or expository essay that focuses specifically on script analysis? *Analyzing Drama: A Student Casebook* especially addresses the third of these questions by giving multiple examples of script-analysis-based essays. This feature alone would make the book valuable as a required or recommended resource in upper division and graduate courses. No competing volume presents multiple examples of script-analysis-based essays like those in *Analyzing Drama*—something that truly sets Russo's book apart."

DR. NORMAN BERT, Texas Tech University, United States

ANALYZING Drama
A student casebook

JAMES R. RUSSO

sussex
ACADEMIC
PRESS
Brighton • Chicago • Toronto

Copyright © James R. Russo 2022.

The right of James R. Russo to be identified as Author of this work has been asserted in accordance with the Copyright, Designs and Patents Act 1988.

2 4 6 8 10 9 7 5 3 1

First published 2022 in Great Britain by
SUSSEX ACADEMIC PRESS
PO Box 139
Eastbourne BN24 9BP

Distributed in North America by
SUSSEX ACADEMIC PRESS
Independent Publishers Group
814 N. Franklin Street, Chicago, IL 60610

All rights reserved. Except for the quotation of short passages for the purposes of criticism and review, no part of this publication may be reproduced, stored in a retrieval system, or transmitted, in any form or by any means, electronic, mechanical, photocopying, recording or otherwise, without the prior permission of the publisher.

British Library Cataloguing in Publication Data
A CIP catalogue record for this book is available from the British Library.

Library of Congress Cataloging-in-Publication Data
To be applied for.

Hardcover ISBN 978-1-78976-111-5

Paperback ISBN 978-1-78976-111-2

Typeset & designed by Sussex Academic Press, Brighton & Eastbourne.
Printed by TJ Books Ltd, Padstow, Cornwall.

Contents

Introduction	1
A STEP-BY-STEP APPROACH TO SCRIPT ANALYSIS	7
1. Analysis of Plot and Action	7
2. Analysis of Character	8
3. Analysis of Language	9
4. General Analysis	11
MODEL ESSAYS	14
1. Style and Genre	14
2. Method and Manner	40
3. Character and Role	65
4. Drama and Film	89
5. Comparison and Contrast	113
6. Names and Titles	130
7. Nature, Landscape, and Setting	140
8. Form and Structure	160
GLOSSARY OF DRAMATIC TERMS	185
STUDY GUIDES	208
1. The Parts of Drama (After Aristotle)	208
2. Table of Contrasts: Theater and Film	211
3. Table of Contrasts: Tragedy, Comedy, and Farce	213
4. Table of Contrasts: Realism and Naturalism	214
5. Types of Theater Or Production Criticism	215
TOPICS FOR WRITING AND DISCUSSION	217
Bibliographical Resources	224
Online Resources	235
Professional Associations	237
Index	239

Introduction

From the fifty short essays included in this book, one will quickly discover that my preoccupations as a critic are not theoretical. I am, rather, a "close reader" committed to a detailed yet objective examination of the structure, style, imagery, characterization, and language of a play. As someone who once regularly worked in the theater as a dramaturg, moreover, I am concerned chiefly with dramatic analysis that can be of benefit not only to students, playreaders, and theatergoers, but also to directors, designers, and even actors—that is, with analysis of character, action, dialogue, and setting that can be translated into concepts for theatrical production, or that can at least provide the kind of understanding of a play with which a theater practitioner could fruitfully quarrel. Many of the plays considered in this volume are regularly produced, especially by university theaters, and it is my hope that these explicatory essays and notes will in some small way make a contribution to future stagings. A number of these dramas—such as *Hamlet, Electra, Miss Julie,* and *Death of a Salesman*—are also routinely treated in high school and college courses on dramatic literature, so it is also my hope that the relatively short (and therefore less intimidating, more accessible) pieces contained in *Analyzing Drama: A Student Casebook* will serve students and teachers as models for the writing of play analyses.

What follows is the explication of a method for play-reading and analysis, not in the conviction that such a method will exhaust every value in a play, but in the hope that it will uncover the major areas the reader of plays should consider. Let no one assume that fruitful analysis of plays is a matter of simple enumeration or of filling in blanks on a comprehensive questionnaire. Analysis also involves judgement. There is no shortcut to cultivating an ear for good dialogue, an eye for effective staging, or a feeling for proper balance and structure in the work as a whole. Just as the reader will better understand what a play is by reading and seeing as many plays as possible, so will he or she better analyze and interpret plays by having read, seen, *and* extensively thought about them. All I can do here is to cite some of the approaches that have proved useful to readers in the past.

Although some beginning readers assume a hostility between reading and analysis, I must stress that the two activities are thoroughly compatible. Indeed, beginning students sometimes evidence a mistrust of any kind of literary analysis. It gains expression in the form of such statements as "I enjoyed the work for itself. Why spoil it by taking it apart?" Analysis, literary criticism, and the consideration and discussion of ideas are not designed, however, to spoil literary works; they are intended to widen and deepen our appreciation of those works. We may even say that consideration and discussion are different stages in the same process: that of enjoying and understanding a play. Good analysis grows out of a thorough and informed reading and only out of such a reading.

Aids in Interpretation

Plays, like all other works of art, occur in definite times and places and bear upon them the marks of a specific culture and set of circumstances. Great interest attaches to such matters of context because they often contribute to our understanding of works from the past. But beginning students are sometimes distrustful of this interest. As they distrust analysis and abstraction for their presumed deadening effect on the work of art, so too do they distrust "external" considerations for their presumed irrelevance. Both suspicions are misplaced, at least as far as the sincere and measured lover of literature is concerned. We do not want "the tail to wag the dog" in this instance, but neither do we want to chop the tail off. We must keep in mind that the reason we do not always have to read social history or literary biography or comparative religion to understand the latest novel is simply that it is of our own time. However, once the concerns of a period transform themselves into other concerns—that is, once current events become history—the same problems that beset us in reading older literary works will present themselves to our descendants when they read the works of our day. These supposedly external matters, then, are actually part of the culture that any writer assumes as he or she writes.

The problem for students of literature is in knowing what else to study and how to evaluate it. Each work of art will present different problems because some works will be more complex than others. Countless periods and times come under our scrutiny, and each play will make different demands on our knowledge and offer different rewards. This is precisely why the study of literature, dramatic or otherwise, is so fundamentally humanizing: it constantly directs the student to wider fields of investigation and thus to a wider understanding of life. I shall now briefly review the areas that frequently impinge on literature in order to suggest the scope of possible auxiliary study.

Literary history and biography. Literary history, broadly construed, is the study of literature as an extended body of material with innumerable interconnections among its constituent parts (individual works) and innumerable influences and parallels that exhibit a continuity and pattern over time. Besides being an individual literary work, every play occupies a place in literary (not to speak of theatrical) history. Literary history is that discipline concerned with establishing the context in which a work appears, that is, the shifts in taste and practice that have exerted influence on writers at different times. Plays can frequently be better understood when we know something about their literary context. Biographies of authors, in turn, arise from our interest in literary works and the men and women who produced them. Occasionally, biographical information will illuminate a literary work, although extreme caution must be urged on the beginner not to treat an individual play as a biographical document. For the most part, the non-specialist will derive the greatest assistance from what we may call literary biography, or an understanding of the author's literary development, his or her interest in certain themes, styles, and the like at various points in his or her career. The application of personal biography to literature is perhaps nowhere so delicate as in the drama, where an autobiographical spokesperson for the author is even rarer than an ideological spokesperson. Still, a knowledge of literary history and literary biography will contribute considerably to our understanding of the development of drama in general and of the place a particular play occupies in that development, as well as in the culture at large.

Political and social history. Since the drama inevitably reflects life, it does so in terms of a particular time, a particular place, and particular issues. Indeed, a knowledge of the political and social conditions of the time of the play can be so important as to be indispensable to an understanding of an individual work. (Non-literary historical elements are similarly important in considering the various playhouses that have been used throughout the evolution of the drama, for the design of a theater can become a matter of literary consequence as well.) Generally, the more one knows about life and society during the period in which a play was written, the greater will be one's comprehension of the work itself. Of course, we do not want history, as such, to usurp the place of the literary artefact; as in all such auxiliary studies,

INTRODUCTION

one investigates the social and political history of the period in which a play was written so as to understand the work better.

Other disciplines. There are any number of other disciplines that we can call upon in interpreting plays, in particular, and literary works in general. Again, these disciplines should be approached with caution. Yet plays do treat human psychology; they have social dimensions; and they may embody certain religious tenets or philosophical beliefs. They may even have affinities with other arts or literary types. Verse plays, for example, are also poetry and can be looked at from the perspective of poetry. Many critics approach all literary works from one or another point of view. Some apply Freudian or Freudian-based psychology in their interpretations; some consider certain plays as an expression of existentialist philosophy and other plays as exemplars of the Christian religion; others see all literary works in terms of their attitude toward social classes. Since dramatists frequently treat psychological, social, political, and religious matters in their plays, we can hardly rule out the aid derived from disciplines like psychology, sociology, religion, philosophy, and arts other than theater when we examine plays. As always, the key lies in maintaining a proper perspective on the literary work so that it does not become a mere excuse for our discovery of a favored theory or doctrine—Marxist, feminist, post-colonial, and the like.

A Note on Organization

Since, in introductory as well as advanced classes, students typically get writing assignments of the following kind, *Analyzing Drama: A Student Casebook* is designed to show them how, through carefully grouped, concrete essay-examples, they might set about completing such assignments:

1. "Choose an important character in such-and-such a play and analyze his or her dramatic function. That is, why is this character in the play and what does he or she contribute to the development of its theme?" (See 3, "Character and Role.")
2. "What type of structure does such-and-such a play have: climactic, episodic, or cyclical? From a thematic point of view, why did the playwright use such a structure?" (See 8, "Form and Structure.")
3. "Choose two plays that are similar in style, structure, or meaning and compare, as well as contrast, them. Has one play directly (or

indirectly) influenced the other, as in the case of a drama made into a film? What are the differences in socio-historical context between the two plays if they are from different periods? Is one of these dramas superior to the other, and, if so, why?" (See 5, "Comparison and Contrast.")

Since *Analyzing Drama: A Student Casebook* is divided into the sections "Style and Genre," "Method and Manner," "Character and Role," "Drama and Film," "Comparison and Contrast," "Names and Titles," "Nature, Landscape, and Setting," and "Form and Structure" (naturally, with some overlap among the sections), the reader can easily go to the appropriate section and find a number of specific examples of the kind of essay he or she has been assigned to write. Supplementing the essays in this book is a useful critical apparatus consisting of a Step-by-Step Approach to Play Analysis, a Glossary of Dramatic Terms, Study Guides, Topics for Writing and Discussion, a list of Bibliographical and Online Resources, and a comprehensive index.

The plays analyzed here have been selected on the basis of their familiarity (a number of well-known works, mingled with some lesser-known ones); geographical representativeness (within the Western canon); aesthetic representativeness (tragedy, comedy, farce, etc.); thematic, stylistic, and linguistic variety; and their modernity or post-modernity (with the exception of one ancient Greek drama and a few works from the Elizabethan era). Some plays are featured in more than one section (some even make two appearances in one section), which is to say that—instructively, I trust—each of them is approached from more than one angle. The sections themselves are more or less self-explanatory. Each one is preceded by a key analytical question so as to guide students in their selective reading, and each, in the end, is concerned with the subject of thesis, thought, or idea—that is, with a play's meaning and how to arrive at it.

A penultimate word, if I may, on the nature, or distinctiveness, of *Analyzing Drama: A Student Casebook*. Play-analysis texts, in general, are books about the methods and techniques of play analysis but contain few (if any) actual play analyses. My book describes the methods and techniques of play analysis at the same time as it provides numerous examples of just such analysis. As for play anthologies themselves, they are just that—anthologies or play collections, not guides to play analysis. Although some anthologies do contain information on dramatic forms, terms, styles, and genres, few offer more than a couple of analyses in the form of student papers—certainly nothing like the fifty essays included in this text. Finally, we must remember that good theatrical productions—the ultimate aim of any written drama (apart from the closet variety)—themselves are the result of intelligent readings. There is, finally, an advantage enjoyed by the reader of plays. Once the performance is over, "these our actors," as Prospero says in Shakespeare's *Tempest* (1611), prove to be ". . . all spirits, and / Are melted into air, into thin air" (IV.i.148–150; Greenblatt, 3095). For the reader, they may come back to life again, and again, on the printed page.

Work Cited

Greenblatt, Stephen, et al., eds. *The Norton Shakespeare.* New York: W. W. Norton, 1997.

A STEP-BY-STEP APPROACH TO SCRIPT ANALYSIS

In order to analyze a play fully, one must begin with its major components: plot or action, character, and language. Then one can move to more general areas such as perspective or point of view, style, and genre. In other words, what happens during the play and who does it? Where does the play occur, when does it occur, and how does it all happen or come about? As you read or see the play, take brief notes and keep the following, more specific questions in mind; when you finish reading (or seeing) the play, try to answer as many of the questions as possible. "Seeing" naturally means seeing on DVD as well as in the theater. A number of plays discussed in this volume have been adapted to film (see "Topics for Writing and Discussion," #38), and are therefore accessible on DVD.

1 Analysis of Plot and Action

1. What are the given circumstances of the play's action? Geographical location? Historical period? Time of day? Economic environment? Political situation? Social milieu? Religious system?

2. From what perspective do we see the events of the play? Psychological? Ethical? Heroic? Religious? Political?

3. What has the dramatist selected of the possible events of the story to put into actual scenes? Which events are simply reported or revealed through exposition?

4. Drama is action and the essence of action is conflict. Insofar as a situation contains conflict, it is dramatic: no conflict, no drama. Drama is the process of *resolving* conflict, or of suggesting that the conflict will continue. (For example, in the last scene of *Hamlet*, Fortinbras of Norway will now be the ruler of Denmark, as the entire Danish royal family has been wiped out by its own internecine conflict. But for many

A STEP-BY-STEP APPROACH TO SCRIPT ANALYSIS

readers or viewers, this conclusion is inconclusive: will the Danes accept Norwegian suzerainty?) What is most important in script analysis is to perceive the conflict inherent in the play. Conflict creates characters, or characters—their opposing desires or needs—create conflict. To understand a dramatic text or playscript, it is necessary to discover and expose the conflict. What, then, is the conflict in the play in terms of opposing principles? What kinds of qualities are associated with either side, or with *all* sides? Or, considering the principal characters as "ideas" or ethical/moral agents, into what sort of dialectic can you convert the plot? What is opposing what?

5. Where has the dramatist pitched the emphasis in his or her story, as an unfolding action? (For example, the long and careful approach to the "kill" in *Hamlet* versus the relatively quick "kill" followed by the long and haunted aftermath in *Macbeth*.) What has happened before the play, and what happens during the play? (For instance, the late point of attack in *Oedipus Tyrannos*, whose plot has a considerable past, versus the early point of attack in *King Lear*, in which the past is virtually non-existent.)

6. How many acts and scenes are there? Did the play's author note them or were these divisions added later? What motivates the divisions of the play and how are they marked (curtains, blackouts, etc.)?

7. Are there subplots? If so, how is each related to the main action?

8. What alignments, parallels, or repetitions do you notice? (For example, the triple revenge plot in *Hamlet*; the blind Teiresias who can really "see" from the start as contrasted with the blind Oedipus who can really "see" only at the end of the play.)

9. What general or universal experience does the plot seem to be dramatizing?

2 Analysis of Character

1. Assuming that each character is *necessary* to the plot, what is the dramatic function of each? (For instance, why does Shakespeare give Hamlet a close friend, but no friend to Macbeth or Othello?)

2. Do several characters participate in the same "flaw" or kind of

A STEP-BY-STEP APPROACH TO SCRIPT ANALYSIS

fallibility? (For example, Gloucester and Lear are both blind to the true nature of filial love.)

3. Is there a wide range of character "positions" respecting such antitheses as innocence–guilt, good–evil, honorableness–dishonorableness, reason–irrationality, etc.?

4. What qualities or aspects of character are stressed: the physical, the social, the psychological, or the moral or ethical? (For instance, Ibsen's "ethical" character versus Chekhov's character of "mood" or frustrated sensibility: Aeschylus's "grand," sculptural character versus Euripides' "psychopathic" character.)

5. How is character revealed? By symbols and imagery (Macbeth's preoccupation with blood and time)? By interaction with various other characters (Hamlet with Horatio and Ophelia)? By what the character says? By what others say about the character? By what the character does? (the most important). By descriptions of the character in the stage directions?

6. How do character traits activate the drama? (Note how a character's traits are invariably involved in his or her acts as motives for, or causes of, those acts.)

7. Consider each character as a "voice" in the play's overall dialectic, contributing to theme, idea, or meaning.

8. What evidence of change can you detect? What seems to have been the source of this change, and what does it signify for the play's theme or the final nature of the character's identity?

9. How is the character's change expressed dramatically? (For example, in a "recognition" speech, in a newfound attitude, in a behavioral gesture, etc.)

3 Analysis of Language

1. The dialogue is the primary means by which a play implies the total makeup of its imaginative world and describes the behavior of all the characters that populate that world. For any one passage of dialogue in a play, ask yourself the following questions:

A STEP-BY-STEP APPROACH TO SCRIPT ANALYSIS

- What happens during this dialogue and as a result of this dialogue?
- What does this passage reveal about the inner life and motives of each character?
- What does this scene reveal about the relationships of the characters to each other?
- What does this section reveal about the plot or about any of the circumstances contributing to the complication or resolution of the plot?
- What are the most notable moments or statements in this dialogue?
- Are there any implicit or unspoken matters in this scene that deserve attention?
- What facial expressions, physical gestures, or bodily movements are implied by the dialogue?
- What props or set pieces are explicitly or implicitly called for in the dialogue or the stage directions?
- What vocal inflexions or tone of voice does a line suggest?
- Where might the characters increase or decrease the volume or speed of their delivery?
- Where might the characters pause in delivering their lines?
- Where might the characters stand onstage and in relation to each other at the beginning of the scene and at later points in the same scene?

2. Do all the characters use language in much the same way, or does each have his or her own verbal characteristics?

3. What are the dominant image patterns? (For instance, disease-decay-death imagery in *Hamlet*.)
Do characters seem to share a particular pattern, or is it exclusive to one character? (For example, Othello gradually begins to pick up Iago's sexual-bestial imagery as he becomes more convinced of Desdemona's guilt.)

4. What combinations or conflations of image patterns can you detect? (For instance, in *Hamlet*, in the lines "By the o'ergrowth of some complexion, / Oft breaking down the pales and forts of reason," the imagery of cancer, or pollution by "overgrowth," is conflated with military imagery.)

5. Explain the presence of such rhetorical devices as: sudden shifts from verse to prose; rhymed couplets, which indicate the conclusion of

a particular scene; "set" speeches that give the appearance of being standard or conventional (Polonius's advice to Laertes in *Hamlet*); choral speeches; formal "debates"; etc. These devices are often used to emphasize, or italicize, certain aspects of meaning and theme. Since Shakespeare's stage, for one, had no curtain, rhyming couplets performed its function, as in these lines from *Macbeth*: "Fair is foul, and foul is fair: / Hover through the fog and filthy air."

6. How, generally, would you distinguish the use of language and imagery in any play under consideration from that of other plays? (For example, dramatic verse speech tends, on the whole, to "recite" the content directly and faithfully, presenting all the implications on the word-surface; but as dialogue in plays becomes more realistic— becomes prose, that is—particularly from the nineteenth century forward, there is an increasing rift between what is actually said and what is implied, or latent, in the language.)

7. In what ways does the language of the play—its imagery; style; tempo or rhythm; tone; descriptive, informational, or ideational content; and level of probability or internal consistency—help to create the sense of a unique "world," or circumscribed space, appropriate to this play and no other? (For instance, *Macbeth*'s dark, "metaphysical" space versus *Hamlet*'s dense and various world of objects, people, animals, and processes.)

4 General Analysis

1. What is the dramatist's attitude toward the materials of his or her play? What tone does he or she take toward the action and the characters? (Skeptical? Critical? Ironic? Sympathetic? Neutral or objective? Etc.).

2. What features or elements of the play seem to be the source of the dramatist's attitude? (A reasonable or reasoning character you can trust? A choral element? A didactic voice detectable in the content as a whole? An allegorical quality? The way in which the incidents are arranged? A set of symbols? A balance or equilibrium of opposed readings of the world?)

3. What is the nature of the play's world order? (Fatalistic? Benign? Malignant? Just? Neutral?) Another way of asking this: Are there

A STEP-BY-STEP APPROACH TO SCRIPT ANALYSIS

operative gods, and what share of the responsibility for events do they hold?

4. What is the source of your impression of this world order? Remember that meaning in drama is usually *implied,* rather than stated directly. It is suggested by the relationships among the characters; the ideas associated with unsympathetic and sympathetic characters; the conflicts and their resolution; and such devices as spectacle, music, and song. What, then, is the source of your impression of the play's meaning?

5. If the play departs from realism or representationalism, what devices are used to establish the internal logic of the action?

6. Are changes in the dramatic action paralleled by changes in visual elements such as lighting, costume, make-up, and scenery? How important is such visual detail to the dramatic action?

7. For what kind of theatrical space was the play intended by its author? Are some of the play's characteristics the result of dramatic conventions in use at the time the work was written?

8. How extensive are the stage directions? Were they written by the author or interpolated by someone else? What type of information do they convey? Are they important to the dramatic action?

9. Is the play a translation? Can you compare it to the original? Can you compare it with other translations? Are there significant differences between the source and a translation, such as the rendering of the author's original French verse in English prose?

10. Is there any difference between playing time (the time it takes to perform the play) and illusory time (the time the action is supposed to take)? What is the relationship between the two, if any?

11. Is there anything special about the title? Does it focus on a character, the setting, or a theme? Is it taken from a quotation or is it an allusion? Does the title contain a point of view, suggest a mood, or otherwise "organize" the action of the play?

12. Does the play clearly fall into one of the major dramatic categories (tragedy, comedy, etc.)? What conventional features of its type does

the play exhibit (subject matter, situations, character types)? Does knowledge of the genre contribute to an understanding of this play?

MODEL ESSAYS

1. Style and Genre

This section consists of short model, or sample, essays on the subject of dramatic style or genre. Treated here are such styles as expressionism, futurism, and Absurdism, as well as such genres as farce, tragicomedy, and the grotesque. The following plays have been chosen for their representativeness, modernity, variety, and quality:

1. Eugene O'Neill's *The Hairy Ape*
2. Joe Orton's *Entertaining Mr. Sloane*
3. Orton's *Loot*
4. David Mamet's *Edmond*
5. Carlo Terron's *The Trial of the Innocents* and *Arsenic, Tonight!*
6. O'Neill's *The Hairy Ape*
7. Arthur Adamov's *Invasion*

For reading and learning purposes, the "Key Analytical Question" below can be applied to any of the above plays or all of them.

Key Analytical Question: "What is the style or genre of a particular play, and why did the playwright use such a style or genre to express the theme?"

"Futurism and O'Neill's *The Hairy Ape*"

Robert "Yank" Smith of *The Hairy Ape* (1922) is meant—if only by Eugene O'Neill's choice of his nickname, together with his melting pot of a "language," Brooklynese—to be the archetypal American, analogous to the archetypal Italian of futurist drama. (Futurist drama was still being produced in Italy at the same time as *The Hairy Ape*—which is otherwise a quasi-expressionist, German-influenced work—was being staged in New York.) The central preoccupations of the futurists were speed and technology; like Yank, they were particularly drawn to

14

the intoxicating power of machines, as Yank himself describes it in the following speech from early in the play:

> Sure I'm part of de engines! . . . Dey move, don't dey? Dey're speed, ain't dey? Dey smash trou, don't dey? . . . Dat's new stuff! Dat belongs! . . . I start somep'n and de woild moves! . . . I'm de ting in coal dat makes it boin; I'm steam and oil for de engines; I'm de ting in noise dat makes yuh hear it; I'm smoke and express trains and steamers and factory whistles . . . And I'm what makes iron into steel! Steel, dat stands for de whole ting! And I'm steel—steel—steel! (176–177)

The futurists welcomed steel and all the other products of industrial society—with its electricity, urbanization, and revolution in the means of transport and communication—with an all-embracing optimism, for they saw them as the means by which people would be able to dominate their environment totally. The speed, change, and motion of the industrial age were also fundamental to the futurists' love of the modern and their rejection of the static, lethargic past—the very "natural" past about which Paddy rhapsodizes in Scene 1 of O'Neill's play. As these Italians realized—in such plays as *Genius and Culture* (1915, by Umberto Boccioni), *The Arrest* (1916, by F. T. Marinetti), and *Lights* (1922, by Francesco Cangiullo)—the effects of the speed of transport and communication on modern sensibility were such that people were aware not just of their immediate surroundings but of the whole world.

In essence, then, the limits of time and space had been transcended—as they are, in a sense, in any production of *The Hairy Ape*, which moves from a transatlantic ocean liner bound for Southampton, England, to several locations on the streets of New York, and which takes place over a period of two months. Now it was possible to live through events both distant and near at hand: in fact, to be everywhere at the same time. Accordingly, Marinetti and his followers held that the speed of modern life called for a corresponding speed of communication in contemporary art, which should—unlike the conventional theater—be far briefer and more compressed or synthesized than even *The Hairy Ape*, yet at the same time incorporate simultaneous action occurring in different places or at different times.

Futurism took hold in Italy—and, in somewhat different, more metaphorical, as well as more short-lived, theatrical form, in the former U.S.S.R. (which, unlike soon-to-be Fascist Italy, restricted or completely suppressed the freedom even of those artists, like the Russian futurists, who supported the Communist revolution)—as in no other Western nation partly because this country, like the Soviet Union, underwent industrialization (as well as nationalization or consolidation) much later than, say, the United States. For this reason, Italian futurists embraced the machine age and all that it made possible—including war, which they labeled the supreme, health-bestowing activity—to an extent unknown in American artistic circles. Indeed, Yank's nickname—commonly used at the time to refer to an American soldier in World War I (which ended only three years before the writing of *The Hairy Ape*)—may have been bestowed on him by his ship's largely immigrant or European crew, including Italians (see the "Voices" on 168–169), because he was a recently returned war veteran. This would have made him the ideal dramatic hero, in the futurists' view—especially as one who had served in the first fully mechanized global conflict—but it could also lead the attentive reader or spectator to see Yank's self-proclaimed machine-like state at least in part as a kind of shell-shocked alienation of which he himself is blithely unaware.

Witness O'Neill's overall treatment of his protagonist in *The Hairy Ape*, where Yank Smith becomes representative of the displacement of modern humanity in general: of people who, in the Marxist sense, become alienated from themselves because their work is not part of their life; because their work (particularly the all-consuming "work" of war) takes over their life entirely, as in the case of Yank; or, in the case of the idle, upper-class Mildred, as opposed to an unemployed member of the underclass, because work is something that they do not even want. As a result, these people find themselves alienated from other human beings as well, with whom they no longer share a social essence or to whose society they no longer feel they belong.

In Yank's case, that alienation translates into a kind of permanent, fatal existentialism—a paralyzing clash, if you will, between Dante's medieval-cum-Renaissance Christianity and Marinetti's twentieth-century, totalitarian godlessness (or elevation of science and technology to godlike status). And the very structure of *The Hairy Ape* reveals this clash, which itself, in a sense, prevents Yank from moving either backward or forward, on to the past or back to the future. For, on the one hand, the episodic form of the play may be conducive to the illustration of a progressive if incremental journey toward spiritual wholeness or organicity; on the other hand, however, that same episodic form, in the rapidity with which it can transcend or condense time and place, suggests the Machine Age of which Yank is a part, with its ease of transport, atomization of human existence, speed of tempo, and even simultaneity of experience.

Looked at another way, the eight scenes of the play break down half & half between modernism in the form of futurism and medievalism in the form of the stations-of-the-cross drama. The first part of *The Hairy Ape*, all on the ship, is "modern." Here, the principles of Marinetti's futurism seem evident in the stokehole as Yank and his cohorts feed the machine at the same time they are, in a way, fed by it. The stokers' language in Scene 1, for example, incorporates simultaneous speech during which they "talk over" one another, and actions themselves occur simultaneously when, in Scene 2, the men (whom we should be able to see on stage) work below in the stokehole even as Mildred and her aunt are visible on top on the ocean liner's promenade deck.

After Mildred meets the "filthy beast," of course, the play completely changes. Following one more scene aboard ship, Scene 4, the underlying structure of *The Hairy Ape* switches to that of a medieval station drama, relying now upon sequence rather than simultaneity. Thus, just as the play's own dramatic journey moves away from the modern and into the past, Yank devolves to see himself ultimately as the Hairy Ape (in both his description and in O'Neill's final stage direction [232]). The fateful meeting with Mildred, one could say, is the end of modernism-cum-futurism for him: "thought" or (self-) reflection kills Yank's forward movement in the present, and then in Scenes 5–8 he learns that, although he may call himself a "Hairy Ape," he can't go back in time, either.

Work Cited
O'Neill, Eugene. *Three Plays:* Anna Christie, The Emperor Jones, *and* The Hairy Ape. New York: Vintage 1972.

"Conception in Orton's *Entertaining Mr. Sloane*"

Joe Orton did not begin by writing the anarchic farces for which he has become best known, *Loot* (1964) and *What the Butler Saw* (1967). His first plays, *The Ruffian on the Stair* (1963) and *Entertaining Mr. Sloane* (1963), were black comedies written under the influence of Harold Pinter and Samuel Beckett. They poke fun at the volatile, confusing, neurotic, and diminished world of contemporary existence, yet their characters nonetheless possess an emotional dimension— unlike those in *Loot* and *What the Butler Saw*.

Sloane, for instance, has no relatives and was orphaned at the age of eight by parents who both died at the same time—and therefore seem to have committed suicide. "It was the lack of privacy [in the orphanage] I found most trying," he says, "and the lack of real love" (67). Tellingly, the only husband and wife mentioned in the play are Sloane's parents.

Kemp is Kath and Ed's father, but he and his son haven't spoken for twenty years, and his daughter treats him as if he were a naughty little boy. Kath and Ed allow Sloane to get away with killing their father in return for sexual favors: he will spend six months of the year with Kath and six months with Ed "as long as the agreement lasts" (148). The first man Sloane killed was Kemp's boss, who was apparently a homosexual. Sloane says that the boss "wanted to photo me. For certain interesting features I had that he wanted the exclusive right of preserving. You know how it is. I didn't like to refuse. No harm in it I suppose. But then I got to thinking" (125).

Kath, at forty-one or forty-two years old, is old enough to be Sloane's mother. In fact, she had a son when she was young by Tommy, Ed's best friend and lover at the time. She says to Sloane, "You're almost the same age as he would be" (68). Kath gave the boy up for adoption and she and Tommy never married. The implication is that Sloane is in fact her son. Sloane, Ed's new lover, himself gets Kath pregnant; they won't marry, either, and she will probably give her baby up for adoption. Ed arranged the adoption of Tommy's son, and there is no reason to believe that he will not do the same for Sloane's—a fetus that Ed predictably refers to as "him" (147).

In his introduction to *Joe Orton: The Complete Plays,* John Lahr wrote that "Sloane feels no guilt and his refusal to experience shame is what disturbs and amuses audiences. Sloane is a survivor whose egotism is rewarded, not punished" (16). Sloane's excessive ego—perhaps the byproduct of his being orphaned at an early age—is rewarded by other egotistical, unloved characters. All three, Sloane, Ed, and Kath, substitute sex for love. It is no accident that the Kemp home stands alone in the midst of a rubbish dump—"it was intended to be the first of a row," says the old man (72). It is a home without love that begets a bastard who himself begets a bastard.

Lahr said that Orton, in his depiction of characters like Kath, Ed, and Sloane, "was not being heartless, merely accurate" (16): in their rapaciousness, ignorance, and violence, these people are the representative products of our age. No wonder Orton has an old woman make "a special trip [all the way from Woolwich] with her daughter in order to dump a bedstead" (72) outside the Kemp house. It is as if the woman is exhorting her daughter not to risk the marriage bed in times inhospitable to families and children—times peopled by the likes of this dwelling's occupants.

In her last conversation with Ed, the pregnant Kath, wanting to spend time with Sloane that should be allotted to Ed according to their agreement, says, "It deepens the relationship if the father is there [present at the birth of his child]." Ed replies, "It's all any reasonable child can expect if the dad is present at the conception. Let's hear no more of it" (149). This is wildly funny. But it is also profoundly disturbing, because prophetic: writing a parody on the Oedipal theme in 1963, Orton foresaw at the same time the age of test-tube babies, sperm banks, surrogate mothers, single-parent families, and adoptive gay or lesbian couples—the very age in which we are now living.

Works Cited

Lahr, John, intro. *Joe Orton: The Complete Plays*. New York: Grove Press, 1976.

Orton, Joe. *Entertaining Mr. Sloane*. In *The Complete Plays of Joe Orton*. New York: Grove Press, 1976. 63–149.

"Money and Evil in Orton's *Loot*"

The continued reluctance of some to value Joe Orton's art is comparable to the reluctance of critics, then and now, to esteem Restoration comedy, its nearest generic ancestor before the comedies of Oscar Wilde. Orton's plays—like William Congreve's and William Wycherley's and later Wilde's, to whose *Importance of Being Earnest* (1895) Orton's *What the Butler Saw* (1967) is close in spirit and sometimes in detail—are designed to negate the conventional assurances of art and to corrode the link between that art and the assumptions of liberal humanism. In fact the work of all four dramatists is a form of social criticism, but through subversion of conventional morality, not through a call for the correction of societal abuses: that is why their plays are sometimes criticized.

Orton's *Loot* (1964), for example, may satirize institutions such as the police and the Catholic Church, but what is important is that the vehicles of this satire themselves remain unaffected by it. Indeed, the play could be said to dramatize the triumph of evil: of greed, corruption, brutality, immorality or amorality, and sacrilege.

Truscott and Hal, for instance, get no comeuppance in the end, which is what makes *Loot* so unsettling. Orton fiendishly satirizes authority through Truscott, yet Truscott—at once the object and vehicle of the playwright's scorn—gets away easily with beating suspects, taking bribes, and in general abusing his power. He may be stupid in some ways, but his stupidity never gets him into any real trouble. And I think that this is Orton's point: the Truscotts of this world need to be satirized, yet it must also simultaneously be pointed out that the Truscotts of this world often go completely unpunished for their crimes. Orton thus makes us laugh at Truscott at the same time as he makes us realize that a Truscott is oblivious to our laughter, and will continue in his corrupt ways well beyond the confines of the drama.

This British dramatist has gone beyond farce in *Loot* in the sense that he has exploited the attractiveness of evil for audiences—paradoxically, the same bourgeois audiences at whom he is striking back. Orton has proved to us that we can be amused by behavior we would normally deplore, and that we can even attend raptly as evil goes unpunished. There are dire consequences in *Loot*, as there are not in traditional farce—Hal gets a severe beating, Mr. McLeavy will probably die (of old age) in prison for a crime he did not commit—and Orton's art, or dramatic sleight of hand, is to make us *not care* while we are watching. We think about what we have witnessed only later, after we've been "taken"—like Hal, Fay, and Dennis at the conclusion of the play. Truscott leaves with the money, and these characters are left to wonder if they will ever see any of it again, or how he managed to walk off with it all in the first place.

What Orton shows us, then, in *Loot*, as in other of his plays, is that evil, in the right amounts, has the power to arrest for our delight certain bold lines of force which goodness simply doesn't possess. Good, as such, is boring, because it is relatively undramatic; evil, by contrast, is endlessly fascinating and suspenseful. Good is self-sustaining, whereas evil is self-destructive: there is always the possibility that two evils will cancel each other out and that we will be left with—nothing. This is one of the reasons we attend to evil, anticipating its sudden and spectacular demise.

What playwrights like Joe Orton and his "serious" counterpart, Harold Pinter, do for evil is almost to remove it from the sphere of morality and raise it to the level of respectability, as something worthy of careful examination. (Orton claimed that the subversively sexual nature of Pinter's *The Homecoming* [1965] was influenced by his first two plays, *The Ruffian on the Stair* [1963] and *Entertaining Mr. Sloane* [1963].) We don't judge evil: we watch it do its work. I don't know that we can speak of this kind of dramatic writing as morally good or bad. But it *is* a kind of achievement, the using up of one more artistic possibility.

In reality *Loot* is a reaction against, nearly a destruction of, artistic forms that have preceded it—traditional farce and satire, on the one hand, and melodrama with its happy ending and omniscient authority figure, on the other—and thus it is always in danger, like the evil it portrays, of going too far and destroying *itself*. One gets the uncanny feeling throughout a reading or production of *Loot* that the next line or next bit of action will simply be too much and the play will end abruptly and abortively. It never does, of course, but the play's very potential for suddenly "exploding" its form keeps us on the very edge of our seats, waiting and watching in utter astonishment.

Joe Orton may be telling us basic things in *Loot* about the ways in which art works, or the ways in which we respond to art, that we didn't know before or haven't considered in a long time. Surely Orton did not count on this response to his work—in his own day his plays were either liked or loathed for their *satirical* stance. Just as surely, he would have been tickled by such a favorable reaction, for it is at a far remove from the liberal humanist conception of the response that "vile art" should engender.

Work Cited
Orton, Joe. *Loot*. In *The Complete Plays of Joe Orton*. New York: Grove Press, 1976. 193–275.

"Mamet's *Edmond* and German Expressionism"

Originally produced as a long one-act play in 1982, *Edmond* is an underrated piece, having been written between Mamet's stellar (and original) screenplay for *The Verdict* (1982) and his best drama, *Glengarry Glen Ross* (1984), and consequently having suffered in comparison with those two highly publicized works. But *Edmond* stands on its own two feet, in part because it points up—as none of Mamet's other plays do—an aspect of his writing style that, like this particular drama itself, has been neglected. I mean the fact that Mamet's staccato or minimalist dialogue, with its occasional explosions, is essentially expressionistic, even when the plays themselves are not thoroughgoing expressionist works.

Mamet's language thus underscores the paradox of verism-cum-abstraction that inheres in all his work. The general linguistic texture is naturalistic, nearly stenographic—the broken sentences, the repetitions, the litanies of the everyday; then, suddenly, with a telegraphic word or phrase, and especially with an entire quizzical or contorted sentence, the vernacular lifts into an arch. As in, "The path of some crazed lunatic sees you as an invasion of his personal domain" (85, *American Buffalo* [1975]). Or, "People used to say that there are numbers of such magnitude that multiplying them by two made no difference" (52, *Glengarry Glen Ross*). And, from *Edmond*: "[God] may love the weak, but he protects the strong" (266). With a lesser writer, such lines might seem to be fissures in verism; but Mamet otherwise so thoroughly certifies the accuracy of his ear that in these instances we feel we are flying past the character's actual powers of expression into the thoughts in him that he isn't always able to express. In this way the real is lifted into the abstract—or what I am calling the expressionistic.

That *Edmond* appears more expressionistic than David Mamet's other plays stems less from its disgorged or deracinated language than from its episodic form. It is what the Germans call both a "station" drama and a *Wandlungsdrama*, a drama of transformation-cum-regeneration that is composed of a series of stations, or stages (twenty-three brief scenes in *Edmond*'s case), through which a character progresses as he takes the moral, spiritual, and emotional journey of his life. (A product of European religious drama of the Middle Ages, the original station play consisted of stations that were sometimes literally stations of the cross.) Several commentators have compared *Edmond* to Georg Büchner's proto-expressionistic play *Woyzeck* (1836), but Mamet's drama has more in common with Georg Kaiser's lesser-known expressionistic work *From Morn to Midnight* (1912).

In this play, a bank cashier, whose humanity has been crushed beneath the social conventions, economic system, and political structure of Wilhelminian Germany, succumbs to sexual temptation and both robs his bank and leaves his wife—to embark on a pilgrimage (to a bordello for some sensual fulfillment, to a sports stadium for some passionate gambling, to the Salvation Army for some soulful religion) in search of something beyond the material, the profane, the mechanized, the quotidian. When he does not find what he is looking for, he kills himself rather than be imprisoned for his crime. Mamet's own play covers more than the twelve or so hours of *From Morn to Midnight*, but it, too, is about a character in desperate search of some new intensity, truth, or meaning in his life.

Edmund Burke is a forty-seven-year-old New York stockbroker on his way home early from work after a meeting has been re-scheduled. A quick quarrel with his wife discloses that Edmond has not loved her for years and does not think she is attractive. For her part, the wife seems angered less by the bad news than by her husband's detached manner in delivering it. Edmond does not care: he just turns his back and walks out on her—and on his mechanical, workaday existence. *Edmond* thus takes place, as it were, after the romance of the archetypal romantic comedy is over—when, in the absence of idealized, romantic love, a desire for a different kind of union or devotion takes over.

In Edmond's case, at least initially, that desire is for sheer sex, primarily of the oral kind. One of his stops after leaving his wife is a strip club where he thinks he can slake his sexual needs. When a pretty, amiable B-girl there tells him her fee for oral sex and also asks him to buy an exorbitantly priced drink, he becomes incensed. Soon Edmond's gotten himself tossed out—the start of a long round of explosive confrontations with hookers, grifters, and pimps in which he keeps heatedly complaining about the cost, naïvely trying to apply bourgeois standards to an inherently corrupt underworld into which he nevertheless keeps sinking deeper and deeper.

His odyssey through New York's seedy underbelly takes Edmond to a peep show next and then to a massage parlor, before he decides to try to get his satisfaction out of a hand of three-card monte. When he accuses the dealer of running a crooked game, however, the dealer and his shills pull him into an alley, beat him up, and steal his money. So Edmond goes to a pawnshop to trade his wedding ring for some cash— and with no such prior plan, comes out with a knife (unlike Woyzeck, who goes to a pawnshop expressly to buy a knife with which to kill his common-law wife). Thus armed, he first threatens a woman on a subway platform, then uses the knife on a leering, gold-toothed pimp who promises to take him to a prostitute but tries to hold him up instead—and in return gets a "knife-whipping" from Edmond that leaves this black man half dead.

Invigorated by this act of violence and experiencing the delirious liberation of living in the moment for the first time in his life, Edmond goes on a manic jag during which he is unable to keep his mouth shut as he babbles first to this stranger, then to that. One of those strangers turns out to be Glenna, a twenty-three-year-old waitress in a coffee-house, whom he successfully propositions and whom he tells, in a highly racialized speech, how alive beating the pimp has made him feel. An aspiring actress, Glenna—the only named character besides Edmond because, apart from him and in contrast to the generic secondary characters of expressionistic drama in general, she is the most humanized—compares his feeling of almost Dionysian ecstasy to the one she gets when she is acting. She thus fits into, shares, or even becomes a projection of, Edmond's narcissistic framework, but only for a time, since Glenna proves to have a slightly different frame of reference from his. To wit: she refuses to join him in "leaving normal" and renouncing the past.

This provokes Edmond's rage and he kills her with his knife, as the fever of his quest for a higher reality, which has been burning through everything he has been doing, propels him past the rational into the hierophantic, the exalted, the truth. The truth, that is, according to Edmond Burke, but a grotesque compound of his lifelong frustrations by any other name. (Does Mamet call him by this name in order to connect his reactionary thought with that of his real-life namesake, Edmund Burke [1729–1797], often regarded as the father of Anglo-American conservatism?) After he leaves Glenna's apartment, Edmond goes (like the Cashier in *From Morn to Midnight* after his bordello-visit) to a religious mission to hear a minister preach another kind of truth: that every soul can be redeemed through faith. But before he gets a chance to make his testament in front of all those assembled, Edmond is identified by the woman he accosted in the subway and arrested. And after a short reunion with his wife, who serves him with divorce papers, he ends up in a prison cell.

A big black man is assigned to his cell, and Edmond expresses conciliatory feelings toward this African-American as well as blacks in general. Uninterested, his cellmate beats Edmond into granting him sexual favors. In the last scene, the two men are simply living together, affectionately; and the film ends as Edmond says "good night," kisses the other man, then turns over and goes to sleep. He thus ends in an unforeseen domesticity, enforced but safe, yet a domesticity, paradoxically, through which he reaches his apotheosis—and finds the gateway to spiritual freedom, inner peace, and personal transcendence.

Mamet's theme is not that we all share Edmond Burke's particular frustrations and hungers, but that we all have them in one form or another and can be interested in a man who not only discovers his own, but does so in such a way as to set himself *apart* from us—by feeling nothing beyond his own suffering. In this he again resembles Kaiser's Cashier, who never wastes a thought on the feelings or troubles of the wife and family he abandons, the waiter he cheats, the whores he abuses, the stadium spectator whose death he engineers. Ironically, the Cashier indirectly compares himself to Christ with his last words, "Ecce homo" ("Behold the man," the same words as those uttered by Pilate, in John 19:5, immediately before Jesus' crucifixion), though *Ecce homo* was also the title of the 1888 book in which Nietzsche unfavorably contrasted Christian ideals with his own superior ideal of the *Übermensch*, or superman. A cashier, of course, is no superman, but this cashier is not (or has not behaved like) a Christian, either—which is precisely Kaiser's point in having him utter words that simultaneously call to mind the Bible and Friedrich Nietzsche.

The same goes for Edmond Burke: he is a slave by the end of *Edmond*, not a superman and not even a Christian slave, and he finds himself in a hell of his own, self-satisfied creation. If Edmond is a martyr of a kind, moreover, he is a martyr, not for mankind, like Christ, but for men—specifically for American men of the 1980s, when the straight white male was reeling from his loss of potency at the hands of women, gays, and especially blacks in a climate of rigid political correctness as well as institutionalized affirmative action. So, after sacrificing a female waitress and an African-American pimp, Edmond sacrifices himself: to the woman who identified him as her (and the pimp's) assailant, to the wife who divorces him, and finally to the black who sodomizes him.

Edmond, like *American Buffalo*, to name only Mamet's second-best drama, is above all a species of incantation: profane, yes, but so desperate in its profanity as to take on spiritual overtones. Edmond may not be as vacuous as Don and Teach in *American Buffalo*, but, even as they do, he tries to create through language some sense of autonomous being. The difference is that the middle-class Edmond is reaching for a higher or more authentic being—hence the more singular and expressionistic his search as well as his speech; whereas Don and Teach (and to a lesser extent young Bobby, the third character in *American Buffalo*) are trying to create through their dialogue only some sense of their lowly—and shared—being, a verbal environment in which that being can at least subsist.

There is nothing romantic about *American Buffalo*, then; it is solely (if superbly) an instance of dramatic naturalism. *Edmond* begins in domestic naturalism but quickly extends beyond it, into a kind of super- or supra-naturalism that I am calling expressionism. In the process Mamet's play invokes the spirit (if not religion itself), or the spiritual search for order, meaning, and harmony, in part through its very form, that of a morality or mystery play. Thus are we indirectly reminded that the theater began as a sacred event and eventually came to include the profane. But, in *Edmond*'s case, paradoxically, we are talking about profanation of a very high order.

Works Cited

Büchner, Georg. *Woyzeck*. Trans. Carl Richard Mueller. In *The Modern Theater*. Ed. Robert Corrigan. New York: Macmillan, 1964. 7–19.

Kaiser, Georg. *From Morn to Midnight*. Trans. Ashley Dukes. In *Masters of Modern Drama*. Eds. Haskell Block & Robert Shedd. New York: Random House, 1962. 489–507.

Mamet, David. *American Buffalo*. New York: Grove Press, 1977.

——. *Edmond*. New York: Grove Press, 983.

——. *Glengarry Glen Ross*. New York: Grove Press, 1984.

"The Grotesque in Terron's *The Trial of the Innocents* and *Arsenic, Tonight!*"

In their focus upon similar moral issues and even their occasional deployment of the trial or investigative format, the plays of Carlo Terron may be compared to those of both Ugo Betti and Diego Fabbri, as well as Pirandello. Terron's theater is perhaps the most varied of his generation; his flexible talent makes each of his dramas a new experiment that reveals an intellectual faculty not bound by schemata or preconceptions. His works range from the grotesque to the sublime, from psychological drama to allegorical farce, and it is partly because of its range or scope, together with its freedom from ideological tendentiousness and its ties to the theatrical avant-garde, that Terron's work deserves attention and reevaluation. Whether it takes the form of comedy or tragedy, however, his *oeuvre* is essentially concerned with an investigation of the roots of guilt, and as such it reflects the moral climate of post-World War II Italy. (This is a period, I might add, that many Italians as well as other Europeans understandably do not wish to dwell on—which, aside from their complexity and lack of commercial appeal, might explain why Terron's plays are seldom produced in Italy or translated into other European languages.) In most of his plays Terron used his training as a psychiatrist to provide the intellectual framework for a world view in which human motives for action are seen as being so intertwined with the complex nature of life that it is almost impossible to fix individual moral responsibility.

In its exploration of the complexity and even inscrutability of human behavior, Terron's drama thus has something in common with Pirandello's "theater of the grotesque." For such a theater not only investigates the gap or disjuncture between appearance and reality, it also questions—like Terron—whether a more reliable truth can indeed be found after life's masks are stripped away. Personality for these dramatists becomes the rigid (yet comic) mask we place over our features in order to placate the busybody's—*everybody's*—hunger to define and classify, while character itself is the suffering (and tragic) face: spontaneous, evanescent, finally unknowable. Thus realistic *personae*, dialogue, and detail or design are the tools of grotesque drama but not its material. With these tools, writers like Pirandello and Terron shaped a new dramatic world in which realism is only the play's surface, just as appearance is life's surface.

Beneath the apparent realism—the illusion of reality, as it were—of this dramatic world whirl the depths of chaos, contradiction, and paradox, ready to rear up at any moment and prove reality a lie—or to reveal the reality of illusion. The same was true of the theatrical avant-garde in Europe from the late nineteenth century on: for these dramatists—whose metaphysical themes, if not whose dramatic means, Terron and Pirandello share—the nature of reality itself became the prime subject of plays because of a loss of confidence in the presumed model for dramatizing human behavior and thinking about human existence. In other words, the representation of the illusion of reality onstage, through bourgeois realism or proletarian naturalism, became the demonstration of the reality of the illusion-making capacity, illusion-projecting essence, or illusion-dwelling tendency of the human mind by such movements as symbolism, surrealism, expressionism, and futurism.

The main thematic thrust in Terron's drama is to undermine the traditional antinomy of appearance and reality with the nihilistic paradox that appearance *is* reality: there is not really anything more to life than meets the eye. An ethic can be derived from this: be content with what meets your eye, be tolerant of what meets other people's eyes, and don't ask more of life. A defeatist metaphysic thus joins hands with a sad belief in the few human realities that are left when God and an intelligible universe are torn away—such realities as compassion and family piety. In the long run, however, as befitting someone who trained to be a psychiatrist, Terron's philosophy and ethics are less significant than his psychology—that is, his presentation of inner experience. If Ibsen presented an image of the modern person as neurotic, Terron, like Pirandello before him, tends to see that person as verging upon psychosis if not actually tumbling into it.

If Terron's protagonists understandably reject judgment by others in such a quasi-absurdist world, where identity and truth are relative or subjective, they are very quick to accuse themselves; indeed, the theme of self-judgment and self-punishment was established in one of his earliest plays, *Liberty* (1943). Unable to resist the temptation to steal an old woman's watch in this one-act comedy, Memmo Ventura afterward escapes from the police who caught him. Naturally, he does so in order to maintain his sense of freedom; but, ironically, Memmo then exercises his free will by turning up at the local jail and condemning himself to a year's sentence. Thus has he come to understand the true nature of liberty, guilt, and punishment—not to speak of his own inner or private truth, to which the hasty action of a moment's confusion, or a moment's clarity, has provided him access.

The theme of self-judgment equally pervades the drama whose production in 1950 cemented Terron's reputation as a playwright: *Judith*, which transposes the tale of the Biblical heroine to the time of the Italian Resistance. When German troops are quartered in her house, Judith finds in their general someone whose life, like her own, is in the service of the ideal of war. But whereas the General sees war as a political and racial affirmation, Judith sees it as a means to combat the very essence of war. She and the General are nevertheless drawn to each other, and she ends up becoming his mistress. Yet neither is able to forgive himself or herself for this abdication of moral principles; and the result is that Judith poisons the General at his own instigation, then arranges to have her other, Partisan lover kill her.

Don Juan's Wife (1944) continues Terron's own drama of paradox as it presents a humorous situation in which a wife guarantees "possession" of her husband by pushing him into the arms of other women. *No Peace for the Ancient Faun* (1951) itself is a hilarious comedy concerning a male ballet dancer whose immorality is seen as "constitutional amorality," and who paradoxically ends in bourgeois respectability—surrounded by the 163 children he had fathered in a Damascus harem. *I Had More Respect for Hydrogen* (1953) is another "happy comedy," according to Terron: it shows scientists at the mercy, in war, of their own discoveries and inventions, and the play concludes in universal destruction. *Lavinia Among the Damned* (1958) returns Terron to a more "serious" mood, as Lavinia's illicit compulsions (to poison her husband, to make love to the priest who is her husband's brother) destroy both her and her seemingly united, harmonious family by bringing to light the fear as well as the loathing behind each member's social mask.

Two of his best and most representative works are *The Trial of the Innocents* (1950) and *Arsenic, Tonight!* (1967), each in its own way a Pirandellian drama of the grotesque. "In this hell," Terron has one of his characters in *The Trial of the Innocents* say, "there is no guilty party, only victims" (Terron 58). Some of those victims are brilliantly on display in *The Trial of the Innocents* and *Arsenic, Tonight!*, each of which is composed in a Shavian linguistic style that diabolically mixes lucidity and intelligence with irony, allusion, and even subversiveness. In the earlier drama, written in three acts, a "respectable" woman's grown children discover that she has a young lover; they then begin to investigate her dubious past, which has been concealed until now beneath the mask of "mother." By the time the "trial" is over, accusers and accused find themselves inescapably linked by the fatefulness of the human condition, which forces contradiction and uncertainty upon everyone.

The very title *Arsenic, Tonight!* invites uncertainty and contradiction: arsenic for whom? For the audience? For the characters? Or arsenic for everybody? And why such a declaration or exclamation, as if some delicious specialty were being served for dinner? In *Arsenic, Tonight!*, billed by Terron as a comedy in two acts, but something closer to a tragic-farce or tragic-grotesque, an apparently happy, middle-class couple are living in a Strindbergian hell: the wife is at once a workaholic and a nymphomaniac who operates her own funeral home, while the husband is an introspective bookworm who, though he has become sexually impotent due to his wife's persistent criticism as well as her rampant unfaithfulness, manages nonetheless to play an active role in the running of her business. Together they remain prisoners of a marriage—ironically, the nucleus on which both the family and society are founded—in which each member both hates and loves, role-plays and acts out, simultaneously attempting to destroy the other and to rediscover the passion that originally brought the two of them together.

Although Terron's fluid dialogue in *Arsenic, Tonight!* and other plays is suspenseful, allusive, and brimming with an intentionality that loads the words with manifold meaning, he, like many another Italian dramatist, has been accused of a linguistic artificiality that robs his characters of life. While this artificiality probably doesn't come across as greatly in translation, it—or the issue of dialectal versus literary language in Italian—points up the larger conflict between the demand for realism (which in Italy requires the use of a regional dialect) and the quest for universality (which requires a more literary or standard speech).

Work Cited

Terron, Carlo. *The Trial of the Innocents*. In *The Theater of Carlo Terron: Two Plays*: The Trial of the Innocents *and* Arsenic, Tonight! Trans. & ed. R. J. Cardullo. Amherst, NY: Cambria Press, 2008. 21–89.

"Tragicomedy in O'Neill's *The Hairy Ape*"

Eugene O'Neill describes his naturalist-expressionist play *The Hairy Ape* (1921) as a comedy in the its subtitle, "A Comedy of Ancient and Modern Life in Eight Scenes," and in the process ironically invokes Dante's *Divine Comedy* (1321). Originally called simply *Commedia*, like *The Hairy Ape*'s own subtitle, "A Comedy," Dante's masterpiece was reissued in Venice in 1555 with the adjective *divina* applied to the work's title for the first time, thus resulting in the title still used today. The characters whom Dante meets on his journey in the *Commedia*, moreover, are drawn largely from ancient Roman as well as recent Italian history and even from contemporary Italian life. Hence this narrative poem could itself be called "A Comedy of Ancient and Modern Life," just as O'Neill describes his play.

Additionally, even as O'Neill succeeded in *The Hairy Ape* in forging an urban American argot that assimilates the spoken English of immigrant Germans, Jews, Scandinavians, Frenchmen, Dutchmen, Italians, Cockneys, and Irishmen, so too, from a reverse angle, did Dante enrich courtly Italian with his native Tuscan dialect to create a serious literary language that would take the place of Latin and become the ancestor of modern Italian. In fact, Dante's use of language was one of the reasons for the "low" title of *Commedia*, for in this work he treated a serious subject, the redemption of man—one normally reserved for "high" tragedy—in the low and vulgar language of Italian, not Latin as one might expect.

Finally, although in structure a journey to, or through, the Beyond of hell, purgatory, and paradise, the *Commedia* is actually a realistic picture and intense analysis of earthly human life. But Dante's literal journey, of course, is also a spiritual one: an allegory of the progress of the individual soul toward God and of the progress of sociopolitical mankind toward peace on earth—hence the "comedy," or happy-cum-heavenly ending, of the poem. Similarly, Yank takes a literal as well as figurative journey in *The Hairy Ape*. Like Dante, he also begins in hell—the inferno-like bowels of the stokehole of a transatlantic liner, as O'Neill describes it in Scene 3:

> The stokehole.... murky air laden with coal dust... masses of shadows everywhere... [The men] use... shovels to throw open the furnace doors. Then from these fiery round holes in the black, a flood of terrific light and heat pours full upon the men... [as they] hurl [coal] into the flaming mouths before them. (187)

It is in hell, furthermore (a hell, appropriately, where men seem condemned or cursed to an eternity of hard labor, in the sweat from which they will slowly roast), that Yank meets Mildred—or, it could be said, that this Adam ("naked and shameless" [191]) meets his Eve ("dressed all in white" [180]), who turns out to be something other than Dante's idealized Beatrice. For Mildred not only violates the atavistic, animalistic Yank's territorial space, she also gives Yank knowledge or consciousness of himself—or of himself as others view him—for the first time, and with it the power to think. But "Thinkin' is hard" (230) for Yank, so hard that at least five times in the play, subsequent to his single encounter with Mildred, O'Neill has his protagonist sit "in the exact attitude of Rodin's 'The Thinker'" (193). This 1881 sculpture is often considered to be optimistic, even uplifting—the epitome of contemplative, intelligent man—but one must not forget that Rodin designed it as the central piece of his monumental work *The Gates of Hell* (1880–1917), which would portray brutish man attempting to puzzle out the truth and meaning of human existence. So construed, thought or self-reflection is a kind of hell that separates or alienates humanity from nature, in contrast to the union with nature enjoyed by all other animals.

Yank, however, is identified with the machine or the machine age; he "belongs" (one of his favorite words) to the age of steam, power, and speed. In the stokehole of this particular ship, moreover, he is the supreme being and unquestioned ruler—"fiercer, more truculent, more powerful, more sure of himself than the rest" (166). Or at least he was until Mildred's simple look of revulsion and her words "Oh, the filthy beast!" (192) topple Yank's confidence and self-respect, completely changing his perspective on his life and work. Just as Mildred descends the evolutionary ladder, so to speak, to see "how the other half lives" (184) in the nether regions of the ocean liner, so too does Yank ascend from the bowels of the ship, shortly after his encounter with her, to discover a world on high he never knew really existed and in which he does not fit. To be sure, he begins his actual as well as metaphoric journey in a quest, at first, for revenge against Mildred's upper class, only to have that journey become, more and more, a search for self.

His journey takes Yank from hell progressively back through the evolutionary scale to four places on "earth," in New York City—Fifth Avenue, the prison on what was then known as Blackwell's Island (Roosevelt Island today), the meeting hall of the International Workers of the World on the Brooklyn waterfront, and the (Central Park?) zoo—purgatories, all, that lead to physical punishment, as opposed to spiritual penance, for Yank's "sins" and ultimately to his death. "I ain't on oith and I ain't in heaven', get me?" Yank tells a gorilla at the zoo—his closest "relative" in terms of appearance, strength, and outlook, and what the "evolved" but overbred Mildred saw in the stokehole when she looked into Yank's "gorilla face" (191)—"I'm in the middle tryin' to separate 'em, takin' all de woist punches from bot' of 'em. Maybe dat's what dey call hell, huh?" (230–231). Maybe, but it could just as well be what they call purgatory.

"Christ," Yank asks as he is dying at the hands of the uncaged gorilla, "Where do I get off at? Where do I fit in?" (232). The answer lies, not in the uniting of his immortal soul (if he has one) with God, but in the freeing of Yank from the prison-house of self and the reunion of his mortal body with the elements of nature. After what he has been through, one could say, this is heaven enough. As O'Neill himself once explained, Yank *while alive* had "lost his old harmony with nature, the harmony which he used to have as an animal"—and that the stoker Paddy thinks was the ancient order of things on sailing ships, when "a ship was part of the sea, and a man was part of a ship, and the sea joined all together and made it one" (175).

Why so lowly a naturalistic character as Yank, in the first place, as symbolic protagonist of this drama? Because, in his utter identification with the machine, he is as close as we can get in a modern character to primitive or prehistoric man's union with nature, on the one hand, and the communion of a Christian saint, martyr, or "mere" true believer with God, on the other hand. He is what Emerson, already in the mid-nineteenth century, was calling the machine man, "metamorphosed into a thing" (64). And it is precisely because of such utter identification that Yank's eventual alienation from the machine (something not foreseen by the Italian futurists in their attempt to fashion man himself as the most superior of machines)—his fall, as it were—is rendered more dramatic, more effective, than it would be for a character not so closely identified. When Yank loses this identification, he has nothing left to fall back on: certainly not God or nature, nor, obviously, is his mind sophisticated enough to embrace secular humanism. He becomes like a puppet without his deterministic strings—one who can no longer be "yanked," if you will. Moreover, as O'Neill himself points out above, even when Yank tries to commune with his "brother" ape, his evolutionary ancestor, he is rejected. He dies in a cage of steel as night falls on the Central Park Zoo, without a future of either a material or a spiritual kind.

We may feel superior to this "comic" character, as we do to comic characters in general from our objective viewpoint, but we laugh at him at our own peril—unless, that is, our laughter is accompanied by the smile of recognition. For Robert "Yank" Smith is an alienated Everyman—*in nuce*, every Robert Smith in America, then as now—or he is no one. O'Neill's discovery, you see—and the discovery of other American dramatists at this time—was that "small" events in the lives of "small" people like Yank could be presented so that they reflected the wider world outside a ship's boiler room, or a home's living room. A national literature of plays thus set in bourgeois living rooms or proletarian workplaces is a deeply democratic literature, one which assumes that the important subjects are those that manifest themselves in the daily lives of ordinary (not "noble" or "heroic") people like Yank Smith.

Common man or not, Yank certainly has his stature increased by O'Neill's use of the equivalent of Greek choruses throughout *The Hairy*

Ape. In the stokehole scenes, the forecastle scene, the Fifth-Avenue scene, the I.W.W. scene, the jail scene, and the zoo scene—indeed, every scene except the second one between Mildred and her aunt, in which Yank does not appear—O'Neill introduced the clamor and chatter of people or animals to set the tone and milieu of his drama; to indicate the masses from whom Yank stands out, to remind us of the essentially social nature of human experience at the same time as we are supplied with a host of witnesses to Yank's private or individual suffering; and to provide us with a kind of frame or lens through which to view Yank as he undergoes his *agon*.

That frame or lens was heightened in the original New York production during the Fifth-Avenue scene because the actors playing rich people wore Greek-like masks (the first use of masks in a serious play on Broadway, where *The Hairy Ape* was moved from the Provincetown Playhouse, also in New York)—a device that O'Neill later regretted he had not used in the stokehole scene and other scenes as well. Our sociochoral perspective on Yank might thus be derisive or dismissive, depending on the "chorus" and its mask. Then again, it could be a combination of the reverential and the fearful, as it is in the case of the stokers in Scenes 1 and 3; or it could be lamentatory, as in the case of the "chattering, whimpering wail" (232) of the monkeys at the end of the play, after Yank has expired).

Whether we view Yank as a fully tragic character in the classical sense seems to me less important, however, than the fact that O'Neill has bestowed on so lowly a figure a number of characteristics we traditionally associate with tragedy. To wit: a kind of freedom of action that enables Yank to choose his course without much restriction, at the same time as we sense the tragic irony of his choices; his own crude proletarian idiom, which, like verse, sets him apart and has a peculiar evocativeness, even exaltation; a life lived, not in a home (let alone with a wife and children), but outside in something akin to a public arena (on a "public" ship and in other such places), which publicness itself— like Yank's choral witnesses—confers moral, spiritual, and philosophical significance on his actions; a hubris in his superior physical strength, which is contrasted with Yank's often-named bewilderment (192, 196, 225, 232) at almost everything that happens to him subsequent to his encounter with Mildred; and, finally, Yank's consciousness or understanding of *what* has happened to him and *why*, which is summed up in a concluding recognition speech that forever removes this character from the realm of the pathetic, the uninitiated, the witless, or the merely animalistic at the same time as it confers on him tragic dignity.

Ironically, Yank's consciousness was "given" to him by his nemesis Mildred, and it is fully expressed, ultimately, not to another human being but only to a gorilla and a chorus of monkeys:

> So yuh're what she seen when she looked at me, de white-faced tart! I was you to her, get me? On'y outa de cage—broke out—free to moider her, see? Sure! Dat's what she tought. She wasn't wise dat I was in a cage, too—worser'n yours—sure—a damn sight—'cause you got some chanct to bust loose—but me—. . . Youse can sit and dope dream in de past, green woods, de jungle and de rest of it. Den yuh belong and dey don't. . . . Sure, you're de best off! Yuh can't tink, can yuh? Yuh can't talk neider. But I kin make a bluff at talkin' and tinkin'—a'most git away wit it—a'most!—and dat's where de joker comes in. (229–230)

It is shortly after he speaks these words of recognition that Yank dies in the gorilla's cage of the Central Park Zoo, never having returned to the security of the stokehole on his ship: an alternative that was open to him but which he bravely did not, could not, or would not take. To the prison-house of self, in life, Yank seems to prefer death in a cage at the hands of a creature not quite of his own kind—yet still very much like him.

Works Cited

Emerson, Ralph Waldo. "The American Scholar." Address delivered before the Phi Beta Kappa Society, Cambridge, Mass., 31 Aug. 1837. In *Selections from Ralph Waldo Emerson: An Organic Anthology*. Ed. Stephen E. Whichler. New York: Houghton Mifflin, 1957. 63–80.

O'Neill, Eugene. *The Hairy Ape*. Three Plays: *Anna Christie, The Emperor Jones*, and *The Hairy Ape*. New York: Vintage, 1972. 161–232.

"Adamov's *Invasion* and the Absurd"

Arthur Adamov's second play, *The Invasion*, was written in 1948–1949 and published along with his first play, *The Parody* (written between 1945 and 1947), in 1950. It was Jean Vilar who recommended to the young author that he use the publication of the two works as a means of making a reputation for himself. The strategy worked and Adamov's name began to be known in literary circles. Through the patronage of wealthy benefactors, two of his plays were presented at the same time in Paris: directed by Vilar, *The Invasion* was performed at the Studio des Champs-Elysées on November 14, 1950, three days after the presentation of *The Large and the Small Maneuver* (1950),

Adamov's third work (whose title refers to the "small maneuver" of social disorder in contrast to the "large maneuver" of the human condition itself), at the Théâtre des Noctambules, directed by Jean-Marie Serreau.

With his second play, Adamov made a decided attempt to create characters who were more human and less schematic. The inspiration for the play may have come from a number of sources. The basic subject, that of a man trying to decipher the manuscript of a friend who has died, could very well have come from the death of Adamov's close acquaintance, Roger Gilbert-Lecomte. According to Roger Blin, Adamov had tried to gather together Gilbert-Lecomte's papers after his death but had found the task perplexing and, eventually, impossible (Gaudy, 32). It is also significant that Adamov was writing this play at the time of the death of Artaud (on March 4, 1948), and this, too, may have provided some of the inspiration. Or, as Geneviève Serreau suggests, Adamov may have thought of the case of Max Brod, who took charge of the writings of Kafka after he died in 1924 (Serreau, 71).

In this second work, the playwright is still pursuing the themes of *The Parody*, stressing again the lack of communication between people in this alien world, pointing out that the quest for meaning in life, or the meaning *of* life, is hopeless and that any search for a sense of metaphysical direction is a waste of time. Just as *The Parody* shows that all paths lead to failure, *The Invasion* takes up a variation on the theme, demonstrating that any specific effort by man to understand his earthly existence ends as an absurd act. This second play, richer and more human than the first work, is, as a result, more accessible also. Whereas *The Parody* is an abstract, almost lifeless presentation of an idea, *The Invasion* is a more direct, more immediate expression of the playwright's feelings. In an obvious self-criticism, Adamov emphasizes here the destructiveness of man's obsessions, which take hold of his life and make him useless. And the author individualizes the play more through limiting his subject to the family circle and underlining the plight of the writer who is rendered creatively and psychologically impotent by the "invasion" into his life of relatives and friends.

In *The Invasion*, Adamov follows a more traditional dramatic technique than he did in *The Parody*. The plot has a sense of progression and the characters are more substantial, although the dramatist makes no attempt to give them the solidity that they might possess in psychologically motivated drama. The action centers on the members of a family and the disruption in their lives caused by the manuscript of a writer, Jean, who has recently died. Jean has left his papers to Pierre, the husband of Jean's sister, Agnes. It is Pierre's responsibility to decipher the manuscript, but the task proves impossible: much of the writing is illegible or has simply faded with the passage of time. In addition, Tradel, Pierre's friend, who is also working on the project, does not mind inventing whatever he cannot understand, leaving the real interpretation more hopelessly jumbled than ever. While Pierre is entangled in this insurmountable project, his personal life has become a nightmare because of the never-ending "invasion" by others. His household is a series of disorders—seemingly caused by his wife, who is in constant conflict with Pierre's mother.

In the midst of all this, a man appears, looking for someone in the residence next door. This man, identified only as "the first one who comes along" or the First Caller (Doan, 64), stays in the apartment, invading Pierre's privacy even more. In an attempt to work in quiet, Pierre retreats first to a café, then to his room in the back of the apartment. At this point Agnes leaves her husband, setting out with "the first one who comes along." With this departure, order has been reestablished and the mother has become the dominant figure. However, Pierre has now decided to abandon his work. In an effort to show the complete futility of all that he has been doing, he tears up the manuscript and returns to his room, once again withdrawing from society. As he does so, Agnes reappears, asking to borrow his typewriter in addition to mentioning that her life with her lover has not worked out well, for he has fallen sick and she cannot manage his business. The mother refuses to allow Agnes to take the typewriter and the latter leaves. Tradel, in search of Pierre, finds him dead in his room, a suicide.

The Invasion may be a play about the hopeless search for ultimate meaning, but it is also concerned with order and disorder in society as well as the family. Agnes herself seems to stand for disorder. Has Pierre, in marrying her, not at the same time married her dead brother with his confused papers? When she initially leaves, order does return—and disorder as well as business failure enter the household of the man whose mistress she has become. Yet when Pierre subsequently abandons work on the manuscript, he dies. Moreover, he loses Agnes to "the first one who comes along" because he is retreating more and more from human contact. So the disorder that Agnes brings also represents the inevitably bewildering nature of reality and of relationships with other human beings, which Pierre is unable to cope with. He withdraws from contact with others because he finds communication more and more difficult.

Pierre even goes so far as to beg his mother, who will bring him his food in his room, never to speak to him—a sure sign of his complete withdrawal. It is only when he abandons his attitude of withdrawal, when he decides that he wants to lead a life like everyone else, that Pierre learns that Agnes has left him. "She left too late, or too soon. If she had had a little more patience, we could've begun again" (Doan, 73), he says, and returns to his room—to die, just missing Agnes, who comes to ask to borrow the typewriter (in a sterling instance of indirect dialogue) yet is clearly begging to be taken back. But Pierre's mother does not, or does not want to, understand, and fails to call Pierre. Here the tragedy turns on a misunderstanding, willful or not. Had Pierre's mother not taken Agnes's request for the typewriter literally, rather than as a symbolic entreaty to be taken back into the family, Pierre might not have died rejected and unloved.

In any event, it is the dead writer's manuscript that remains the center (like Lili, who acted as the axis in *The Parody*) around which the characters of *The Invasion* revolve. In essence, the manuscript is the image of the tragic situation of man, a symbol of what Richard Sherrell calls "the indiscernible meaning which invades life at its core" (Sherrell, 402). Or the manuscript symbolizes the unanswerable questions that haunt human life, such as: Why do we exist? Is there a God? And what is the purpose of life, its ultimate or transcendent meaning? Jean's papers represent just such a vain, disheartening quest for meaning in life. Pierre cannot determine what the man wrote, for the handwriting is unclear, and even if a sentence can be deciphered, it must be placed in the total context of the otherwise complete disordered papers. There is even the strong suggestion that if Pierre were to make some sense of the manuscript, such final "sense" might nonetheless be absurd or meaningless.

In addition, these papers have become an invasion of Pierre's own life. In his determination to understand their meaning, he is spending his time on what has become an unreasonable project, an obsession. Adamov implies that Jean's work is not meant to be deciphered, and, more significantly, Pierre does not even plan to publish his results if he were able to complete the task. In this way, the playwright expresses the total futility of an exaggerated devotion to an idea that harms the individual involved and that is of no benefit to others. The idea of being obsessed with something to the point of not functioning adequately as a human being—a topic most pertinent to Adamov's own life—would be repeated by the dramatist in later plays, notably in *Ping-Pong* (a 1955 commentary on mechanized society and the deification of the machine). At one moment, Pierre himself refers to this when he indicates his wish to lead a normal human existence again. Adamov thus seems to be pointing out that such a quest for meaning (i.e., the obsession to decipher the manuscript) becomes a means of escape rather than a way of living one's life. It is a flight from reality, an attempt to cover up the difficulties of existence.

The playwright also suggests that the manuscript's invasion of Pierre's life is reciprocated in turn by Pierre's own violation of Jean's past existence through his persistence in trying to understand the words of the dead writer. Jean wanted to destroy his own manuscript because it reminded him of what he had suffered. And it is in this context that we can understand Pierre's comment at the end of *The Invasion*, while tearing up the manuscript: "Forgive me for not having understood you sooner" (Doan, 73). It is also possible to interpret the sentence as an indication of Pierre's realization of the message that Jean might have wished to convey: the meaninglessness of everything in life, including the manuscript.

Pierre's work on the manuscript has been a series of frustrations and defeats, even more so because his life has been invaded on all levels, for all reasons: by his wife, who brings disorder; by his mother, who struggles with the wife for domination; by Tradel, who only adds imprecision to the difficult task of deciphering the manuscript; by the relatives of the dead man, who are suing over the use of Jean's papers; by "the first one who comes along," who takes Agnes away. The audience is meant to see, in a concrete, physical manner, this intrusion into Pierre's personal world and the disorder that it has created. Following Artaud's concept of filling up theatrical space—in which he maintained that "the stage is a tangible, physical place that needs to be filled, and it ought to be allowed to speak its own concrete language" (Artaud, 27) through "spatial poetry" (Artaud, 28) rather than through the merely spoken poetry of traditional drama—and Adamov's own desire to express verbal concepts through visual means, the playwright has indicated that the first sight the audience will see on stage is the complete untidiness and disarray of items, the visual aspect expressing the disorder in the situation and in the mind of Pierre. This confusion is then reflected in the use of language, which itself becomes more and more incomprehensible, seemingly disintegrating before Pierre's eyes, as he is unable to make any sense of what he is doing: "Why does one say: 'He is coming'? Who is this 'he'—what's he got to do with me? Why does one say: 'on' time, rather than 'at the' time? I've lost too much time thinking about such things. . . . I'm not going to look for anything anymore" (Doan, 70).

Yet, in this quest for normalcy, it is clear that order is not going to bring Pierre the peace of mind that he needs. With order comes the visible control of his mother, a control suggested on stage by her "voluminous" armchair, which becomes, little by little, the dominant, all-enveloping piece of furniture. Once the mother has rid the family of Agnes, the social fabric of the country has also rid itself of all of the "immigrants" who are crossing the border (themselves symbolic of social disorder), an ironical twist that Adamov must have inserted while thinking of his own days as an immigrant and meditating on the narrow-mindedness of those people who are afraid of others who are different. And with order comes a sense of sterility and hopelessness, perhaps even more agonizing than that associated with disorder. Now that Agnes apparently no longer has any use for Pierre, and now that he discovers that the manuscript can no longer be used as a basis for deciphering some sort of sense in life, existence holds not even a minimal sort of meaning, and Pierre's only response is suicide.

In this respect, *The Invasion* reflects Adamov's ambivalence about his own life. While seeking a rational, stable, day-to-day life, the writer also recognized that the very elements that might cause the disorder and seemingly stifle creativity were those which were also most needed for an artist's development. To a great extent, Pierre needs Agnes in spite of the chaos that she may bring with her, because, as noted, she also represents the very difficult, but necessary, world of human relationships. To attempt to be free of her, to rid oneself of human contact, particularly with a woman, is to deform the nature of the real world, in a sense to reenter the mother's womb. Such a situation is a flight from maturity, and for Pierre, like Adamov himself, this can only be a frightening experience. Indeed, much of the power of *The Invasion* comes from the combination of fear and frustration, adding up to despair, that Adamov created in Pierre—a despair that reflected the playwright's own tortured response to life.

The Invasion is a haunting drama. André Gide himself was deeply impressed by it; he felt that the play dealt with the greatness of a dead writer and the process by which his influence and power gradually fade away—surely a curious misunderstanding on the part of the venerable old man of letters, applying the conceptions of his own generation to the works of a new age. (Gide's tribute to Adamov, together with comments by other distinguished literary and stage figures like René Clair, Jacques Prévert, Roger Blin, and Jean Vilar, is contained in the slim volume *La Parodie, L'Invasion*, which, in the spring of 1950, presented Adamov's first two plays to the public before they were performed on the stage.) To a contemporary reader or spectator, by contrast, the most striking feature of *The Invasion* is precisely the unreality of the dead hero, the fact that his much vaunted message is essentially meaningless—absurd.

Works Cited

Adamov, Arthur. *La Parodie, L'Invasion*. Paris: Charlot, 1950.

Artaud, Antonin. *The Theater and Its Double*. Trans. Victor Corti. London: John Calder, 1970.

Doan, Robert J., trans. *The Invasion*, by Arthur Adamov. *Modern International Drama*, 22. 1 (1968): 59–75.

Gaudy, René. *Arthur Adamov*. Paris: Théâtre Ouvert, 1971.

Serreau, Geneviève. *Histoire du "nouveau theater"*. Paris: Gallimard, 1966.

Sherrell, Richard E. "Arthur Adamov and Invaded Man." *Modern Drama*, 7.4 (1965): 399–404.

2 Method and Manner

This section consists of short model, or sample, essays on the subject of dramatic method or manner. Treated here are the use of such devices as poetry, time, documentary, movement, and song in the advancing of a drama's action. The following plays have been chosen for their representativeness, variety, quality, and modernity (relative in the case of *A Yorkshire Tragedy*):

1. Bertolt Brecht's *Mother Courage, The Good Person of Setzuan, The Caucasian Chalk Circle,* and *Life of Galileo*
2. Harold Pinter's *The Birthday Party* and *Old Times*
3. Brendan Behan's *The Hostage*
4. Sam Shepard's *Curse of the Starving Class*
5. Anonymous's *A Yorkshire Tragedy*
6. Bernard Shaw's *Major Barbara*
7. Tennessee Williams' *A Streetcar Named Desire*

For reading and learning purposes, the "Key Analytical Question" below can be applied to any of the above plays or all of them.

Key Analytical Question: "How does a play use dramatic method—a manner of advancing its action through certain devices, techniques, and strategies—to create thematic meaning?"

"The Poetic Principle in Brecht's *Mother Courage, The Good Person of Setzuan, The Caucasian Chalk Circle,* and *Life of Galileo*"

"Monstrously delicate" is how Brecht described his poetry (Bentley, 8). The same might be said of Brecht's plays. I want to bring up this matter here, because it is extremely important for an appreciation of Brecht's work but one that has been given only scattered attention. I am speaking specifically of Brecht's *theatrical* poetry, his poetry of the theater, in Francis Fergusson's phrase (590 et passim), a poetry of theatrical elements and effects rather than words. Beyond the symbolic use of *mise-en-scène*, there are symbolic tropes and patterns of reference, some of which echo from one play to the next and reinforce each other's meaning. There are, for example, the recurring images of the cross and crucifixion in *Mother Courage and Her Children* (1941); the image returns in the flier's scene in *The Good Person of Setzuan* (1940) and in the Christ imagery that surrounds the beaten and bloody Azdak in the final scene of *The Caucasian Chalk Circle* (1945), giving Brecht access to received images of martyrdom, which he can then deploy in unexpected and partly ironic ways. In fact, Christian images abound in Brecht, not least in the holy-family echoes in the latter play and in its baptismal scene of Grusche's washing and dressing the child; Brecht's fascination with maternal instinct is thereby colored with a displaced religious reverence.

Not all these motifs can be said to have a precise denotation; some operate affectively and by intuition. There is, for example, the ominous motif of white faces, the origin of which (a suggestion by Karl Valentin) has been frequently repeated; it appears in Begbick's cosmetics in *Rise and Fall of the City of Mahagonny* (1930), in the faces of the soldiers in the prologue scenes of *The Good Soldier Schweik* (1943), in *Coriolanus* (1953), and elsewhere, as well as in Brecht's early poetry, where it is always associated with decay and death. Moreover, some of the symbols, or motifs, seem to change meaning from one play to another: milk and cheese are reminders of Galileo's unidealistic materiality, an aspect of his moral decline, yet the same products signify nurturing and protection in *The Caucasian Chalk Circle*—a play that dwells much on recurring images of milk, blood, and water: a maternalized poetic vocabulary for a play about maternalism. *Life of Galileo* (1939), too, claims its own symbolic tropes, appropriate to its subject: the sun and all other sources of light are used throughout as precise symbols of truth. Galileo's daughter—who at one point carries a shaded candle—faints at the sight of the sun when it is optically magnified and projected on a wall; and Galileo himself symbolically loses his capacity to see the light after his recantation.

One symbol that is put to exquisite use through intertextuality is that of snow. In *The Tutor* (1950), it serves as an explicit sign of the desire to let problems be covered up, concealed, and left uncorrected—an image of vicious complacency. Always, snow has a threatening quality.

It is a symbolic (as well as a physical) opponent to the hero in *The Good Soldier Schweik*, as is the wintry chill of *Mother Courage and Her Children*. Only once does snow become an affirmative presence—at the moment in *The Caucasian Chalk Circle* when Grusche, having rescued the child and fully realized its importance to her, describes the world with the eyes of one who has become newly maternal, and entirely generous:

> *Grusche (looking around at Michael)*: Never be afraid of the wind, it's only a poor devil like us. His job is pushing the clouds and he gets colder than anybody.
> (*Snow begins to fall.*)
> The snow isn't so bad either, Michael. Its job is covering the little fir trees so the winter won't kill them. And now I'll sing a song for you. Listen!
> (*Sings.*)
>
> Your father is a bandit
> And your mother is a whore
> Every nobleman and honest
> Will bow as you pass
> The tiger's son will
> Feed the little foals his brothers
> The child of the serpent
> Bring milk to the mothers. (177, *Collected Plays*, Vol. 7 [1971])

With this peculiar, unaccompanied song, Brecht shows a miracle beginning: imaginatively, Grusche's love transforms the world's evil into a momentary, idyllic vision, in a brilliantly composed and affecting image—made more powerful by its compression and by its subtle reference to related figures in other Brecht plays.

In fact, a fuller understanding of Brecht's stage will demand that we see it as a fully symbolized sphere, in which any routine element may unexpectedly take on special meaning, such as Mother Courage's non-progress on the moving turntable floor, or Galileo's Pope exiting into darkness. Like Ibsen, Brecht moved from a boldly poeticized language in his early plays to an apparent realism that nevertheless functions as a transmogrified poetry, a seemingly conventional dramaturgy internally polarized by ideational schemes and complex revelations of an "inner" meaning. For Ibsen, a spiritual meaning is evoked, whereas for Brecht it is more a vision of concrete social facts, but each is reached through a subtle and complex theatrical poetry that has been too long ignored.

Works Cited

Bentley, Eric. "The Brecht Memoir." *Theater*, 14.2 (Spring 1983): 4–26.

Brecht, Bertolt. *Collected Plays*. 9 vols. Ed. Ralph Manheim & John Willett. London: Methuen, 1977 (1970–2004).

Fergusson, Francis. "Poetry in the Theater and Poetry of the Theater: Cocteau's *Infernal Machine*" (1950). In *Literary Criticism—Idea and Act: The English Institute, 1939–1972; Selected Essays*. Ed. William K. Wimsatt. Berkeley: University of California Press, 1974. 590–601.

"Drama and Poetry in Pinter's *The Birthday Party* and *Old Times*"

More than most plays, Harold Pinter's *The Birthday Party* (1958) seems, finally, to be about six characters with secret knowledge about themselves and only partial knowledge of others and the world. These six meet and interact in the living room of the Boles house over a twenty-four-hour period, but nobody really gets to know anyone better and no character learns the reason for Goldberg and McCann's mission. Precisely because no character gets to know another one well and no character finds out or reveals what (if anything) Stanley has done wrong, the reader or spectator is held more by the characters themselves, by their elusiveness, than by the overt drama—the abduction of Stanley. The abduction of Stanley becomes an excuse, if you will, for displaying the characters' inscrutability. This inscrutability takes its extreme form in the anonymous "duets" of Goldberg and McCann, where Pinter blurs the identities of the two and multiplies their charges against Stanley, in order to discourage the audience from blaming the men individually for Stanley's abduction and from seeking to know the reason for it.

But inscrutability also takes subtle form in the speeches of four characters. Stanley, Meg, Goldberg, and McCann all speak about their pasts. Goldberg does this the most, Stanley a few times. Meg and McCann speak of their pasts once, in tandem, during the party:

> *McCann*: I know a place. Roscrea. Mother Nolan's.
> *Meg*: There was a night-light in my room, when I was a little girl.
> *McCann*: One time I stayed there all night with the boys. Singing and drinking all night.
> *Meg*: And my Nanny used to sit up with me, and sing songs to me.
> *McCann*: And a plate of fry in the morning. Now where am I?
> *Meg*: My little room was pink. I had a pink carpet and pink curtains, and I had musical boxes all over the room. And they played me to sleep. And my father was a very big doctor. That's why I never had any complaints.

> I was cared for, and I had little sisters and brothers in other rooms, all different colors. Tullamore, where are you? (60)

Paradoxically, speeches like these, in revealing something about the characters' pasts, reveal how little we actually know about these people, how much they keep to themselves. Ironically, Lulu and Petey, who do not speak of their pasts at all, seem the most knowable, the most familiar. They are never onstage together in *The Birthday Party*, and one suspects that this is through the playwright's design. If they were onstage together right before Stanley's departure, one would expect them to question Goldberg and McCann more incisively than each does alone and perhaps to get an answer or two. But it is not to Pinter's point to reveal why Goldberg and McCann have come to get Stanley or what Stanley has done to deserve abduction, so he keeps apart the two characters interested in obtaining this information. He is concerned above all to map his characters' opaqueness or mystery. To this end, he makes Lulu and Petey unknown to each other: neither speaks the other's name, and neither hears the other's name spoken. It is as if they come to the play from separate worlds. In the world of the play, they take their place among characters who call attention to one another by contrast rather than illuminate one another through conflict and disputation. Pinter wrote a poem titled "A View of the Party" (1958) about *The Birthday Party*:

> The thought that Goldberg was
> A man she might have known
> Never crossed Meg's words
> That morning in the room.
> . . .
> The thought that Goldberg was
> A man to dread and know
> Jarred Stanley in the blood
> When, still, he heard his name.
>
> While Petey knew, not then,
> But later, when the light
> Full up upon their scene,
> He looked into the room.
> . . .
> The thought that Goldberg was
> Sat in the center of the room,
> A man of weight and time,

> . . .
> And Stanley sat—alone,
> A man he might have known,
> Triumphant on his hearth,
> Which never was his own.
> . . .   (*Poems*, 34–36)

I would emphasize the title of this poem: "A *View* of the Party"; and I would also emphasize that Pinter felt the need to envision, or create an image of, his play in poetic form. This poem paints a word-picture of the Boles living room and its occupants. Poems, and paintings, can create images of action or behavior without having to explain the causes and effects. Plays have a harder time doing this, obviously, because in a play events occur in a certain order and spectators automatically look for connections in that order (as in "this happens because that happened"). One cannot help but feel that Pinter wrote a poem about *The Birthday Party* because he wished his play to be seen as a poem, as the *image* of an action rather than the *imitation* of one. "Image" here implies simultaneity, "imitation," sequentiality. And Pinter would probably compress the entire action of *The Birthday Party* into a single moment if he could, so that we would concentrate above all not on the "becauses" of, or reasons for, the drama, but on the simultaneous irreducibility and appeal of its characters and the topography of their relations. Just as Stanley seems to be an artist out of his element, Pinter seems in this play to be an artist out of his. Unlike Stanley, however, who fails to impose his will on hostile surroundings, the playwright successfully struggles to impose his painterly or poetic vision on a recalcitrant dramatic form.

Pinter also wrote a poem about *Old Times* (1971), called "All of That" (1971), which could be spoken by either of the play's three characters (Deeley, his wife Kate, and their visitor Anna) or by all of them at once:

> All of that I made
> And, making, lied.
> And all of that I hid
> Pretended dead.
>
> But all of that I hid
> Was always said,
> But, hidden, spied
> On others' good.

> And all of that I led
> By nose to bed
> And, bedding, said
> Of what I did
>
> To all of that that cried!
> Behind my head
> And, crying, died
> And is not dead.   (*Poems*, 39)

This poem compresses the action of *Old Times* into four stanzas; the phrase "all of that" occurs in each one (twice in the first stanza) and, through repetition, itself becomes the dominant image. (In "A View of the Party" the *characters*, in the living room, were the dominant image.) But of what is it an image? The sense of sex power over lives—shaking and shaming and exalting them—seems to be what remains after the play. The agony of affinities, unchosen but irresistible, is apparently what Pinter has caught in the slender filaments of his exquisitely distilled dialogue, his pauses and silences. Deeley and Kate and Anna are very much themselves; but they are also manifestations of a giant invisible force. And Pinter's writing is like a series of colored markers sent up to the surface of a sea by a deep danger below, the mere surface index of a huge, buried presence in us that has nothing to do with reason or explanation.

Yet even the mysteries of sexual desire don't encompass the huge, buried presence in *Old Time*s, and to call this presence "sexual," as I do above, is to clarify the stakes involved in Anna and Deeley's conflict, which are as elusive as they are deeply felt (by both the characters and the audience). A major source of difficulty for both critics and actors of this play is that Kate, Deeley, and Anna reveal an ambiguous past while interacting in a setting that suggests a real place:

> *A converted farmhouse.*
>
> *A long window up center. Bedroom door up left.*
>
> *Front door up right.*
>
> *Spare modern furniture.*
>
> *Two sofas. An armchair.* (6)

In this realistic setting we expect characters to provide substantial evidence of their pasts and of their relationships to one another in the past and present. Typically the past is ambiguous in Pinter's plays, so we may not expect to get all the answers we get in, say, Ibsen. But the very dramatic procedure of *Old Times* is that of unfolding the ambiguous past, and the play's subject is memory. We find the procedure and the subject disconcerting because the play's set is realistic. As we observe Deeley, Kate, and Anna "merely" talk to one another in Deeley and Kate's living room (and, in the second act, their bedroom), we want to piece together the information they reveal into the story of their lives. Indeed, the contradictions between Anna's and Deeley's memories heighten this tendency: we think we are working out a kind of puzzle of character histories and relationships.

To treat *Old Times* as a puzzle, however, is to try to resolve a tension fundamental to the play's mysteries, a tension between real space and other, figurative spaces that are this work's main concern: the space between self and being, between being and being with others, between being and having been with others. Pinter sustains this tension between real and what might be called ontological space in order to fuel the interaction among Anna, Kate, and Deeley and to transform them into figures in a drama about the essence of experience. The "spare modern furniture" of Kate and Deeley's home incarnates life pared down to that essence. And *Old Times* is best served by a set that suggests an actual country home without seeming to *be* that home. Such a set intimates that what is being dramatized does indeed occur in such homes, is true to the actuality of our experience, and yet takes place in virtually imperceptible realms of that experience.

Of special relevance to our experience of what I am calling this drama of essence or even of the invisible is that we must attend to its motions and not meanings; we must observe its figures of action without supplying a "ground" that explains their motion. We must stay with what emerges before us; we must remain *within* the play, allowing its tensions to work on us. The invisible drama of *Old Times* arises from the interaction of words and silences, which build upon one another to bring a heightened world into being. If we fill in information that we don't learn from what Anna, Deeley, and Kate say, we do so at the risk of deadening our capacity to respond to that world. For Pinter has written the play as if it were a test for the *audience's* poetic imagination, for the kind of patience required to witness and experience fully a poem that creates itself word by word, line by line.

"All of That," Pinter's poem about *Old Times*, itself is just such a poetic vision of the giant invisible force I have spoken of. And Deeley, Kate, and Anna are the "colored markers" of it; like figures in a painting, they suggest more than they can ever reveal. Like Stanley,

Deeley (who is a film director) is an artist out of his element—in this case, nudged out of it by Anna in the struggle for possession of Kate. Like the Pinter of *The Birthday Party,* the Pinter of *Old Times* seems to be an artist out of *his* element, again imposing a painterly or poetic vision, one of evocation instead of revelation, on the dramatic form.

Pinter did not write poems about all his plays, but, I would submit, much of his work can be looked at as poetic or painterly, as an attempt to delineate rather than explain. Thus one can speak, as I have done, of *Old Times* as dramatizing not so much the inexplicable as the invisible. And *The Birthday Party* might best be described as dramatizing the unknowable, the impenetrable. Indeed, I don't think it is any accident that the more we have come to realize—from, say, the 1990s to the second decade of the twenty-first century—that much about the world defies explanation (including, most obviously, its ultimate reason for being) even if human existence itself is not "absurd," the less popular Pinter has become. (He had begun writing plays in the late 1950s.) His later plays appear tired and repetitive (when not being overtly political), as if they were telling us something that we already knew. We did, of course, thanks in large part to Harold Pinter.

Works Cited

Pinter, Harold. *The Birthday Party* and *The Room*. New York: Grove Press, 1968.

——. *Old Times*. London: Methuen, 1971.

——. *Poems*. London: Enitharmon Press, 1971.

"Time in Behan's *The Hostage*"

Set in a Dublin brothel in the late 1950s, Brendan Behan's *The Hostage* (1958) in fact satirizes the Irish Republican Army's fanatical nationalism and senseless glorification of the past, while asserting through song, dance, and love (between the Irish maid Teresa and the English soldier Leslie) the worth and community of all human souls. Leslie, the hostage of the title, is to be shot in reprisal by the I.R.A. (Irish Republican Army) if one of its members being held in Belfast Jail is executed by the British. Leslie's captors themselves are hostages of the past, of a political program that has lost its urgency in a world threatened by economic depression, on the one hand, and nuclear destruction, on the other. (That the I.R.A.'s headquarters in *The Hostage* is a brothel, moreover, is its own comment on the iniquity and frivolousness of this organization's cause.)

Ironically, Leslie is killed by a random bullet at the end of play, in a gunfight between rebels and the police: in other words, by the situation as a whole that exists between England and Ireland, and between the legal government of Ireland and the Irish Republican Army. The former I.R.A. soldier Pat is mistaken, however, when he responds to Teresa's line, "But [Leslie's] dead," with, "So is the boy in Belfast Jail" (182). The boy in Belfast Jail is *not* dead yet; he will not be executed until 8 A.M (92). This is important, because it means that Leslie died *before* he was supposed to, according to the rules of reprisal, and that, whether Leslie was randomly killed or not, the I.R.A is still responsible for his (premature) death.

What time is it at the end of *The Hostage*? Teresa says that it is only 11 P.M. (177); Pat says that it is closer to 1 A.M. (177). Either way, it is not 8 A.M. or later—stage time is not *that* flexible—and Leslie has died before his time.

Work Cited
Behan, Brendan. *The Quare Fellow* and *The Hostage*. New York: Grove Press, 1964.

"Sleep and Shepard's *Curse of the Starving Class*"

For long periods of time in Sam Shepard's *Curse of the Starving Class* (1976), either Weston or Ella lies asleep onstage while the action of the play continues unabated. Weston, very drunk after a night away from home, falls asleep on the kitchen table in Act II; Ella, exhausted after a night spent in jail attending to her daughter, Emma, falls asleep on the same kitchen table in Act III.

Having a character fall asleep onstage and remain out of the way of the other characters, so as not to draw focus, is one thing; having a character fall asleep center stage, as Shepard does, so *as* to draw focus, is quite another. The fact that shouting and arguing go on around both sleeping characters draws attention all the more to their dormant condition, since neither awakens. Both Weston and Ella are apparently deep sleepers; either that, or Shepard is using their sleep as a metaphor, making them sleep through shouting and arguing so as to suggest something about the way in which this husband and wife have conducted their lives up to the point where the play begins.

The point, actually, is less that Weston and Ella sleep through shouting and arguing than that they sleep imperviously through some events that will have a major effect on their lives. While Weston is asleep, for example, Ella returns from a night out, presumably with the lawyer Taylor, thinking that she has sold the family property right out from under her husband; then Ellis, the bar owner, appears with the money he agreed to pay *Weston* for the property, keeping that money—which would have got Weston out of debt—when he discovers that Emma has severely damaged his bar in a retaliatory shooting spree. While Ella is asleep, Weston leaves for Mexico to escape his creditors, and Emma steals her mother's money and her car so that she can begin a life of crime. (The hoodlums Emerson and Slater blow up the car, and Emma with it, because the car has never been paid for in full.)

Weston and Ella thus sleep through events that will profoundly impact their lives, even as, Shepard suggests, they have "slept through" important events or decisions in their lives in the past. That is why they are in the position in which they find themselves at the start of *Curse of the Starving Class*: their marriage is a shambles, they are in heavy debt, and each dreams of escape: Weston to Mexico and Ella to Europe. One could even say that these two have slept through their own relationship, for they don't communicate with each other—or with the world, for that matter. To underline the lack of communication between Weston and Ella, Shepard gives them only one scene in which they actually speak to each other. It comes in Act III, after their son, Wesley, has gone to take a bath; the rest of the time, they're either not in each other's presence or, as I point out above, one is asleep and the other is not.

Both Weston and Ella wake up from their deep sleeps in what might be construed a contrived fashion. Weston just happens to wake up at the end of Act II, after Taylor has run off, Ellis has left with the money and Wesley has chased after him, and Ella has decided to go to the police station to retrieve Emma. Ella, for her part, just happens to wake up after Weston has left her and his children for good and Emma has fled with her mother's money. I myself, however, view these awakenings as dramatic device rather than artistic contrivance. That is, the awakenings of Weston and Ella, just moments too late, hint that these two have habitually "awakened" to their problems too late—and that they've awakened to their situation in the play, if they can be said to have really awakened to it at all, too late.

Work Cited
Shepard, Sam. *Curse of the Starving Class*. In Shepard's *Seven Plays*. New York: Bantam, 1981. 133–200.

"Docudrama, God, and *A Yorkshire Tragedy*"

Modern though the earliest domestic tragedies are, from a journalistic point of view, they are not modern in the same sense as realistic and naturalistic social-problem plays. For, although the former are concerned with middle-class family relationships that are unhappy enough to end in disaster, their action is contained within a Christian frame of reference in which God's providence and justice are paramount, rather than a socio-psychological one that examines the earthly causes of adultery, alcoholism, gambling, and the like. This summary definition applies equally to the anonymous *A Yorkshire Tragedy* (1605–8), on the one hand, and to the anonymous *Arden of Faversham* (1592) and Thomas Heywood's *A Woman Killed with Kindness* (1603), on the other. Yet there is a notable difference between *A Yorkshire Tragedy* and the other two plays. For *Arden of Faversham* and Heywood's drama are influenced by the tradition of Catholic moral drama, as they are directed toward penitence and the hope of salvation.

In these works the expected mercy of a loving God makes the disaster—whether it is the destruction of human life or the violation of the sanctity of marriage—terrestrial and finite. The earthly tragedy dissolves in the light of eternity, since the soul's salvation is assured for those who truly repent, even for those who commit the crime of murder. *A Yorkshire Tragedy*, however, is altogether different in purpose, for it is a drama of the soul's damnation. The tragedy, beginning in this world and lasting for all eternity, is devastatingly complete. This kind of play, which dramatizes the ultimate Christian tragedy, also belongs to a tradition—the aforementioned one of "warning" literature, or teaching by negative example. Already established in the Cain, Herod, and Judgment plays of the fifteenth-century Catholic Biblical cycles, this tradition re-emerged in sixteenth-century Protestant morality plays such as William Wager's *Enough Is as Good as a Feast* (ca. 1570). The full flowering of the tradition is subsequently found in Christopher Marlowe's *Doctor Faustus* (1592).

A Yorkshire Tragedy's "negative example" was Walter Calverley, called only the Husband in the play (perhaps out of fear of offending the families involved in the actual tragedy, but also from the desire to create a homiletic "type" out of him). Head of a well-known Yorkshire family, Calverley (born 1579) had, on April 23, 1605, killed his two, older sons, one not yet five years old and the other but a year-and-a-half. Moreover, he had seriously wounded his wife and set out to kill his remaining son, who was being nursed some miles away. Walter was apprehended, however, before he could bring his plan to completion.

He was then brought before two Justices of the Peace, to whom he stated as his motive for murder the suspected infidelity of his wife and illegitimacy of her children. Yet, at his trial Walter stood mute and would make no plea. He was therefore forced to undergo *la peine forte et dure* ("strong and hard punishment"). This was because British law, until well into the eighteenth century, required that a defendant charged with a felony enter a plea of guilty or not guilty before the trial could proceed: if he did not so plead, he was stretched out and pressed with heavy stones or iron weights until he either pleaded or died. So it was that Walter Calverley remained silent and was pressed to death on August 5, 1605.

In June 1605, a pamphlet appeared recounting his crime and ending with the fact of the murderer's imprisonment. The extant pamphlet, the anonymous *Two Most Unnaturall and Bloodie Murthers*, tells the Calverley story in its first half and in its second recounts a similar matter involving a Mistress Browne who murdered her husband. The Calverley narrative begins with Walter's betrothal to the daughter of his neighbor and tells how he was forced by his guardian instead to marry his guardian's niece. This aspect of the story has been shown to be historically untrue, but it was this aspect that most interested George Wilkins, the author of the other play on the Calverley theme, *The Miseries of Enforced Marriage*, published in 1607.

Wilkins' play is a sociological treatise of sorts on the subject of its title: the hero, Scarborrow (a.k.a. Calverley), mistreats his family and treads a prodigal path because of the enforced marriage. But, despite being described in *The Stationers' Register* as "A tragedie" on July 31, 1607, *The Miseries of Enforced Marriage* is a tragi*comedy*. A tragic climax, in which Scarborrow murders spouse and children, is miraculously averted at the last moment by the arrival of the news that he has inherited a fortune from his guardian. Husband and wife are then reconciled and all ends happily.

All does not end happily in *A Yorkshire Tragedy*, although it, too, like the pamphlet *Two Most Unnaturall and Bloodie Murthers*, concludes on a note of indecision, with Calverley being led off to prison to await trial, and with his wife resolving to do all she can to save her husband from execution. At some stage, in fact, *A Yorkshire Tragedy* was created directly out of the pamphlet, being directly dependent on it not only for episodes and details from the story but also for its phrasing and vocabulary. Except in its superfluous first scene (of low comedy), the play has turned third-person narrative into dialogue with slavish fidelity, often merely versifying the original. It is reasonable, then, to infer that the play was written and staged before the end of the story was known—that is, within three months of the actual murders. In any event, the date of composition of *A Yorkshire Tragedy* is firmly bracketed between June 12, 1605, when its prose source was entered in *The Stationers' Register*, and May 2, 1608, when the play itself was entered.

Although the drama owes its structure and much of its wording to its prose source, the best things in it are the playwright's own. In various ways he contrives to transform a humdrum tale of murder into a short, swift play of tragic force. One way in which he does this is to deal with both place and time in a more concentrated fashion than the writer of the pamphlet. In the pamphlet the action begins "within the Countie of Yorke, not farre from Wakefield" (Sturgess, 10), moves to London with Calverley's departure and subsequent marriage to his guardian's niece, and returns at some unspecified time to Yorkshire, where it stays except for Mistress Calverley's visit to her uncle in London. The playwright, by contrast, localizes all the action "i'th' country" (i.62; 55), either in the Husband's house or its vicinity; and there is a gain in intensity through the restriction of the play's action to the house until after the murders.

Moreover, *Two Most Unnaturall and Bloodie Murthers* covers a period of about four years, beginning while Calverley is still a ward and lasting until the eldest of his three children is four years old. Scene i of *A Yorkshire Tragedy* indicates the passage of the preceding four years by getting Sam to tell his fellow servants that their young master's marriage has produced "two or three children" (i.40; 54). From Scene ii onward the speed of events never slackens: the scenes all follow hard on one another, and even the Wife's visit to her uncle, by being reported, is not allowed to slow down the action. This telescoping of events has the effect of giving not only speed, but also urgency to the action. In addition, the reported visit allows a fierce irony to be achieved through the juxtaposition of the Husband's brutal threats at the end of Scene ii with the Wife's newfound optimism in the reporting speech that opens Scene iii.

The playwright amplifies as well as abbreviates his source material, however, and his amplifications have two effects. One is the strengthening of the characterization of both the Wife and the Husband. This the author does through the convention of the "lament," the set-piece speech of lamentation that is a widespread feature of Elizabethan drama and which, at its most characteristic, makes use of a series of accepted formulas and rhetorical figures. There are four laments in *A Yorkshire Tragedy*: the Wife's soliloquy with which Scene ii opens (ii.1–24; 57–58); another soliloquy by the Wife at the end of Scene iii (iii.78–94; 71–72); the Husband's soliloquy in Scene iv, which is the turning point of the play (iv.55–91; 75–77); and the Husband's speeches of lamentation and repentance in the last scene as he mourns over his dead children and injured wife.

These "laments" raise the emotional tone of the tragedy and heighten the characterization, by making articulate the otherwise unvoiced anxieties and sorrows of the characters' inner selves (though in the interest of moral exposition or expostulation, not of realistic character portrayal as such). Compare, for just one example, the fluent paternal grief of the last scene with the pamphlet's description of Walter Calverley upon seeing his dead little boys: "He was melted into water and had not power to take any farewell of them but only in tears" (Sturgess, 32). *Two Most Unnaturall and Bloodie Murthers* is true to life, then; but *A Yorkshire Tragedy* is true to dramatic representation.

The second and most significant effect of the dramatist's amplifications is the development of the theme of diabolic possession. The title page of *Two Most Unnaturall and Bloodie Murthers* presents a woodcut of the murder scene: Calverley inappropriately wields a club, his wife and two children lie prostrate, and a dog slinks away in the background. But, most interestingly, on the left side of the picture is a devil figure surveying the action. Surprisingly, the pamphlet itself makes no mention of the demonic possession of Calverley, though this is a recurrent motif in other "warning" literature. The theory of demonic possession, besides being good theology and ethics, was also good psychology: it could account for fits, neuroses, and implacable evil with the same satisfying swiftness. The author of *A Yorkshire Tragedy* has incorporated this idea carefully and consistently, so that it becomes a theme of the play and an analysis or explanation of the Husband's behavior.

The idea of the devil's work is hinted at in Scene ii (ii.146; 65), and it is taken up by the servingman of Scene iii (iii.24–26; 69). The "lusty" servant of Scene v gives added force to the idea in his struggle with the Husband (v.35; 80), and he finds no other explanation than diabolic possession for the Husband's strength (v.40; 81). The devil's presence is also noted by the soliloquizing servant of Scene vii (vii.2–6; 82), by the same servant to the Wife (vii.27–28; 83), and by the Knight (ix.7; 87). In the last scene, the Husband himself recognizes the fact of his possession and vividly describes being freed from it:

> [N]ow glides the devil from me,
> Departs at every joint, heaves up my nails.
> Oh, catch him new torments that were ne'er invented;
> Bind him one thousand more, you blessed angels,

> In that pit bottomless. Let him not rise
> To make man act unnatural tragedies[.]
>
> (x.18–23; 90)

Here, then, is the dominant theme of *A Yorkshire Tragedy*: the Husband's spiritual consumption, which is first detected by his wife (ii.16–21; 58) and which suggests to her the possibility of demonic possession. The source pamphlet has all the other themes of the play—the Husband's squandering of his money as well as his good name on dicing and dissoluteness, his groundless suspicion and brutal treatment of his wife, the beggaring of his children, his unnatural conduct toward his brother—but the theme of spiritual beggary and diabolic possession represents the playwright's own attempt to account for the prodigal husband's behavior. The writer of the pamphlet makes clear that Calverley commits his monstrous crime in a fit of madness; but to the dramatist the Husband is suffering from a disease worse than madness. His malady is identified by his wife as "beggary of the soul" (ii.36; 59), and it is she who first observes that her husband behaves "as if some vexed spirit / Had got his form upon him" (ii.38–39; 59).

The devil presumably begins to take possession of the Husband some time after Scene ii, and probably does so because of the Husband's crazy desire for revenge on a completely innocent person: his wife (ii.180–183; 67). (Up to the end of this scene he still has his normal strength, as he is wounded and brought to the ground by the Gentleman.) And the process of possession probably becomes complete in Scene iv, just after the meeting between the Husband and the Master of the College, and right before the murders are committed. The Husband has been physically humiliated by the Gentleman, who spares his life but makes him listen, at sword's point, to a homily on his sins; and he has been spiritually humiliated by the Master, whose solemn diatribe on the Husband's shameful treatment of his brother fills him with self-loathing. Now at his lowest ebb, morally as well as materially, the Husband is thus ripe for possession. The devil has been on his lips before (ii.52, 60; iii.70, 71), but here, for the first time, he is willing to "take up money upon his soul, / Pawn his salvation" (iv.88–89; 77). In effect, he pawns his soul to the devil; the murders immediately follow; and the Husband displays a new, monstrous strength that only the devil can have given him.

He may be dispossessed of that strength, and the devil, in the final scene; he may have achieved spiritual illumination and a return to humanity, largely because of his wife's unexpected kindness toward him. But the Husband's hopelessness and boundless despair remain.

MODEL ESSAYS

(On these matters, and certainly on the matter of dispossession, *Two Most Unnaturall and Bloodie Murthers* does not touch.) It is not simply that his position is hopeless in this world—his children dead, his wife lost to him, and execution waiting. The Husband's despair stretches from this world to the next, for he is guilty of the deadly sin of despairing of God's grace (x.36–42, 91; x.47–48, 91; x.52, 92; x.57–58, 92). He has no hope of escaping eternal punishment for his crime, since his repentance, although it includes acknowledgment of sin and contrition for it, excludes the trust in God's mercy that is needed to make atonement complete. Like Marlowe's Faustus, the Husband believes himself to be damned, and sees no loophole through which his soul can escape to salvation. He is freed from diabolic influence, then, but his spiritual defeat endures.

By emphasizing the Husband's acceptance of eternal damnation as his lot, *A Yorkshire Tragedy* departs not only from the source pamphlet, but also from such a murder play as the anonymous *Two Lamentable Tragedies* (1601). The latter ends with scaffold speeches of repentance in which the murderers, before paying the extreme worldly penalty for their crime, express trust in divine mercy. Plays like *Two Lamentable Tragedies* are basically moral in outlook; they are Christian penitential works that stress the efficacy of full and sincere repentance. Dramas of this kind cannot be tragedies, unless the term "tragedy" is applied to any play that ends in death for the protagonist. For they offer clear, obvious solutions to the problem of man's relation to God and show the way to escape the ultimate Christian tragedy of the soul's damnation.

A Yorkshire Tragedy, however, sets out to dramatize this very tragedy: the devil supplants God in the Husband's soul and body; the Husband lives for a time in a world of violent words as well as actions; and from him is exacted in the end the double penalty of the body's death and the soul's extinction. Superficially, this play may seem to have the conventional morality pattern of sin, even sin intensified or magnified, followed by final repentance. But in fact there is nothing resembling true or perfect repentance at the end of *A Yorkshire Tragedy*. In one sense it is a grim parody of the morality play, for it shows what may happen in real life, as distinct from what is made to happen in the carefully composed, compensatory or wish-fulfilling picture of life presented by the moral dramatist. In any event, *A Yorkshire Tragedy* looks for a theological explanation for Calverley's ruinous course—not a sociological one.

Works Cited

Anonymous. *Two Most Unnaturall and Bloodie Murthers*. London: V. Simmes & Nathanael Butler, 1605.

Arber, Edward, ed. *A Transcript of the Registers of the Company of Stationers of London 1554–1640 A.D.* 5 vols. London: Privately printed, 1875–94.

Sturgess, Keith, ed. & intro. *Three Elizabethan Domestic Tragedies*. 1969. Harmondsworth, UK: Penguin, 2012.

Wilkins, George. *The Miseries of Enforced Marriage*. 1607. New York: AMS Press, 1970.

A Yorkshire Tragedy. Ed. A. C. Cawley & Barry Gaines. Manchester, UK: Manchester University Press, 1986.

"Transfiguration and Ascent in Shaw's *Major Barbara*"

Deeply embedded in Christian theology is a tension between life in the world and life beyond it. Christ, as the manifestation of God, enters the world in the humblest form imaginable to live among human beings as a teacher and healer; however, underlying the story of his Passion—by far the most dramatic portion of his life—is the impulse to escape this world for another, more satisfying one. The flogging and crucifixion underscore the "man-ness," some would say "mean-ness," of Christ's existence on earth, but the resurrection and ascension point toward deliverance from worldly constraints. The belief that ascent towards God, in the "other world," is humanity's natural destination finds reflection in the medieval chain of being, which is organized hierarchically from the natural to the supernatural. Man, in imitation of Christ, must operate in the world but at the same time seeks ultimately to leave it, and, cleansed of his sins, his departure is always seen as an ascent—a release from the earth's gravity.

Bernard Shaw's plays themselves—among them *Major Barbara* (1905), *Misalliance* (1910), and *Saint Joan* (1923)—sometimes reflect the tension between gravity and ascent that makes up so much of the legacy of Christian thought. The use of these motifs should not be surprising in the work of a dramatist whom J. Percy Smith has described as "not only a profoundly religious man but a profoundly religious playwright" (74). Their presence in his plays, however, also suggests something of the inner conflict of the artist who would transcend his art—become, as it were, his own audience—at the same that he creates it. Comedy requires more detachment from life, or more objectivity toward it, than most forms of art, as many critics have observed, and Shaw's own detachment, his would-be transcendence, results in a comic style that is more remotely contemplative than directly experiential. Even at the height of emotional involvement, his characters are able to pull up short in order to speculate about their own condition or to question the nature of their next action. Not every rhetorical or "set" speech in Shaw's *oeuvre* is an instance of a character's transcendence to a higher realm of the intellect or the spirit, but these speeches nonetheless are often evidence of a schism between a character and the world of his or her play—a schism that deepens as Shaw's theory of Creative Evolution, with its own schism between Darwinism and mystical will, begins to take shape.

My purpose is not to trace Shaw's relationship with Christianity, yet I must emphasize that the theater for Shaw was more than a means toward social progress. It was, Shaw wrote in *Our Theatres in the Nineties*, "a temple of the Ascent of Man" (vi), a place "where two or three are gathered together" (Preface to *Major Barbara*, 1009). In the lay sermon "The New Theology," which he delivered in London on May 16, 1907, Shaw outlined a religious hierarchy of being that has its origins in his own plays:

> If there are three orders of existence—man as we know him, the angels higher than man, and God higher than the angels—why did God first create something lower than himself, the angels, and then actually create something lower than the angels, man? I cannot believe in a God who would do that. If I were God, I should try to create something higher than myself, and then something higher than that, so that, beginning with a God the higher thing in creation, I should end with a God the lowest thing in creation. (312)

This is, of course, a radical inversion of other systems of belief, but Shaw's model still retains a vertical quality. Unfortunately, as he writes further in "The New Theology," the "continual struggle to create something higher and higher," to make social as well as spiritual progress, has been marred by "innumerable experiments and innumerable mistakes" (313), such that the tension between gravity and ascent has continued to inhere in human existence. My interest here is in some of the moments in Shaw's dramaturgy, specifically in *Major Barbara*, when the balance between these two forces cannot be sustained, and the impulse toward escape or release catapults his characters upward into a realm of "otherness."

Since I use the word "transfiguration" in my title, however, it is necessary to return to Christian theology in order to define this term more completely. The story of Christ's transfiguration is told in three of the Gospels (Matthew 17:1–9, Mark 9:2–8, and Luke 9:28–36) and varies little from version to version. The chief points worth noting about this event are that it begins in prayer at a high place, on a mountain, and that it grows into an intense religious experience—during which Jesus speaks with Moses and Elijah and is called "Son" by a voice in the sky assumed to be God the Father—only dimly perceived by the apostles Peter, John, and James. The aura of unnatural brilliance that surrounds Christ at the moment of transfiguration (he takes on, in all three Gospels, an "unearthly appearance") foreshadows his appearance as the Messiah after the resurrection. But just as important as the transfiguration itself is the event's context within Christ's tenure on earth. The transfiguration follows directly after the feeding of the multitudes and the healing of the blind man. It is one of the few moments of meditative escape from the constant activity surrounding Christ before his entrance into Jerusalem; as soon as he descends from the mountain, he is again caught up in the sickness of the world as he is called upon to cast out the demon from an epileptic boy.

Two contrasting views of the transfiguration can be found in Fra Angelico's and Raphael's paintings, the one a static presentation of the event, the other a dramatic representation of it. Fra Angelico's Christ stands on sculptured rock, surrounded by an aura of pure white, with his hands outspread in prefiguration of the crucifixion to come. His separation from the kneeling apostles here is complete, except for a downward glance that suggests his continuing attachment to the beings who cower in terror below him. This *Transfiguration* (1438–1445)—painted as a fresco for an individual cell in the Monastery of San Marco—presents a single, contemplative subject from which the rest of the world is in retreat. Raphael's *Transfiguration of Christ* (1517), by contrast, depicts both Jesus's glory and his gloom, or the gloom that continues to pervade his life on earth. Christ is in mid-air, his arms and head raised to the heavens as if to greet the divinity above him. But down below, the windswept apostles, in the foreground, impatiently await his return as their confused gesturing envelops the demon-possessed boy and his father. The world beneath Christ in this instance is dark—only half-lit by the radiance of his transfiguration.

Raphael's version of the transfiguration, then, more dramatically captures the eruption of the spirit toward privacy or solitude, away from the strictures of the demanding society of men. A similar moment is captured in the last scene of *Major Barbara* as the now enlightened Barbara, stripped both of her uniform and her idealism by her realist father, begins her new mission of saving human souls without the "bribe of bread" (1055). Shaw describes a scene of visual contrast here: "an emplacement of concrete, with a firestep, and a parapet which suggests a fortification" (1047), overlooks the town of Perivale St. Andrews, which is spotlessly clean and "only needs a cathedral to be a heavenly city instead of a hellish one" (1047). Included in this otherwise pristine picture are the instruments of war—a huge cannon, sheds for explosives, and dummy soldiers who, "more or less mutilated, with straw protruding from their gashes" (1047) and strewn about like grotesque corpses, are constant reminders of the destructive forces controlled by the gigantic "creative" will of which Andrew Undershaft is a part.

Barbara herself stands on the firestep, "looking over the parapet towards the town" (1047). Often during the scene she is above the action, and at one point she steps onto the mounted cannon so that her father must reach up to grasp her hand. Shaw's placement of Barbara on the parapet and on the cannon, where she is above the earthly powers at her feet yet still connected to them, suggests the imprisonment (by her father) in a tower of the Christian saint of the same name. And it is no accident that these two Barbaras are linked, for St. Barbara is the patron saint of the hour of death and liberation from the prison-house of earth.

Barbara is silent in this scene until Cusins declares the circumstances of his birth, but her presence is noted by Shaw as Undershaft announces the death of 300 soldiers and follows this announcement by "kicking a prostrate dummy brutally out of his way" (1047). At this moment Barbara and Cusins exchange glances, and when Cusins sits on the step and buries his face in his hands, "Barbara gravely lays her hand on his shoulder" (1047) in Shaw's stage direction. As Cusins subsequently explains his status as a foundling, Barbara climbs onto the cannon and remains there during most of what has been called "Undershaft's apologia." Only when her father takes her hands and demands a definition of power does Barbara finally confess her anxiety—how she waits in "dread and horror" (1050) for the second shock of the figurative earthquake that has caused her world to reel and crumble around her.

Barbara then reverses herself by erupting with "sudden vehemence" (1051) in response to her father's scoffing remark about her "tinpot tragedy," and demands that he show her "some light through the darkness of this dreadful place" (1051). Shaw has been careful throughout to present this "dreadful place" as beautiful, blemish-free, and enlightened, both in his stage directions and through Sarah's, Stephen's, Lomax's, and Lady Britomart's surprised and even possessive approval of Perivale St. Andrews. But Barbara, the divine spark in the play (Cusins declares, "I adored what was divine in her, and was therefore a true worshipper" [1049]), reveals the correct perception of this gleaming factory town. Though it may bask in middle-class morality and the respectability that comes with it, Perivale St. Andrews remains the home of a dreadful factory of death and destruction. By the end of the play, though, it will have become the object of Barbara's energy, the demonic child from which she herself will cast out the devil.

Barbara's relative silence during this scene, in contrast with Undershaft's and Cusins' loquacity, suggests that her focus is turning inward. Her responses become increasingly reflective, seeming to arise out of a sedate, even somber mood—and responses like this from a character who, for the two previous acts, has been vigorously outspoken, rhetorically persuasive, and charmingly humorous. When Lady Britomart demands that they leave, since the father of the family is obviously "wickeder than ever" (1052), Barbara's rejoinder is simple and soft-spoken: "It's no use running away from wicked people, mamma" (1052). The word "wicked" is repeated here, though subtly altered, as Shaw contrasts Lady Britomart's superficial objection to Undershaft's social behavior with Barbara's heartfelt insight not only into her father's character, but into the major premise of the play—that "there is no wicked side. Life is all one" (1054).

In the final scene the trio of Undershaft, Barbara, and Cusins is reduced to a duet, yet Barbara's questions and responses continue to give no hint of what her final action will be. Cusins' own rationalized defense of his decision to join Undershaft grows more and more assertive, until his final cry is characterized by the repeated use of the first person: "Dare I make war on war? I dare. I must. I will" (1054). When he then turns and asks Barbara if their relationship is over, in "evident dread of her answer" (according to Shaw's stage direction [1054]), she replies, "Silly baby Dolly! How could it be!" (1054). She has answered Cusins' weakness in the only way her nurturing nature will allow, but the "levity" (1054) of his response, as Shaw describes it (and which understandably would follow his previous dread) is too indelicate for the intensity of the moment. Accordingly, Barbara reacts by transcending in word and thought the "mereness" of the world: "Oh, if only I could get away from you and from father and from it all! if I could have the wings of a dove and fly away to heaven!" (1054).

Barbara is thus gradually transfigured, as the pull of her mission raises her above the paltry concerns of her family and lover to reveal the agony of the soul who finally faces evil without illusions, who must endure evil "whether it be sin or suffering" (1054). The second act of this play has removed the "bribe of bread," and in her transfiguration in Act III Barbara dismisses the "bribe of heaven" (1055), for God's work is to be done "for its own sake" (1055). Moreover, in indirect reference to the quotation above from Shaw's unique "new theology," Barbara vows that she will forgive God—an inversion that places her higher than the Creator, since He will now be in her debt.

Like the apostles in the Raphael painting, Cusins has become a disciple at her feet, and his question, "Then the way of life lies through the factory of death?" (1055) elicits from Barbara the mystical outpouring that has puzzled so many, and that can itself be explained as a gloss on Shaw's new hierarchy of being: "Yes, through the raising of hell to heaven and of man to God, through the unveiling of an eternal light in the Valley of The Shadow" (1055). Her religious ecstasy here oddly parallels Luke's own at the transfiguration of Christ, when he speaks of clouds, God, man, and revelation:

> ... a cloud came and overshadowed them; and they were afraid as they entered the cloud. And a voice came out of the cloud, saying, "This is my Son, my Chosen; listen to him!" And when the voice had spoken, Jesus was found alone. (9:34–36; 1258)

Eric Bentley once said of Vivie at the end of *Mrs. Warren's Profession* (1893): "A soul is born" (107). A description of Barbara at the end of *Major Barbara* might be: A soul is illuminated. Fighting the limitations of the world and seeking escape through meditation, she reaches out in the end toward the eternal, only to find it in herself. Barbara's return from the metaphorical mountain (the parapet of the gun factory) results in marriage to Cusins and not only the start of a new dynasty and the continuation of the Undershaft inheritance, but also the start of new spiritual mission—proof of Shaw's abiding optimism in 1905, before world war would change him, his art, and the world forever.

Works Cited

Bentley, Eric. *Bernard Shaw, A Reconsideration*. New York: New Directions, 1947.
Luke 9:34–36. In *The New Oxford Annotated Bible*. New York: Oxford University Press, 1977.
Shaw, George Bernard. *Our Theatres in the Nineties*. London: Constable, 1932.
———. "The New Theology." In *The Portable Bernard Shaw*. Ed. Stanley Weintraub. New York: Penguin, 1977. 304–315.
———. *Major Barbara*. In *The Longman Anthology of Drama and Theater: A Global Perspective*. Ed. Michael L. Greenwald et al. New York: Pearson/Longman, 2001. 1020–1055.
———. "Preface to *Major Barbara*." In *The Longman Anthology of Drama and*

Theater: A Global Perspective. Ed. Michael L. Greenwald et al. New York: Pearson/Longman, 2001. 1005–1019.

Smith, J. Percy. "The New Woman and the Old Goddess: The Shaping of Shaw's Mythology." In *Women in Irish Legend, Life, and Literature*. Ed. S. F. Gallagher. Totowa, New Jersey: Barnes and Noble, 1983. 74–90.

"The 'Paper Moon' Song in Williams' *A Streetcar Named Desire*"

Through much of Scene 7 in *A Streetcar Named Desire*, Tennessee Williams interweaves Blanche's singing of "It's Only a Paper Moon" in the bathroom while Stanley reveals her lurid past to Stella in the kitchen. Of course, this juxtaposition is immediately comic: the gruff Stanley complains to the quiet Stella about all the lies Blanche has been telling, at the same time as Blanche herself sings *"blithely"* of love, according to Williams' stage direction (360), and thoroughly enjoys her bath. Stanley Kowalski and Blanche DuBois are so different, it seems, that their very presence together on the same stage is funny, and it is even funnier here since Blanche is oblivious to Stanley's revelations about her past and, later, his need to use his own bathroom.

Williams is trying to do more in this scene, however, than create a comic juxtaposition. The content of the song Blanche sings is as important to an interpretation of the scene as the fact that she is singing blithely. Blanche sings the following verses from "It's Only a Paper Moon," a popular song by Harold Arlen that was published in 1933, with lyrics by E. Y. Harburg and Billy Rose:

> Say, it's only a paper moon,
> Sailing over a cardboard sea—
> But it wouldn't be make-believe
> If you believed in me!   (360)
>
> It's a Barnum and Bailey world,
> Just as phony as it can be—
> But it wouldn't be make-believe
> If you believed in me!   (360)
>
> Without your love,
> It's a honky-tonk parade!
> Without your love,
> It's a melody played
> In a penny arcade ...   (361)

It is no accident that Williams chooses this song for Blanche to sing. It is her birthday, and a birthday supper is planned at Stanley and Stella's apartment, to which Mitch is invited. (The day is September 15th, and Blanche and Mitch have been dating for some time.) Blanche is singing on one level of her hope that Mitch will believe in her, that he will love and marry her. The world that Blanche has created for Mitch *is* "make-believe" and "phony" (360): she has lied to him about her past, painting a portrait of herself as an old-fashioned girl with high ideals and strict morals. But Blanche suggests that this world would not be make-believe if Mitch believed in and married her. Then she would truly become what she has pretended she is: a proper, loving, faithful woman. Blanche thus hopes to celebrate the day of her birth as the day of her rebirth through union with Mitch. She bathes in this scene—as she does many other times during her stay with the Kowalskis—not only to cool off from the heat, but also to cleanse or purify herself, in a sense, of her past sexual indiscretions, to be reborn as it were. After her bath in Scene 2, for example, she declares to Stanley, "Here I am, all freshly bathed and scented, and feeling like a brand new human being!" (276).

The comedy in Scene 7 is undercut by our knowledge that, even as Blanche sings her love song, Stanley is telling Stella, as he has already told Mitch, of the "phony" image Blanche has been presenting all summer. Stanley has made sure that Mitch will not be coming over for supper, and Stanley will soon give Blanche her only birthday present: a bus ticket back to the real world of her past, in Laurel, Mississippi, which she has been trying to deny since arriving in New Orleans. At the end of Scene 8, after the birthday supper unattended by Mitch, Stella's labor pains begin and Stanley rushes her to the hospital: the imminent birth of their child has, in this way, substituted for Blanche's failed rebirth.

Without Mitch's love, Blanche's world will become a kind of "honky-tonk parade," a "melody played in a penny arcade" (361): accordingly, during the rape in Scene 10, we hear the "*Blue Piano*," drums, and a "*hot trumpet*" (401–402); and as Blanche is being led away to an insane asylum in Scene 11, we hear "*the swelling music of the 'Blue Piano' and the muted trumpet*" (419). Without Mitch's love, Blanche's world will also become "make-believe" and "phony" in another sense: she will lose her mind and believe that the Doctor who has come to get her is her old beau Shep Huntleigh, with whom she will embark shortly on a Caribbean cruise—a different kind of soak in a bathtub.

Work Cited
Williams, Tennessee. *A Streetcar Named Desire* (1947). In Williams' *The Theater of Tennessee Williams*. Vol. 1 of 8 vols. New York: New Directions, 1971 (1971–2001). 239–419.

3 Character and Role

This section consists of short model, or sample, essays on the subject of dramatic character, or how character functions to advance a play's theme. The following plays, including some by Shakespeare, have been chosen for their representativeness, variety, and quality:

1. Bernard Shaw's *Candida*
2. Sam Shepard's *Curse of the Starving Class*
3. Falstaff's Dramatic Character in the Plays of William Shakespeare
4. Shakespeare's *Hamlet*
5. Shakespeare's *Romeo and Juliet*
6. Tennessee Williams' A Streetcar Named Desire
7. Harold Pinter's *The Homecoming*

For reading and learning purposes, the "Key Analytical Question" below can be applied to any of the above plays or all of them.

Key Analytical Question: "What is the dramatic function of a particular character: why is this character in the play, and what does he or she contribute to the development of its theme?"

"Burgess in Shaw's *Candida*"

The devilish Burgess, as the Christ-like Marchbanks's opposite in Bernard Shaw's *Candida* (1894), deserves discussion unto himself. Jacob H. Adler, sensing the mystery of the young poet Eugene Marchbanks's disruption of the Morell household, has written that "Shaw's whole story is very close to much ado about nothing" (57). Adler adds that "the presence of a character [Burgess] who feels this way himself is disarming" (57). Burgess's response to Reverend Morell's sermonizing, Marchbanks's "poetic horrors" (which he gets when he realizes that Candida, Morell's wife and Burgess's daughter, does menial chores along with the servants; *Candida*, 248), and

Candida's independence of mind is to conclude that all three characters are mad, since they grossly overstate their complaints or opinions. He thus functions as a comic devil who cannot take seriously the "mysteries" unfolding before him, or who simply does not understand them. Candida's father is funny precisely because he combines equal amounts of ignorance and arrogance in the same character.

Like the devil figures of medieval mystery plays, who often were composites of the worst sins that the audience could commit, Burgess is a stand-in for any audience of *Candida*, from Shaw's day to our own, as his name indicates. *Les bourgeois* identify with Burgess. (The archaic meaning of "burgess," derived from Middle English, is "an inhabitant of a town or borough with full rights of citizenship.") This is not to say we completely identify with his point of view on the action—we cannot, the most important reason for this being that he is not onstage at the crucial moments in the Marchbanks–Morell–Candida story. What Burgess does is to drain off our own devilish disbelief in the feasibility of Marchbanks's assault on the Morell marriage. As Adler puts it, "Paradoxically enough, the audience can take events [onstage] more seriously, precisely because Burgess does not" (57). He pulls us back from the action, so that we can observe it for the insights it contains into marriage—between male and female, on the one hand, and between the artist and his muse, on the other.

If Burgess pulls us back from the action, representing the comically objective point of view on it, Marchbanks takes us into the action, personifying subjective submersion in it. Their opposition is reinforced, paradoxically, by their similarities: both are outsiders—Burgess by virtue of having been estranged from his daughter and her family for three years—and both are alone. Marchbanks is estranged from his own family and has been living outdoors; Burgess has been living by himself in the house he once shared with Candida. (He never mentions his wife, who we may assume is dead, or any other family members.) The two men are at opposite ends of the play's social ladder, however, with the young aristocrat at the top and the old Cockney at the bottom. And they pursue mutually exclusive interests: the one, art for humanity's sake; the other, commerce for money's sake. When they meet for the first time, Marchbanks nearly runs away from Burgess, so dissimilar are they in motive, temperament, appearance, and social station.

Marchbanks has been sleeping on the Embankment (a road and river-walk along the north bank of the River Thames in London), and "in [his] garments he has apparently lain in the heather and waded through the waters" (*Candida*, 226). He was originally called

Majoribanks, but this was shortened by Shaw to what would be heard in normal pronunciation (Weintraub, 97). "Majoribanks," it's true, would have offered upper-class echoes to Shaw's audiences, since the name was a familiar one in Victorian life, in both society and government; that Eugene was the nephew of an earl would nonetheless have been believable from his name, despite its blurring by Shaw for the sake of production.

Burgess is clearly Marchbanks's opposite in origin, a Cockney elevated by money into a petty bourgeois. He has been sleeping in his own large house, attended by a servant: the petty bourgeois has enclosed himself in comfort and plenty. (Another origin of "burgess" is the old French "burgeis," meaning a castle or fortified town.) Whereas Burgess dismisses as madness what he cannot understand about his daughter and her husband, Marchbanks takes Morell and Candida very seriously and finally penetrates to their core. He is utterly sincere and completely without humor, Burgess, by contrast, is most insincere and likes a good laugh. Ironically, Marchbanks forgets, in his worship of Candida, that she is a Burgess—her father's daughter, and so named before she acquired through marriage the surname of Morell. It would not have occurred to Eugene that the Virgin Mother herself—to whose level he raises Candida, or his Madonna, during the play—was of lowly birth, but it would have occurred to Shaw.

Candida, finally, is not an apology for Burgess's capitalism, but it is also not a denunciation of his money-grabbing in favor of selfless devotion to a higher cause. Rather, the play's balanced, humanitarian view simultaneously stresses the necessity of the comparative safety and restricted bliss of domestic life for some people (Morell and Candida), and the requirement of others (Marchbanks) that they have the unchecked freedom to plumb the depths of holy, artistic night; the need for some (Lexy, Morell's assistant, and Prossy, Morell's secretary) to live their lives in the service or imitation of another, for others (Burgess) to dedicate their energies to self-aggrandizement, to making themselves wealthy and powerful.

Works Cited

Adler, Jacob H. "Ibsen, Shaw, and *Candida*." *Journal of English and Germanic Philology*, 59.1 (Jan. 1960): 50–58.

Shaw, George Bernard. *Candida* (1894). In Shaw's *Four Pleasant Plays:* You Never Can Tell, Arms and the Man, Candida, The Man of Destiny. London: Grant Richards, 1898. 207–283.

Weintraub, Stanley. *Shaw's People: Victoria to Churchill*. University Park: Pennsylvania State University Press, 1996.

"Wesley's Role in Shepard's *Curse of the Starving Class*"

Wesley: Feet walking toward the door. Feet stopping. Heart pounding. Sound of door not opening. Foot kicking door. Man's voice. Dad's voice. Dad calling Mom. No answer. Foot kicking. Foot kicking harder. Wood splitting. Man's voice. In the night. Foot kicking hard through door. One foot right through door. Bottle crashing. Glass breaking. Fist through door. Man cursing. Man going insane. Feet and hands tearing. Head smashing. Man yelling. Shoulder smashing. Whole body crashing. Woman screaming. Mom screaming. Mom screaming for police. Man throwing wood. Man throwing up. Mom calling cops. Dad crashing away. (137–138)

I excerpt this monologue of Wesley's (600 words in full) from early in Act I in full, not because I intend to explicate it (it is fairly self-explanatory), but in order to illustrate the peculiar ability that the main characters of Sam Shepard's *Curse of the Starving Class* (1976) have to describe their experiences in highly incantatory, almost poetic language. I say "poetic," not dramatic language, because in these instances the characters are not revealing their innermost thoughts for the purpose of advancing the action in some way. They are literally talking out loud to themselves, telling stories in which they are actors or observers, and which—in the case of the tale of the eagle and the cat by Wesley's father, Weston, at the start of Act III—may have metaphorical implications for the play as a whole.

Arguably, Wesley is characterizing himself in the monologue quoted above, if not advancing the dramatic action, but the characterization would come more from the *actor's* dramatizing these words than from the words themselves. In production it is difficult to make this long speech work, precisely because it neither advances the action nor gives audiences much direct information about Wesley. In fact, it usurps one of the audience's traditional roles in the theater: to fill in for itself the details of an event—here, Weston's return home drunk and his breaking down the door—that has been referred to by the characters.

So what, then, are this speech and others like it doing in the play? If Wesley's monologue reveals his ability to describe his experiences in incantatory, nearly poetic language, then we must ask where this ability comes from. I think that it comes from the characters' habit of always talking to themselves and their having to do so in a home and a world devoid of warmth or simple human fellowship. As Weston says, "Always was best at talkin' to myself. Always was the best thing. Nothing like it. Keeps ya' company at least" (192). One of the ideas suggested by the long speeches in *Curse of the Starving Class* is that the gift for language or self-expression may be developed in people—and especially in writers—at the expense of the gift for communion, for communicating with and loving others. On the one hand, the characters' gift for language gives audiences pleasure by painting appealing word-pictures for us. On the other hand, the desperateness of their social situation disconcerts audiences and makes them wonder if something could not have been done to help them.

All that the characters in *Curse of the Starving Class* seem to have left is their imagination, as expressed in words. The play may ask, is that enough? Is it sufficient for continued humane survival? Or will it lead inevitably to the kind of self-obsession that can end only in the destruction of the self and the world? Dramatic form, of course, is itself an act of communion between playwright-cum-players and the audience, and a play such as *Curse* intends to keep up some warm kind of dialogue between human beings, even if it is only the silent type that takes place in the theater. *Curse* also means to warn against the pleasure of the monologue, of its narcissism (in this sense it is representative of Shepard's form of drama)—for the potentially mesmerized spectators as well as for the characters.

The following excerpt from a "duologue" between Wesley and his mother, Ella, about an eagle and a cat—an exchange which comes at the end of the play—is at least a step in the right direction, towards communion:

> *Ella*: And they fight. They fight like crazy in the middle of the sky. That cat's tearing his chest out, and the eagle's trying to drop him, but the cat won't let go because he knows if he falls he'll die.
> *Wesley*: And the eagle's being torn apart in midair. The eagle's trying to free himself from the cat, and the cat won't let go.
> *Ella*: And they come crashing down to earth. Both of them come crashing down. Like one whole thing. (200)

The pleasure of the monologue is the pleasure of art, the artist, and the spectator in isolation. This isolation—lack of communication—is killing us, Shepard suggests. It is no accident that in *Curse of the Starving Class*, Weston's story of the eagle and the cat is not completed until the end of the play, and at that point by two characters, not one. This story is a metaphor for the entire action of *Curse*, and it is important that two people finish telling it to each other, for its lesson is that humans in isolation, not communicating with others, will inevitably destroy themselves and everyone with whom they come into contact.

The eagle and the cat both want the same thing—the lamb, or lamb testes, that Weston throws atop the shed roof (he is castrating lambs in his story)—and they kill each other trying to get it. The "eagles" and the "cats" in *Curse of the Starving Class* do the same; they want the Tate-family land, which is identified with the lamb testes of Weston's story. One clue to this reading is the lamb Wesley brings into the house in Act I, and which Weston returns to the house in Act III after he decides to stay on the land.

The *lamb*, brought into the house to recover from infestation by maggots, is identified with the *land*; like the lamb, the land is diseased or "cursed." When Wesley, in his father's clothes, butchers the lamb in Act III, he symbolically enacts what his father has done over the years: borrow money and thus borrow away, or destroy, the land. Wesley says he killed the lamb because he was hungry, but there is plenty of food in the refrigerator. He wastes the lamb meat, in other words, and the thugs Emerson and Slater remind audiences of this when they bring the discarded lamb carcass into the house late in the play.

The "eagles" and the "cats" in *Curse of the Starving Class* more or less destroy one another in the fight over the Tate land. Weston, an "eagle" (he was a pilot during World War II), fights against Ella, a "cat," and both lose. (When she participates in telling the story of the eagle and the cat at the end of the play, the cat enters the picture for the first time; when Weston tells the story by himself at the start of Act III, he stops before the cat begins to challenge the eagle for the lamb testes.) Weston goes off to Mexico to escape his creditors, and Ella is abandoned by the attorney Taylor and left with nothing. Taylor, the "legal eagle" (he also served in World War II), fights against Ellis, a "cat"—a "meat and blood" man by his own description who preys on unsuspecting drunks at his bar—and they both lose. Taylor himself runs off to Mexico in the end to avoid legal action for selling worthless land (the piece of desert property that Weston bought), and Ellis's "Alibi Club" is badly damaged during a shooting spree by Emma, Wesley's sister.

The eagle and the cat in Weston's story are archetypal loners who kill each other by chance, because they are not natural enemies despite the fact that in this instance they are competing for the same food. Humans, by contrast, are not by nature a loners or self-seekers. Ironically, Shepard gives audiences a family—better yet, a farming family—of loners to point this up all the more. When people attempts to go it alone or are driven to do so, the play implies, they ineluctably destroy themselves and others.

The curse of the starving class—of any social class in American society, in fact—is precisely its spiritual starvation amidst plenty, its neglect of its spiritual needs for satisfaction of material ones, on account of the very existence of such plenty. Thus the catch-22 situation at the start of *Curse of the Starving Class* is that the Tates are in deep financial trouble because, over the years, they have depended too much on credit to satisfy their every material need, to get their share of the American dream. What could get them out of this trouble, or at least get them through it intact as a family, and able to begin again somewhere else, is exactly what they have animalistically sacrificed in their single-minded quest for the material: spiritual communion, or honest, loving, and selfless communication with one another.

Wesley himself is put through an incredible experience in the play, and so are audiences, because they are "spies," as audience members. Audiences are made to live vicariously through what Wesley does (e.g., his first long monologue in Act I) in *Curse of the Starving Class*, if only because he is the character who is onstage the most. He leaves the stage solely for immediately practical reasons: to dump the wheelbarrow (Act I); to feed the sheep (Act I); to escape his father's return home drunk and angry (momentary exit, Act I); to get the $1,500 back from Ellis that the latter agreed to pay for the Tate land (Act II, during which Wesley is otherwise onstage the whole time): and to bathe and to kill the lamb (both in Act III). Shepard identifies audiences with the onstage Wesley in a most striking manner when he stares out the window at the burning car with Emma inside it. There is no stage direction indicating that she dies; audiences presume that she does because she leaves the house with the keys to the only car left on the property—the one that explodes in flames. Nonetheless, audiences must see Emma's demise *through Wesley's eyes*, because he himself does not declare her death, and thus audiences are identified with his point of view.

Finally, Shepard more or less passes judgment on every character *except* Wesley in the play. *Audiences* must pass or reserve judgment on him and decide if he has truly learned anything and will succeed where his father failed: *Curse of the Starving Class* is open-ended in this sense. Wesley is the play's anchor in a sea of hoodlums (Emerson and Slater), con men (Taylor and, to a large extent, Emerson), antiseptic or impotent lawmen (Sgt. Malcolm), and dreamers [Weston and, to a degree, Emma and Ella (e.g., what was going to happen after Ella's trip to Europe? how would she have supported herself and the children?)]. The parable of the play exists in this way almost outside him.

Work Cited
Shepard, Sam. *Curse of the Starving Class*. In his *Seven Plays*. New York: Bantam, 1981. 133–200.

"Falstaff's Dramatic Character in the Plays of Shakespeare"

In Shakespeare's history plays, Falstaff is the central character at the London Eastcheap Tavern habituated by young Hal, Prince of Wales and later King Henry V, estranged from his father Henry IV. For the first half of *Henry IV, Part One* (1597), Falstaff embodies tavern-world "holiday" (I.ii.182; 1164) influences, keeping Hal from helping his father's side as Henry IV faces mounting threats—from rebel forces, particularly—in what has become the everyday world of civil war. Unknown to Falstaff, Hal in an early soliloquy marks his intention of rejecting the tavern crew; and he shows himself largely distinct from them at Gadshill, where Falstaff's band robs a group of pilgrims. In partly comic charade, with Hal playing King Henry to Falstaff as Prince, Hal rejects Falstaff yet then protects him from a tavern search by the law.

The play subsequently traces Hal's turn back toward his father as Falstaff raises troops for the impending, climactic Shrewsbury battle with the rebels. There Hal rescues his father's life and in single combat kills his heroic rebel-rival Harry Hotspur, "king of honour" (*1 Henry IV*, IV.i.10; 1203) in the play. Hotspur's heroic notions of honor are also dangerous, however, as Falstaff makes clear with a realistic if cowardly counter-assessment of their costs: "Can honour set-to a leg? No. Or an arm? No" (*1 Henry IV*, V.i.130–131; 1214). At the play's end, he gains public credit for dispatching Hotspur because Hal is willing to "gild" a lie for Falstaff (V.iv.151; 1221), who knows full well that Hal is due the credit, since he, Falstaff, witnessed the fight while pretending to be dead.

Henry IV, Part Two (1598), with its own near climactic battle against the rebels at Gaultree, repeats some of *Part One's* dramatic structure. Falstaff is faced down by Hal in the Act II, scene iv, tavern scenes of both plays; Hal is again far from his father in the opening acts and once more reconciles with Henry IV at the dying man's bedside in Act IV. And Falstaff is again rejected, now seriously, when Hal become King Henry V in Act V, scene v. The body of *Henry IV, Part Two*, however, shows Falstaff on his own apart from Hal, who is a reduced presence in this play, with only half the lines (9.5%) he had in *Part One* (19%); Falstaff retains his same 20 percent.

Falstaff is a man on the make in *Henry IV, Part Two*, thanks to his Shrewsbury-based soldierly reputation, which allows him to insult England's lord chief justice with impunity; to prey inventively on two rural justices, Shallow and Silence, as he again recruits troops; to lust after the prostitute Doll Tearsheet, who marks the transformation of the Boar's Head Tavern into a brothel; and to capture a Gaultree rebel, who gives up on the strength of Falstaff's fame alone. In public, he speaks for youth and modern fashion, yet privately he worries over age and failing health, admits to Doll that he is old, and arrives not only late but also improperly dressed for Hal's coronation: "O, if I had had time to have made new liveries" (*2 Henry IV*, V.v.10; 1373). Age is his downfall, as the new king's disavowal of Falstaff finds him, together with his former influence, out of date literally and symbolically: "I know thee not, old man" (V.v.45; 1374).

The *Henry IV* plays have several overlapping themes and patterns. There is a conflict between the generations pitting young, virile Hal and Hotspur against sick, past-ridden, crafty, impotent, guilty old men—a conflict parodied by Falstaff as he descends on the travelers in the Gadshill robbery with the cry "They hate us youth" (*1 Henry IV*, II.ii.76; 1175). Each of the fathers, moreover, has a characteristic way of trying to control Hal. Motionless, Henry IV lets the freezing rigidity of his distant majesty break Hal down, whereas Falstaff is constantly moving and shouting at Hal, cajoling and approaching him. There are the equally universal conflicts in these two plays of holiday versus everyday; the individual's need for joy, fluidity, and release against society's need for order, duty and restraint; as well as the desire for power and immortality set against the limitations placed on man by the force of nature.

In the clash of Falstaff and his world with Henry IV and his, we see the former, a man "out of all compass" (*1 Henry IV*, III.iii.17; 1199) in body and spirit—night reveler, punster, protean role-player, court jester, rebel against all limits, an embodiment in short of the comic spirit—come up against everything in life that demands to be taken seriously. Incorporating the Falstaff-theme is the pattern of death and rebirth. Falstaff is a sacrificial figure, heaped with the sins of both his community and the wayward prince, then banished like the human as well as animal victims in J. G. Frazer's *Golden Bough* (1922). For his part Henry IV, having killed Richard the King, suffers and dies (like Oedipus) to rid his kingdom of the plague, to be replaced by the son he feared might kill him. Only thus does spring replace winter and are the curses of disease and sterility removed.

Henry V (1599) bars Falstaff from the stage, but sympathetic reports of his death darken the portrait of heroically—or jingoistically—military Henry V. The new king never asks after his old companion, never even utters Falstaff's name. Henry's retinue, however, reminds the audience (though not Henry) of his rejection of Falstaff, a reminder that contributes to Hal's loss of humanity as king. That loss is connected to the loss of the absolute distinction between high and low that occurs when Falstaff is banished at the end of *Henry IV, Part Two*, in deference to a legalistic conception of social order. Hal, Henry V, thus represents a firm step on the path that will lead, as a character in Stendhal's *The Red and the Black* (1830) laments, to a time when there will be no more kings in Europe—only prime ministers and presidents.

The Merry Wives of Windsor (1597), purportedly fulfilling Queen Elizabeth I's wish to see Falstaff in love, presents a far less resourceful Sir John, one humiliated throughout the play. Impelled by his amorous sense of self and the unreasonably jealous husband Master Ford, Falstaff is duped perpetually both by members of his tavern crew from the histories, who turn upon him as a "varlet vile" (*Merry Wives*, I.iii.84; 1242), and by the faithful Windsor wives Mistresses Ford and Page, upon whom his desire falls. He barely escapes discovery with Mistress Ford twice, once carried away crammed into a wash-basket filled with dirty laundry and thrown into the river Thames, then exiting dressed as an old woman whom Ford cudgels. By the play's end Falstaff is tricked into standing in a forest wearing deer antlers and waiting for yet another assignation, frightened by (play-acting) fairies before he is revealed—"Fie on lust and luxury!" (V.v.91; 1287)—to everyone. Falstaff's final "Use me as you will" both acknowledges conclusive defeat and summarizes his humiliations throughout the play (V.v.153; 1288).

Aging and heirless Elizabeth may have wished to see Falstaff in love, but the late-sixteenth century vogue for onstage histories was probably dictated by the political uncertainty in England during the 1580s and 1590s, when the nation saw no obvious successor to this late representative of the Tudor line. Chief among these histories were plays like *Henry IV, Part One* and *Henry IV, Part Two*, detailing the last era of civil turmoil, the fifteenth-century War of the Roses, which suggested a possibly hopeful pattern surfacing from unrest. That war's vexed succession to the English Crown involved foreign and domestic conflict, but from it finally emerged the strong Tudor line of monarchs, liberally assisted by providence—at least in Tudor propagandistic accounts of the war.

Henry IV, Part One partly stems from a source steeped in providential design—the Prodigal Son story, the most common of earlier morality interludes and plays. Rejecting Falstaff as "that reverend Vice, that grey Iniquity . . . that Vanity in Years" (II.v.413–414; 1187), Hal briefly addresses him in the language usually leveled at Vice in moral drama, after Falstaff himself has threatened Hal with Vice's usual stage prop, the "dagger of lath" (II.v.124; 1181). The Prodigal Son pattern perhaps derives from an earlier, anonymous dramatic version of Hal's story, *The Famous Victories of Henry the Fifth* (1580s), which lacks a separate Vice figure. If so, Falstaff as Vice in the *Henry IV* plays is new, the old play locating a vice in young Hal, who later undergoes a St. Paul-like transformation. Shakespeare shifts culpability to Falstaff and his tavern crew, who thus become convenient scapegoats for Hal's behavior.

Yet Falstaff fails to meet Vice's job description fully. In *Henry IV, Part One* he enters dramatic literature not scheming to corrupt Hal, but fast asleep; in *Part Two* he is hardly around Hal enough to win his spleen, let alone his soul—the two being together in two scenes for 132 lines, 4 percent of the play, contrasted to more than 1,000 lines over the course of eight scenes in *Part One*, almost a third of the play. The aging Falstaff of *Henry IV, Part Two* appears to represent, then, not Vice from morality models but the figure of "Old Morality," a man on his way out despite his arguments for modernization.

Other background information may help to explain Falstaff's departures from simple moral Vice in *Henry IV, Part One* and *Part Two*. Renaissance political theory suggests that Hal is a young prince confronted with models of political virtue and their opposite: Falstaff is a type of dishonorable action set against Hotspur's notion of honor in *Henry IV, Part One*; and in *Part Two* he contrasts with the lord chief justice, an embodiment of legal order. For some, however, Falstaff is more important to Hal's education as prince, for Falstaff is not just a contrast to Hotspur but a corrective to his excessive pursuit of honor. Others find Falstaff to be the stage stereotype of distorted honor, displaying features of the braggart soldier derived from *miles gloriosus* of ancient Roman comedy. Falstaff may even link up with medieval philosophy and linguistics on the subject of honor, for he appears to be tied to nominalism—the denying of meaning to abstract words—as he reduces "honour" to the element producing its sounds in *Henry IV, Part One*: "What is honour? A word. What is in that word 'honour'? What is that 'honour'? Air" (V.i.133–134; 1214).

Biblical tradition could also figure here. There are those who see the plays *Richard II* (1595) to *Henry V* as an analogue to post-Babel linguistic collapse, and Falstaff's nominalism as a logical degenerative stage following on King Richard's earlier worry over adequate nomenclature once a rightful (pre-Edenic) king is deposed. For others, like James L. Calderwood, Falstaff is simply lying's "human form" (68). Religious tradition figures more convincingly in considerations of folk celebrations of Lent, with their ritualistic if reluctant exile of the holiday impulse in expelling celebratory Carnival. The Carnival pageant is always corpulent, as is "fat-kidneyed" (*1 Henry IV*, II.ii.6; 1173) and "fat-guts" (II.ii.29; 1174) Falstaff. Religious tradition even allies with clown theory if Falstaff is regarded as a Christian fool, the spirit of play amid a world of utilitarianism, whose veiled and often scriptural comments reveal Henry IV as thief of the crown, honor as a hollow value, and Hal's claims of repentance as a sham.

The Merry Wives of Windsor barely mentions Falstaff in the company of prince, king, or court, emphasizing domestic—not political—virtue and vice. The political realities of Elizabethan society, however, provide a telling if ambiguous framework for the play. Sixteenth-century patriarchal values dominate *Merry Wives* for feminist critics, who highlight the wives' obsession with demonstrating what their husbands want: chastity. But the women could be said to control the men in this comedy, thereby disrupting male dominance. Successful feminine plotting parallels queen-dominated court politics, which arouses male uneasiness—uneasiness most obviously embodied in Falstaff's onstage humiliation and lengthy, rueful reflections on being "cozened, and beaten too" (IV.v.77; 1281). England's rigid class structure may also be invoked here, with the middle class besting a corrupt aristocracy in Falstaff, the titled knight. Stage tradition, again, could partly account for the Falstaff of *The Merry Wives of Windsor*, given the braggart soldier's conventional pretensions as a lover—especially as we find him incarnated in the *capitano* figure of Italian *commedia dell'arte*. Sexual proclivities, however, appear as well in the likely source of *Merry Wives*, Giovanni Fiorentino's novella *Il pecorone* (*The Simpleton*, 1378), whose oversexed student is a Falstaff prototype. Elizabethan folk practices may also be important to this comedy if one sees Falstaff as a domestic scapegoat, a threatening spirit of fertility symbolically castrated at the end of the play.

After Shakespeare, and in between the high points of Giuseppe Verdi's opera titled *Falstaff* (1893), Fernand Crommelynck's play called *The Knight of the Moon, or Sir John Falstaff* (1954), Orson Welles's play *Five Kings* (1938, 1960), and Welles's film *Chimes at Midnight* (a.k.a. *Falstaff*, 1966), the fortunes of Falstaff have percolated at their own rhythm. His continuing influence was evidenced by Gus van Sant's 1991 movie *My Own Private Idaho*, which grafts a contemporary gay storyline onto the framework of Shakespeare's *Henry IV*,

Part One. But, Shakespeare's drama excluded, Falstaff's legacy goes as far back as the seventeenth century, and can be found in later plays by Samuel Johnson himself (1739) and James Branch Cabell (1906), among numerous others, as well as in novels by Robert Nye (1976) and Jack-Alain Léger (1996), not to speak of a nineteenth-century poem on the Falstaff-theme by Herman Melville.

Among the lesser lesser-known but nonetheless representative plays that center around the character of Sir John, one can discover a 1766 work by the Englishman William Kenrick (1725–79) titled *Falstaff's Wedding: A Comedy*, which was meant as a sequel to *Henry IV, Part Two* in imitation of Shakespeare; a "drollery" called *The Bouncing Knight*, by Francis Kirkman (1632–80), from his Restoration-era collection of twenty-one such drolls called *The Wits, or Sport upon Sport* (1662); *The Death of Falstaff* (1820), a melodrama by the Briton Zachariah Jackson (who in 1818 also wrote a book called *Shakespeare's Genius Justified: A few concise examples of seven hundred errors in Shakespeare's plays, now corrected and elucidated*); and *The Life and Humours of Falstaff* (1829), a comedy by Charles Short formed out of both parts of *Henry IV* and several scenes from *Henry V*.

All the variations on the Falstaff-theme—be they dramatic, novelistic, cinematic, operatic, or poetic—stem in the end from an unflagging Bardolatry and are representative of what is almost a subgenre in itself: Shakespeare imitations. In their own way, they attest to the immense vitality that, over the centuries, has continued to inhabit the rotund figure of a Falstaff who is never out of place in any time. As Dover Wilson aptly put it, Falstaff "is a figure we find in the looking-glass . . . no doubt, but still what it shows us is ourselves. Ourselves, not as we are, but as we can fancy we might have been; expanded, exalted in every direction of bodily life" (9). Falstaff's exalted quality is such that his rivals in Shakespeare are not many: Hamlet, Rosalind, and Cleopatra would complete the list unless we admit the intellectual villains, Iago and Edmund. All six of these have the rhetorical genius to overcome any disputant. Yet Falstaff stands apart from the others because he is older than all of them, and younger than all of them, younger and older even than Cleopatra, who ends in absolute transcendence, whereas Falstaff ends in rejection and grief. For, despite his great wit, he violated the Freudian admonition not to invest too much affection in any one person.

Falstaff's tragedy, then, is one of misplaced love, but Shakespeare does not allow that to be our final sense of his grandest comic creation. Instead, we are given the great vision of the death of Falstaff in *Henry V*, which assures us that he is in Abraham's bosom, in heaven. Playing with flowers, and smiling upon his finger's end, Sir John dies like a child just christened, reminding us again of his total lack of hypocrisy, of what after all makes us love him, of what doubtless first drew the Machiavellian Hal to him. Authentic freedom—freedom from the superego, if you will—is the liberty to play, even as a child plays, in the very act of dying. Falstaff had that freedom, used it abundantly, then quietly departed the scene. His character survives him.

Works Cited
Calderwood, James L. *Metadrama in Shakespeare's Henriad: Richard II to Henry V.* Berkeley: University of California Press, 1979.
Greenblatt, Stephen, et al., eds. *The Norton Shakespeare.* New York: W. W. Norton, 1997. 1157–1222 (*Henry IV, Part One*); 1234–1289 (*The Merry Wives of Windsor*); 1304–1376 (*Henry IV, Part Two*); 1454–1521 (*Henry V*).
Wilson, J. Dover. *The Fortunes of Falstaff.* 1945. Cambridge, UK: Cambridge University Press, 1964.

"Polonius in Shakespeare's *Hamlet*"

In a play built on Hamlet's hesitation or delay, it should come as no surprise that Polonius's own long-winded delays find a home. What is a surprise, however, is the fact that the nature of his delay, as well as its relationship to Hamlet's own, has escaped analysis in the criticism thus far published on Polonius's character.

Polonius hesitates or delays immediately upon entering the play for the first time. Laertes is set to sail for Paris and is about to take his leave from Ophelia when Polonius enters (appropriately, on Laertes' line "I stay too long") and says, at I.iii.55–59:

> Yet here, Laertes? Aboard, aboard, for shame!
> The wind sits in the shoulder of your sail,
> And you are stayed for. There—my blessing with thee,
> And these few precepts in thy memory
> See thou character. (1680)

We expect Polonius to let Laertes go after he gives him his blessing, but father then goes on to give son, in more than twenty lines, the commandments of social living. The whole Polonius–Laertes–Ophelia subplot in *Hamlet*, introduced here for the first time in the play, itself could be looked at as a kind of delaying action—a "pause"—coming as it does right after Hamlet agrees to meet with Horatio and Marcellus on the guard-platform at night to see the Ghost, and preparing us subliminally for the larger delay on Hamlet's part that we are to witness throughout the action.

Polonius's next delay occurs in Act II, scene i. Even as he gave Laertes his blessing and then detained him with the "precepts," so too does Polonius now give his servant Reynaldo "money and notes" to take to Laertes in Paris and then detain *him*, not only by asking Reynaldo to check on his son's behavior, but also by giving him at length the proper strategy for doing so. We might expect the whole exchange of dialogue between Polonius and Reynaldo to go something like this:

> *Polonius*: Give him this money and these notes, Reynaldo.
> *Reynaldo*: I will, my lord.
> *Polonius*: God buy ye, fare ye well.
> *Reynaldo*: Good my lord.

Instead, we do not get Polonius's "Fare ye well" (II.i.69; 1690) until sixty-seven lines after Reynaldo's "I will, my lord" (II.i.2; 1688). And Reynaldo's "Good my lord" is still not the end of it. Polonius then goes on to tell him to be sure to observe Laertes directly as well as to make inquiries about his son to others. In his long-windedness, Polonius seems to have forgotten Reynaldo's original purpose in going to Paris: to give Laertes money and notes, during which time he would surely have the opportunity to observe Laertes directly in *facing* him directly. Finally, Polonius says "fare ye well" and Reynaldo departs. His brevity here is somewhat unexpected after the verbosity that has preceded it— it is also somewhat peremptory—and it is therefore comical.

Moreover, contributing to his delay, Polonius even forgets at one point the instructions he meant to give to Reynaldo:

> *Reynaldo*: Very good, my lord.
> *Polonius*: And then, sir, does he this—he does—what was I about to say?
>   By the mass, I was about to say something. Where did I leave?
> *Reynaldo*: At "closes in the consequence," at "friend, or so," and "gentleman."
> *Polonius*: At "closes in the consequence"—ay, marry . . .
> (II.i.48–54; 1689)

Any number of actors playing Polonius—Michael Redgrave, Ian Holm, and Hume Cronyn, to name only three from the twentieth century—have extended the delay at this point by pausing for a seeming eternity as he loses his place at II.i.50–51, with the lines "what was I about to say? By the mass, I was about to say something. Where did I leave?" (1689).

Perhaps Polonius's most obvious delay comes in Act II, scene ii, when he goes expressly to tell Claudius what he believes to be the cause or origin of Hamlet's "antic disposition" (I.v.173, 1688): Hamlet's unrequited love for Ophelia. Instead of immediately telling the king what he knows, or thinks he knows, Polonius defers to Voltemand and Cornelius, the ambassadors to Norway, who bring the news that young Fortinbras (under orders from old Norway) will not take up arms against Denmark. Then, after the ambassadors have spoken and departed, Polonius delays further. He does not come right out and state, at II.ii.49, what he believes to be "the very cause of Hamlet's lunacy" (1692), but instead characterizes Hamlet as mad—something already more or less known by Claudius and Gertrude—reads a love letter from Hamlet to Ophelia, then finally connects the letter with Ophelia's negative response to Hamlet's love (a response ordered by Polonius himself) and explains Hamlet's madness as the result of his daughter's rebuffs.

All of this is punctuated by Polonius's own ironic "brevity is the soul of wit" (II.ii.91; 1693), Gertrude's "More matter with less art" (II.ii.96; 1693), and Claudius's "But how hath she / Received his love?" (II.ii.128–129; 1694)—the direct answer to which would explain at once the cause of Hamlet's madness from Polonius's point of view. Claudius and Gertrude wait on Polonius, Polonius even waits on himself, as he delays, hesitating to say what he has come to say.

One of the reasons Shakespeare did not have Ophelia accompany Polonius in this scene—and she was to have accompanied him [her father says to her, "Come, go we to the King," at the end of Act II, scene i on line 118 (1691)]—is that she would have prevented his delay, and Polonius's delay is as important to Shakespeare here as Polonius's theory about Hamlet's madness. Ophelia's mere presence, together with Claudius and Gertrude's understandable desire to hear what she has to say, would have made Polonius speak more to the point. The dramatist instead gives Polonius a letter from Hamlet to Ophelia to "speak" for Ophelia, so that she can be dropped out of the scene altogether and Polonius's delay got on with.

Polonius's penultimate delay also occurs in Act II, scene ii. He has suggested to Claudius, at II.ii.165–166, that they spy on Hamlet and Ophelia in the "lobby" in order to discover "If [Hamlet] love[s] her not, / And be not from his reason fall'n thereon" (1694); and Claudius has agreed to this. Then Hamlet enters the "lobby" where Polonius, Claudius, and Gertrude are standing, but, instead of "loosing" Ophelia to him and seeking cover behind an arras with the King so as to "mark the encounter" (1694), as Polonius has just said he would do, he asks Claudius and Gertrude to leave so that he himself may immediately "board" Hamlet. Polonius thus delays. We expect him to act on his original plan, but he does not do so: first he wants to sound Hamlet out himself. Ironically, in abandoning the arras for a direct confrontation with Hamlet, Polonius will himself be "marked" by Hamlet from behind another kind of arras—Hamlet's madness, the very madness that Polonius thinks is real and transparent.

Polonius is no match for Hamlet, naturally, and therefore, at II.ii.209–210, he falls back on the plan he and Claudius had agreed upon: "[Aside] . . . I will leave [Hamlet], and suddenly contrive the means of meeting between him and my daughter" (1696). He cannot do this immediately, however, for Claudius has sent Rosencrantz and Guildenstern to accomplish what Polonius has not been able to accomplish on his own. His plan must wait, or will be delayed, until Rosencrantz and Guildenstern themselves fail, in Claudius's own words at III.i.1–4, by "gift of circumstance / [to] Get from [Hamlet] why he puts on this confusion, / Grating so harshly all his days of quiet / With turbulent and dangerous lunacy" (1704).

Polonius's final delay of the play occurs, or is prepared for, in Act III, scene i, when, after he and Claudius have secretly observed Hamlet and Ophelia in conversation, Polonius suggests that, following the play-within-the-play in Act III, scene ii, he be allowed to observe Gertrude and Hamlet in conversation. Such observation can be construed as a kind of delay on Polonius's part because Claudius has already decided, at III.i.168, to send Hamlet "with speed" (1707) to England, on which journey

> Haply the seas and countries different,
> With variable objects, shall expel
> This something-settled matter in his heart,
> Whereon his brains still beating puts him thus
> From fashion of himself.   (III.i.170–174; 1708)

Polonius's delay in *Hamlet* clearly derives from his need to please or impress Claudius. (Polonius rhetorically asks in Act II, scene ii, at lines 154–156, "Hath there been such a time—I'd fain know that— / That I have positively said, ''Tis so' / When it proved otherwise?" [1694].) It also derives from his need to assert his parental prerogatives before Laertes. Polonius's delay is thus formally comic, because it is designed to accommodate or reconcile him to his society. When he hesitates so long to tell Claudius and Gertrude what he thinks is causing Hamlet's madness, it is not to anger or alienate the King and Queen, but to tease or titillate them with the "facts" (in addition to savoring his own "discovery") that he believes they want so much to hear. When Polonius accosts Hamlet alone in the "lobby," it is to examine Hamlet by himself and, as he himself declares at II.ii.158–160, to "find / Where truth is hid, though it were hid indeed / Within the center" (1694)—and thus to prove once again his value to the King as an "assistant to the state." And when he asks Claudius to let him spy on Gertrude and Hamlet, it is because he wants so very much to prove once again his value to the king as an "assistant for a state" (1695), as he describes his role at II.ii.167.

Unlike Polonius's delay, Hamlet's is designed to separate or distance him from society: in his soliloquies, so that he might examine his thoughts, motives, and doubts as well as his opportunities to act (such as when he comes upon Claudius praying in Act III, scene iii); in his "antic disposition" (I.v.173; 1688), so that through the mask of madness he might examine the thoughts, motives, and potential plans of others. Hamlet delays, not to aggrandize himself like Polonius, but to sacrifice self to other, to suppress his desire for private, criminal revenge and wait for the public, sanctioned moment provided to act. He wishes, in other words, to be an agent or minister of God rather than an aggrandizer or indulger of self.

Indeed, Polonius's delay is intricately wound up with Hamlet's in the play. Polonius may provide us with "comic relief" in *Hamlet*, but it is not of the gratuitous kind. Rather it is structurally necessary: his delay places Hamlet's own tragic delay or hesitation in perspective; and it leads, in the turning point of the drama—the closet scene—to the stunning, fateful meeting of both "delaying" forces. Polonius can delay no more, for he is dead; or rather he delays, even in death, by remaining onstage as a corpse. Hamlet can delay no more, for he has run out of patience, and he kills Polonius, believing him to be Claudius. As Hamlet says to Horatio at V.ii.158–160, right before the climactic duel, "If it be now, 'tis not to come. If it be not to come, it will be now. If it be not now, yet it will come. The readiness is all" (1751). And so, I would add, is the delay.

Work Cited

Shakespeare, William. *The Tragedy of Hamlet, Prince of Denmark* (1601). In *The Norton Shakespeare*. Ed. Stephen Greenblatt et al. New York: W. W. Norton, 1997. 1668–1756.

"The Nurse in Shakespeare's *Romeo and Juliet*"

In a play built on the hastiness or impulsiveness of characters like Romeo and Old Capulet, not to mention Mercutio and Tybalt, it is at first surprising to find the Nurse delaying. In Act II, scene v, for example, the Nurse returns home to give her mistress Romeo's message: Juliet is to ". . . devise / Some means to come to shrift this afternoon, / And there . . . at Friar Laurence's cell / Be shriv'd and married" (II.iv.176–179). But, contrary to our expectations, the Nurse does not give the girl the happy news right away. The scene consists of 79 lines; the Nurse enters on line 17 but does not give her message until lines 69–70. She claims that she is tired and aching and needs to catch her breath; she is also, of course, teasing the impatient Juliet. But the Nurse's behavior here has an underlying meaning: Shakespeare delays the giving of the message as long as possible, in contrast with his hastening the Friar's agreement to marry Romeo and Juliet two scenes earlier, in order to suggest that the message is something Juliet should *not* want to hear and abide by. Marriage to Romeo may mean her doom, in other words, yet she rushes to it: throughout Act II, scene v, Juliet is "hot" to hear what her lover has to say. (The Nurse says to her on line 63, "Are you so hot?"; similarly, later in Act III, Lady Capulet tells her husband, when he is insisting that Juliet marry Paris, "You are too hot" [III.v.175].)

In Act III, scene ii, furthermore, the Nurse hesitates in announcing the sad news of Tybalt's death to Juliet. Although this scene is almost twice as long as scene v of Act II (143 lines to 79), and the Nurse consequently enters on line 31 instead of 17, she waits only until lines 69–70 to give her message—the same point at which she gave her message in Act II, scene v. The Nurse's delay is long enough, however, to provoke this response from Juliet: "What devil art thou that dost torment me thus?" (III.ii.43). The Nurse is naturally in shock here over the death of Tybalt; indeed, she barely acknowledges Juliet upon entering. Shakespeare has her hesitate in giving the news of Tybalt's death, in contrast with his having Friar Laurence rush to get the news of Juliet's seeming death to Romeo four scenes later (IV.i.), in order to connect Juliet's own impulsiveness with Romeo's and to prefigure both their deaths at the end of the play.

The Nurse's delay, then, brings out a quality in Juliet that the Friar's haste brings out in Romeo: for when the Nurse does not immediately reveal who has been slain, Juliet assumes that Romeo is dead and impetuously vows to join him with the lines "Vile earth to earth resign, end motion here, / And thou and Romeo press one heavy bier" (III.ii.59–60). She does not commit suicide until the last scene of the play, of course; at this point Juliet is foreshadowing that suicide and Romeo's own. Wrongly believing her dead because Balthasar reached him and Friar John did not, Romeo poisons himself beside her bier; awakening to find him dead, Juliet mortally wounds herself with his dagger.

The Nurse's delay, unlike Friar Laurence's haste, is not itself lethal. She corrects Juliet's erroneous assumption about Romeo's death and tells her that "Tybalt is gone and Romeo banished. / Romeo that kill'd him, he is banished" (III.ii.69–70). Juliet will live to love Romeo before being parted from him once and for all in Act III, scene v. Once he receives Balthasar's fateful report, Romeo will not live to love her again.

The above explanations of the Nurse's delay connect it directly with the calamitous events that follow. But her behavior can be spoken of in a general sense, also. It makes the haste of the other characters stand out by contrast. And, paradoxically, the delay is a device of suspense as well as one of suspension: it makes us want the Nurse to hurry up at the same time it gives us a brief rest from the headlong action, a slight hint of a world outside the drama where haste and delay translate into frivolity and leisure. This is the world of *play*, of *comedy*, to which a confidante such as the Nurse naturally belongs. Like the subject of *Romeo and Juliet* (1595)—the reconciliation of two feuding houses through marriage—she has been drafted from the comic sphere into the tragic, where she performs in memory of her former self.

Work Cited
Gibbons, Brian, ed. *Romeo and Juliet*, by William Shakespeare. London: Arden/Methuen, 1980.

"The Mexican Woman in Williams' *A Streetcar Named Desire*"

In Scene 9 of Tennessee Williams' *A Streetcar Named Desire* (1947), Harold "Mitch" Mitchell appears and confronts Blanche DuBois about her past, armed with the truth that Stanley Kowalski has provided him. During this confrontation, "*a blind Mexican woman in a dark shawl, carrying bunches of those gaudy tin flowers that lower-class Mexicans display at funerals and other festive occasions*" (387), comes up to the door of the Kowalski apartment trying to sell some of her "flowers for the dead" (*flores para los muertos* [388]). Little attention has been paid by critics to the role of the Mexican Woman Vendor in Scene 9, since it seems fairly obvious that she is meant to be a kind of death figure with whom Blanche comes face to face as the latter is beginning to experience the spiritual death—paradoxically, on her birthday—that will lead to her commitment to an asylum. The Mexican Woman becomes a visual symbol of Blanche's fate, then. But Williams' choice of a *blind Mexican* woman to sell "flowers for the dead"—gaudy tin flowers at that—and his movement of her onto and off the stage greatly enhance the power and richness of this symbol.

The Mexican Woman is not simply a symbol of the death or doom that awaits Blanche. Williams uses this vendor not only to ordain the future, but also to recapitulate the past. She becomes, in her blindness, a symbol of all the deaths at Belle Reve that helped to deplete Blanche's finances and break her will. (Blanche told us in Scene 1 that "the Grim Reaper had put up his tent on our doorstep!" [262].) The blind Mexican Woman finds her way to Blanche's doorstep in Scene 9; she seems to stalk Blanche, even as death blindly stalked the DuBois family at Belle Reve. The moment Blanche slams the door on the Mexican Woman, the former begins talking to an uncomprehending Mitch about all the death that plagued Belle Reve, as if the Mexican Woman herself had suggested the topic for conversation.

The "flowers for the dead" that the Mexican Woman sells are themselves symbolic of the many deaths at Belle Reve that helped to drive the DuBois family into bankruptcy—a symbolism that is underlined by the juxtaposition of the Mexican Woman's calls with Blanche's evocation of the dying that surrounded her:

> *Mexican Woman (she turns away and starts to move down the street)*: Flores. Flores para los muertos . . . (*The polka tune fades in.*)
> *Blanche (as if to herself)*: Crumble and fade and—regrets—recriminations . . . "If you'd done this, it wouldn't've cost me that!"
> *Mexican Woman*: Corones para los muertos. Corones . . .
> *Blanche*: Legacies! Huh. . . . And other things such as blood-stained pillow-slips—"Her linen needs changing"—"Yes, Mother. But couldn't we get a colored girl to do it?" No, we couldn't of course. Everything gone but the—
> *Mexican Woman*: Flores.
> *Blanche*: Death—I used to sit here and she used to sit over there and death was as close as you are. . . . We didn't even dare admit we had ever heard of it! (388–389)

Williams has the Mexican Woman offer "flowers for the dead" to Blanche partly because, were Blanche to die now, she could afford no better flowers for her own funeral. But the flowers are also symbolic, in their gaudy tininess and their display at festive occasions" (387) as

MODEL ESSAYS

well as at funerals, of all the cheap, good times that Blanche enjoyed with strangers, young soldiers, high-school boys. They are symbolic of the desire that finally lost Blanche her job at the high school in Laurel, and also of the larger desire that seems always to have characterized and divided the DuBois family, from the "epic fornications" (284) of the men to her sister Stella's elemental lust for her husband, Stanley. Once Blanche slams the door on the Mexican Woman, she speaks not only of all the death at Belle Reve, but also of all the desire she cultivated in order to forget death. Again, the Mexican Woman, with her "gaudy tin flowers" (387), has provided Blanche with her cue and continues to cue her as she chronicles the slaking of her desire:

> *Mexican Woman*: Flores para los muertos, flores—flores . . .
> *Blanche*: The opposite is desire. So do you wonder? How could you possibly wonder! Not far from Belle Reve, before we had lost Belle Reve, was a camp where they trained young soldiers. On Saturday nights they would go in town to get drunk—
> *Mexican Woman (softly)*: Corones . . .
> *Blanche*: —and on the way back they would stagger onto my lawn and call—"Blanche! Blanche!"—the deaf old lady remaining suspected nothing. But sometimes I slipped outside to answer their calls. . . . Later the paddy-wagon would gather them up like daisies . . . the long way home . . .
> (*The Mexican Woman turns slowly and drifts back off with her soft mournful cries. . . .*) (389)

So Williams has summarized, through the symbol of the Mexican Woman, the forces behind the play's tragedy: the desire of the DuBois men that squandered away the family fortune and deprived the family of love; the sickness and dying that finally bankrupted the family; and the desire that Blanche used to escape death and achieve intimacy with others, however fleeting. When Blanche finishes speaking of death and desire in Scene 9, she is confronted with a Mitch who wants what he has "been missing all summer" (389). She is confronted, in other words, with yet another reminder of her past—a man who wants a cheap, good time. The cheap, good time that Stanley has at Blanche's expense in Scene 10 is, of course, what seals her doom. Her desire will have led to her spiritual death, even as the illicit desire of her forebears led ultimately to the death of the DuBois line and the loss of Belle Reve.

It is entirely appropriate that a Mexican woman of the lower class becomes the cumulative symbol of death and desire in *A Streetcar Named Desire*. The Mexican Woman speaks a foreign language and repeats one sentence over and over again ("Flores [or 'corones'] para los muertos" [388]); Blanche taught English and is highly articulate. The Mexican Woman is poor, and from a poor foreign country; Blanche's family was once wealthy, and Blanche is proud of her Southern aristocratic heritage. The Mexican Woman, probably old and wearing a dark shawl, is anything but sexually attractive; Blanche once prided herself on her ability to attract men with her good looks and nice clothes. The Mexican Woman, then, represents all that Blanche once thought she was above, and all that she has now become: a foreigner of sorts in New Orleans without a penny, whose language is not understood by Stanley and goes unheeded by Stella; a woman whose heavy make-up and costume jewelry can no longer hide her ravaged looks; a silent woman by the end of the play who does not heed Stella's desperate cries and who "allows [the Doctor] to lead her [out of the Kowalski apartment] *as if she were blind*" (418; emphasis mine).

Williams is careful not to have the Mexican Woman appear suddenly at Blanche's door and disappear just as quickly. We hear the Mexican Woman coming in the background, we hear her calls from afar, and we hear her calls as she turns from the apartment and drifts away offstage. Since she is blind, obviously she moves slowly. The effect of the Mexican Woman's movement, combined with her calls, is haunting. It is to make us feel that Blanche is haunted by her past—by the death and desire that the Mexican Woman and her tin flowers represent—that her past can never leave her; and it is to make us feel that her past will inevitably determine, indeed has already determined, her future. The Mexican Woman, in her walk up to and on from the Kowalski apartment, seems to walk out of the past and into the future, into an oblivion that Blanche herself will soon know.

Work Cited
Williams, Tennessee. *A Streetcar Named Desire*. In *The Theater of Tennessee Williams*. Vol. 1 of 8 vols. New York: New Directions, 1971 (1971–2001). 239–419.

"Uncle Sam in Pinter's *The Homecoming*"

At the end of Harold Pinter's *The Homecoming* (1965), right before Teddy leaves, his paternal uncle, Sam, with whom he seems to have a good relationship, "croaks and collapses" (78). Sam is not dead, yet no one does anything to help him, not even Teddy. Max, Lenny, and Joey—Teddy's father and two brothers, respectively—are more interested in whether Teddy's wife, Ruth, will really be remaining with them in England as their mother-whore. (She finally agrees to terms of "employment.") Teddy is so concerned with getting out of the family home and back to his teaching duties, as well as his three sons, in the United States, that he neglects Sam. Now that his wife has joined his father and brothers, he believes he has no alternative but to depart. To remain with the family is to become like them—which is perhaps one of the reasons that, six years before, Teddy left for America in the first place.

That Teddy sacrifices Sam in order to save himself, however, is a sign of the desperateness of his condition and of his family's insidious power to shape his behavior even as he takes steps to preserve his moral autonomy. For it is Sam with whom Teddy is most identified during the play, and whose physical breakdown can therefore be viewed as signifying his nephew's moral breakdown, as opposed to moral self-preservation. Since Teddy, Sam's "favourite" (62), lives and works in the United States, Sam's very title, "Uncle Sam," as well as his job, driving Yankee businessmen around London (12), connects him with his nephew's country of refuge and thus with his nephew himself.

Teddy married but apparently feared bringing his wife home to meet the family, although he finally does so for the first time in the play—after six years. Sam, for his part, never married, partly for fear of having to bring his own bride home to meet the family, as the following exchange with his brother suggests:

> *Max*: When you find the right girl, Sam, let your family know, don't forget, we'll give you a number one send-off, I promise you. You can bring her to live here, she can keep us all happy. We'd take it in turns to give her a walk round the park.
> *Sam*: I wouldn't bring her here.   (15)

After Teddy brings Ruth "home" from America, it is Sam, and only Sam, who insists that "[Teddy is Ruth's] lawful husband. She's his lawful wife" (69), when Max, Lenny, and Joey get the idea of keeping Ruth as their mother-cum-whore. And it is Ruth's coming to a business agreement with her father-in-law and brothers-in-law, together with Teddy's acceptance of that agreement, that in the end drives Sam to collapse: thus is he identified with the very man—his own nephew—who repudiates him.

Work Cited

Pinter, Harold. *The Homecoming*. New York: Grove Press, 1967.

MODEL ESSAYS

4 Drama and Film

This section consists of short model, or sample, essays on the subject of drama and cinema, or the adaptation of plays to film. Considered here are issues of faithfulness, transmutation, and performance. The following plays have been chosen for their representativeness, variety, quality, and modernity (or, in the case of *Electra*, the rationale for a twentieth-century re-working):

1. *Electra*: Euripides and Michael Cacoyannis
2. *The Balcony*: Jean Genet and Joseph Strick
3. *Equus*: Peter Shaffer and Sidney Lumet
4. *The Elephant Man*: Bernard Pomerance and David Lynch
5. *The Crucible*: Arthur Miller and Nicholas Hytner
6. *Miss Julie*: August Strindberg and Mike Figgis
7. *The Cherry Orchard*: Anton Chekhov and Cacoyannis

For reading and learning purposes, the "Key Analytical Question" below can be applied to any of the above plays or all of them.

Key Analytical Question: "How has one work been adapted from another, as in the case of a film made from a play, and to what extent are the changes in the new work aesthetically justified?"

Introduction: Theater into Cinema, or Seven Adaptations (1962–1999)

I shall not discuss here which form is superior, theater or cinema—an issue, at this point, about as meaningful as the old debate on art versus science. The old strictures about films as *against the theater* are still valid, however. A film is created almost as much by technicians (cameraman and cutters) as by artists (actors, writers, directors). The cinema is essentially not congenial to language. (All the Shakespeare films prove this.) Film does not permit sustained acting; further, skillful directors and editors can synthesize a performance where the talent is minimal. (Marilyn Monroe could not have sustained a ten-minute vaudeville sketch, but Billy Wilder wrung a few hundred snippets of scenes out of her and wove them into her amusing vocalist in *Some Like It Hot* [1959].)

But, true though these strictures are, all they do is compare cinema with the theater, and we can no longer use theatrical standards to judge films. It is a historical fallacy. Film, as we all finally know, must be judged by an aesthetic that is consonant with its resources, methods, and highest potentials. To refute the strictures above by *appropriate* argument: there are indeed more technicians in a movie, but the notion that this means the mechanical deep-freeze of art is about as sound as saying that good writing cannot be done on a typewriter. The theater uses some technicians; the cinema uses more. At what precise number does art die? Obviously all that matters is the result. If our bosoms are truly wrung, it is irrelevant to dismiss the work because the sound engineer and special-effects man contributed. We should know how it happened; but how can we claim it *didn't* happen?

By now, moreover, it has become an unwritten law that film is a director's medium and the theater is a writer's medium; but all unwritten laws ought to be written down once in a while so that they can be examined. Some plays make the second part of the proposition worth examining. At least they show how much the playwright is at the mercy of his director, a mercy that is sometimes hard and sometimes helpful. In conventional theater, plays do not begin without a script. Between us and the author are the performers, as boon or blockade; and in the past 150 years or so, the controlling figure of the director has arisen (incidentally, soon after the rise of the virtuoso musical conductor). Nowadays no dramatist comes to us except through the mind and sensibilities of a director. This does not make the theater as much a director's medium as the cinema; one has only to compare film scripts and play scripts to see this quite clearly. But it does often make the director the decisive element in theatrical performance, for good or less good. One advantage of the theater over films—and a factor that swings the theater's balance to the writer—is that a play can survive one production to be produced again. (Hollywood remakes of earlier movies are not really a relevant analogy.)

As for language, if film is not its best medium, still a film can be well written (Orson Welles's *Citizen Kane* [1941] always immediately to come to mind); and film has non-verbal languages of its own that the theater is denied. They include montage; metaphors of motion by which the audience can be transported as easily as the actors; and the art wrung from sheer physical action—from the elemental chase to the scurrying of the tiny car in Jacques Tati's *Mr. Hulot's Holiday* [1953] to Max von Sydow's ritualistic bath-cum-revenge in Ingmar Bergman's *The Virgin Spring* [1960].

However, it is the matter of acting that, even today, is the heart of the theater's assumed superiority. If Monroe's voice in a play could not puff past the tenth row, why is that a relevant criterion for her performances in films? Many a fine singer can "act" well in his singing but is hopelessly ham in his actual acting; no one thinks that nullifies his validity in his own medium. The superiority of theater acting over film acting—sustained work over "piece" work done out of sequence—rests on the false assumption that if acting is not done in the theater *per se*, it is not acting. Film underplaying itself is not, by definition, easier than most contemporary stage playing; it is simply more internal, not non-existent. The ability to jump into the middle of a scene, without build-up, does not demand the power of sustenance of the stage, but it does demand keen powers of concentration and imagination, as any stage actor can testify who has been interrupted in rehearsal, then asked to resume in mid-scene.

Most conclusively, again, the results speak for themselves. The techniques of film may aid screen actors in ways that the stage actor, coached by his director but now alone, is not aided. But the performances of the best film actors are *performances*—designed, projected work, fired by empathy and imagination and the talent of re-creation. I cite, among many from the past, the film acting of Paul Newman, Marcello Mastroianni, Toshiro Mifune, even Jean Simmons. (A double bill of two inferior films, Mervyn LeRoy's *Home Before Dark* [1958] and Stanley Donen's *The Grass Is Greener* [1960], would show how sadly Simmons was underrated.)

In 1936, the film critic Otis Ferguson wrote the following in *Theatre Arts*:

> The movies have had a hard time in the court of criticism, finding themselves generally in the position of being guilty until they prove themselves innocent. . . . The prosecution can always cite ten bad pictures to the one good picture found by the defense . . . Hence pictures as art are simply not, not nearly; and there is nothing left for the defense to say except that art shall not live by its bad works alone, and that anyone in the more established fields who squinted down the tradition and saw only the fertilizer and not the flower would be punished horribly. (137)

This statement could almost be applied to contemporary theater. But never mind, for the theater has always been judged by its best achievements, its potentialities. A case could be made that serious plays, tragic *or* comic, are not wanted by our society today. The writing talents of our time, whether they could succeed dramatically or not, are rarely drawn to plays because they cannot feel that the theater is penetrable by them or important to the audience they want to reach.

Positively speaking, by contrast, the attractions of film to serious writing, directing, and acting talents increased in the second half of the twentieth century because, in the United States and abroad, there was a sense of social response to film, a sense that it was wanted, that it was acutely attuned to the age. (The historical fact seems to be that when a society wants an art form, talent arises to supply the need [painting in the Renaissance, opera in nineteenth-century Italy].) With the interplay of timeliness and talent, all things—though doubtless difficult—were possible.

To put the matter negatively, as film stands now, most of its works are (as ever) ephemeral and bad, as are most works in all arts. Cinema may be free of the shadow of its antecedent art, but its future, once at least as bright as the theater's, is now hamstrung by cable television, digital widescreens, and the rise of the computer, together with the Internet, live-streaming, social media, iPhones, YouTube—as well as the consequent, inevitable disappearance of movie theaters if not of DVDs themselves. The bonds of commercialism thus are no longer worse in the theater than in the cinema.

All of that said, let me look now at seven Euro-American adaptations of plays to film during what I am now calling the Golden Age of Cinema, from the post-World War II period (starting with the rise of Italian neorealism, otherwise not treated here) to the invention and subsequent development first of the videocassette, in 1971, and then of the digital video or versatile disc (DVD) in 1995. I emphasize, in the previous sentence, Golden Age of *Cinema*, for, by contrast, none of the following adaptations is a superior filmic work of art unto itself: by and large, each is too dependent on the form from which it is derived. I treat these works here because, analytically speaking, they reveal—in what can only be called their state of aesthetic limbo—as much about the drama as the cinema.

Electra: Euripides and Cacoyannis

In the early 1960s the question of adaptation broadened out from a matter of form, purely, to include style, as from Greece came two films adapted from classic plays: *Antigone* (1961) and then *Electra* (1962). The second is the more successful because Michael Cacoyannis, its director, is more aware of its inappropriateness. Euripides' play was designed for performance (in masks) to an audience of many thousands, some of whom were a hundred yards away, to be declaimed to music with formal movement, with its cast always seen at one fixed, great distance; the film is seen in distances varying from long shot to close-up, with mixed movements and rhythms and the camera's motion added, with photography insisting on the realism of the individual rather than his or her symbolic reality. Texture is thus drastically altered; the chorus—which, besides its dance and dramatic aspects, was a kind of amplifying system for the back rows—becomes merely a nuisance; and the gods, whose appearance was fitting in the abstraction of the theater and necessary to the themes of any Greek drama, are eliminated as *ex machina*.

In making *Antigone*, the director George Tzavellas himself clung fairly closely to the original of Sophocles and achieved sincere stiltedness. Cacoyannis, a more talented film director, foresees this pitfall and tries to "lick" Euripides. He slims down the dialogue (although he added some reviling of her mother's body by Electra) and beefs up the physical movement wherever possible—even to the point of taking us into the peasant's house with Clytemnestra. (Euripides was a daring innovator but he would have been horrified by that.) Cacoyannis also attempts to preserve style by using attitudes and stately groupings derived from Greek bas-reliefs and urns, but the more he tries, the more it all looks like pretty posing, too studied and statuesque for the busybody camera. Only some arts and styles—ballet, opera, classic theater—were designed to exist at a remove from the audience, in conventions too large for intimacy.

Walter Lassally, the cameraman of Tony Richardson's socially realistic *A Taste of Honey* (1961) and *The Loneliness of the Long Distance Runner* (1962), makes a considerable journey eastward and back in time to photograph *Electra* in steely sun and muted shadows, and gives us the austerity of the Greek landscape. (Some of the scenes in palaces and temples seem odd, however. These buildings weren't ancient at the time; they must have looked new.) Irene Papas, distinguished and smoldering, does her best to sustain a high Handelian line as Electra, as she tried in Tzavellas's *Antigone*, but is cramped and harried by the form itself. Some of her moments, though—like the recognition of Orestes (Yannis Fertis)—strike home.

None of this is to argue that the film form is incapable of tragedy or to say that the cinema will necessarily always be inferior to the great Greek theater. It is only to note—in formal and stylistic comparison—that *Electra* on film is basically as incongruous as Antonioni on stage. One can understand that a Greek film director was tempted by his nation's heritage, even as the English have been tempted by Shakespeare. But from Laurence Olivier's *Henry V* (1944) we remember most vividly the flight of the arrows and the charge of the horses at Agincourt, from *Electra* the stony, shadowed mountains—not

Shakespeare or Euripides. Billy Wilder's *Some Like It Hot* (1959) is better, as film, than either.

The Balcony: Genet and Strick

Jean Genet's play *The Balcony* had a considerable history of adaptation in its early life. It was first published in 1956 in fifteen scenes; it was subsequently published in 1960 in nine scenes. (This is the version available in the U.S. in translation.) Its first production was in English—London, 1957—over the author's violent protests about the way it was produced. *The Balcony* was first presented in New York, Off-Broadway, in March 1960 and was condensed before the opening; it was presented in France the following May and was again condensed—after the opening. In 1963 it was radically adapted for the screen and filmed Off-Hollywood, so to speak.

"The Balcony" is the name of a brothel in an unidentified country that is torn by revolt. This brothel, an imaginatively equipped palace of illusion, is an observation post from which the bloodshed and struggle can be watched; and the fantasies that the clients act out with the girls are caricatures of the world outside. Three regular customers have always enacted a bishop, a judge, and a general, and in a moment of crisis they have to masquerade as such in the real world. The chief of police, busy suppressing the rebels, himself takes time to visit the madam, who is his mistress. One of his frustrations is that no client has yet wanted to impersonate him. The rebel leader appears toward the end and asks to impersonate the chief. At the conclusion of his scene with a girl, the leader castrates himself. The characters disperse. The revolt is either a success or a failure; it is not clear. The madam addresses the audience: "You must now go home, where everything—you can be quite sure—will be even falser than here" (Genet, 96).

Even this stripped-down summary discloses that the play is a fantasy on themes of power and relative values, as mirrored in extreme rituals of sex. Genet's plays were once shoved into the hastily convoked Theater of the Absurd, but they do not belong there. Both before and after *The Balcony*, he showed himself to be a poetic dramatist of social protest. The modes of meaninglessness—of Beckett, Ionesco, Pinter, Adamov—were remote from this man, whose life and work were acts of assault, hatred of degraded ideals. There was cruelty in the Absurdists, but there was little hate. Hate is impossible without ideals, and ideals were not possible in the theater's *reductio ad Absurdum*.

The screenplay of *The Balcony* (1963), by Ben Maddow, tries to slice down to the themes of the original, articulating them somewhat differently. In a narrow sense the script is an improvement. Genet poses vivid situations, then does not develop them dramatically. For example, each of the clients' scenes begins startlingly, but after one has perceived both the fetish and its symbolism, which takes about a minute, nothing further comes of the scene but verbal embroidery on the initial situation. On a larger scale the play could be summed up in the same way: it is a basically startling and promising image that is not successfully developed. One does not ask for copybook maxims from a poetic drama, but, on Genet's own terms, the metaphors do not generate sufficient tension, do not grow and burst, as the act of drama should. The best effects here are those of lyric poetry, which has only to establish striking figures in apposition and need not do much more with them.

Maddow, sensing this, has tried to impose stricter form and direction on the material, has shortened and simplified. Thus some of the theatrical tedium has been excised, but, inevitably, so has much of the imagery and idea. If Genet had shaped the work better, it would be a better play; Maddow's shaping only makes it more streamlined. And, while altering, Maddow has added mere gags (some of which date: the general settles his bill with a credit card); and he has disrupted the tone of the work by fluctuating between bitter fantasy and broad satire. The police chief gives a nonsensical radio address; the three fake officials make a farcical, triumphant tour by car and pay a meaningless visit to the morgue; the castration is omitted, and the chief and the rebel fight—stopped only by the whores' stripping them naked at the madam's orders.

Yet this same script might have become a more satisfying film in the hands of a more gifted director. Joseph Strick, who previously made the sophomoric *Savage Eye* (1960) and *The Big Break* (1953), has little knowledge of acting, a trite pictorial eye, and less sense of tone than his scriptwriter. Under the titles we see a montage of newsreel shots: street riots, raging mobs. From this scary reality we switch to the brothel, which does not seem to be related even in fantasy to this grainy newsreel world. (When the three fakers later ride through the streets, the newsreel shots, which had previously been used with the grimmest reality, are used for Chaplinesque effects.) Within the chimerical brothel itself, the film is handled without evocative poetic effect. The camera is factual, yet it needed the touch of a Cocteau.

Strick cannot help insecure actresses like Joyce Jameson and Arnette Jens, and he has miscast Ruby Dee. Peter Falk, an actor of guttural capabilities, is never allowed to make the police chief either a power symbol with comic facets or a Marx Brothers butt. Shelley Winters, the madam, is much too earthbound to be an Earth Mother; we could believe her as a madam in Toledo or Tulsa, but not as the archetypal madam of Nowhere and Everywhere. However, the film does give substantial opportunity to that shamefully neglected actress, Lee Grant, who plays the madam's lesbian friend. How prodigally wasteful our theater and cinema were (and are), not to have offered fuller scope to this fine actress.

The merits of the picture, which exist, must not be scanted. It is worth applauding the elementary fact that *The Balcony* was made, that something was done at the time—even if it was adapting a French play—to keep American films at least vaguely in touch with what was happening in the rest of the world. (The New American Cinema, only a few years later, would do more such "outreach" in films like *The Pawnbroker* [1965, Sidney Lumet], *The Graduate* [1967, Mike Nichols], and *Medium Cool* [1969, Haskell Wexler].) More positively, after all the faults have been noted, the picture contains a residuum of the suggestive ambiguities of Genet's play. And it conveys some sense of sex as ambience, sex not merely as the pleasures of the bed but as a pervasive force, a medium for mysteries, revelations, fulfilments.

Equus: Shaffer and Lumet

Peter Shaffer's 1973 play *Equus* had been a tremendous success in London at the National Theatre, had been hailed in New York even before it arrived for its middle-seriousness, and had then opened in the City to praise and profits. It's probably still being revived somewhere in the United States. What bothered me was not the play's success—success or failure is not my professional interest—but its ecstatic critical reception. Like all serious critics, I remain naïve in at least one respect: I can never reconcile myself to the fact that inferior work often gets high praise. (I've never known a serious critic who was truly cynical in this regard. The good ones are outraged by bad criticism the thousandth time as much as the first time.)

At least Sidney Lumet's film of *Equus* (1977) exposes the play for the artistic mediocrity—or less—that it is. I had no clue at the time as to whether the film would be a commercial success (it was not), but I risked one prediction: the film would impose less than the play. The acting, even Lumet's direction, might be praised, but the dubiousness of the material would be more apparent. And this drew me to think of past occasions when transposition to film had been like an acid bath revealing the lead in allegedly golden plays—Arthur Miller's *Death of a Salesman* (1949; filmed 1951, Laszlo Benedek) and Arthur Kopit's

Indians (1968; filmed 1976 as *Buffalo Bill and the Indians*, Robert Altman) are only two examples—and then to explore why this happens.

I don't mean plays that make bad films because they're badly filmed: Terrence McNally's *The Ritz* (1975; filmed 1976), for one, is a better-than-average farce, but its better-than-average film director, Richard Lester, didn't know how to handle stage material. I mean plays that make bad or lesser films because they are bad or lesser plays; I'm talking about the way in which film form searches out flabbiness and thinness in subject matter that, in the theater, has been thought substantial. Often this is because techniques that seemed impressive in the theater are stripped away or reduced to commonplaces by the very form of film. The time-interweavings in *Salesman*, the heavy-breathing sleight of hand in *Indians*—these are such commonplaces of film discourse that they couldn't possibly aggrandize the material on screen. So, in the cases of Miller and Kopit, the film medium revealed that the content under the wrappings was: (a) separable from the wrappings, which in good art would not be the case; (b) less than it had seemed when wrapped.

In *Equus* on the stage, the central metaphor was a boxing ring, into which the actors for each scene stepped from the sidelines. The encounters between the psychiatrist and the boy who had blinded six horses were seen as bouts, probably—since the recurrent motif in the doctor's mind is ancient Greece—intended to have some of the flavor of classic pugilism. The horses were represented by six young men in skin-tight costumes with wire-frame horse heads, and all this symbolic accoutrement was necessity-changed-into-device. The boxing ring was a way of theatrical containment and of abstraction. And, since six real horses were somewhat out of the question, the men-as-horses suggested both the sleek physicality of the beasts and the underlay of unacknowledged homosexuality that pervaded the boy's problem.

These devices gave the play, for many, an air of the poetically profound; but these devices were ruled out by the transposition to film. Symbolism has often been used in films and sometimes by masters—Jean Cocteau and Ingmar Bergman come to mind—but usually it has been symbolism conceived in cinematic modes, and it has very rarely been used in expensive pictures aimed at the "massiest" of mass markets. The mass *theater* audience is not only much smaller numerically than the mass film audience, it also begins at a somewhat higher stratum of intellectual-artistic sophistication. (As has often been noted, there is no longer a truly popular theater audience corresponding in kind to the immense broad base of the film audience.) Indeed, the Broadway audience and its counterparts elsewhere rather enjoy, from time to time, a bit of comfy derrière-garde experimentation and non-realism—Michael Cristofer's *The Shadow Box* (1977; filmed 1980, Paul Newman) was a contemporaneous instance. One of the reasons for the success of the play *Equus*, I'm convinced, was its assurance to theater audiences that they had been tested imaginatively—and had passed!

There's none of this in the film version. Not only because the biggest part of the audience would be discomfited by it but also because the film medium itself would be discomfited by it. Nothing is easier to the cinema than to include many places, so the boxing-ring idea would seem artificial. And real horses, easy to manage with cutting and retakes, push the idea of symbolic horses into the trashcan. Even the most subtle viewer would find these symbols hard to credit in a film. So the film of *Equus* is stripped of its theater paraphernalia.

The script must therefore rearrange the time planes. For the most part we don't get the past as, for the most part, we got it in the play: through the boy's remembering "now" of what happened "then." The film goes to the past in conventional flashback, converting the past into another "now." This makes patent nonsense of what was dreamily disguised nonsense in the play. We see the boy—again, as in the play, well acted by Peter Firth—behaving moonily and loonily with real horses *before* he commits the atrocities, instead of remembering his past acts moonily and loonily after he commits them. This is to make the boy a very visible clinical case right from his first appearance. He is so immediately weird that his parents seem dense not to notice it, and the girl's sexual interest in him becomes highly bizarre. The film thus changes the play's intended mystery about the boy's violent explosion into a flat inevitability, highly predictable by everyone around.

The film does even worse, in a different way, for the psychiatrist. (He is played by Richard Burton with more to work on than in the contemporaneous *Exorcist II* [1977, John Boorman], but with about equal professional sincerity.) The play's various devices tried to give the doctor at least a base for his own agony—his envy of the boy's passion. In the film the present-tense re-creation of the past makes the doctor's envy, which was clearly silly to some of us in the theater, now glaringly clear. Here is a doctor a great deal sicker than his patient—not deprived of passion but sick. Because what the doctor is envying here, obviously, is not passion but psychosis. And the loading of the medical dice by the author, Peter Shaffer, is much more conspicuous on screen: the boy has been assigned to a doctor who is having a frigid marital life. In the play it was plain enough that if the doctor were happily married, the whole thesis would crumble. In the movie version, the contrivance of choosing just this one doctor seems much clumsier, and the whole jerry-built pseudo-Lawrentian comment on the lack of ecstasy in modern life utterly collapses.

But the film medium reveals the spuriousness in spurious plays by more than the stripping away of theatrical devices. Sometimes a poor play has no such devices: it tries to make its way by conviction of realism. Then we get such films as *The Subject Was Roses* (1968, Ulu Grosbard) and *The Effect of Gamma Rays on Man-in-the-Moon Marigolds* (1972, Paul Newman)—each made from a Pulitzer-Prize-winning play by Frank D. Gilroy (1964) and Paul Zindel (1970), respectively—where what seemed like verisimilitude in the theater shows up as artifice, or mere banality, on screen. The film medium *begins* realer than the theater: it eats such plays for breakfast before it gets down to the day's realistic work. Before the digital era, it would have been like putting a ten-power photograph under a 1,000-power viewer and discovering that the photo was insufficiently microscopic or even touched up. With *Equus*, it isn't a case of beginning with gritty realism. The necessities of film "reduced" the play to realism, and that second-stage realism simply doesn't stand up under the camera. Put another way, if there had never been a play called *Equus*, the film still wouldn't ring true.

What does this mean about the relative truth and value of the two arts as such? Absolutely nothing. Some good plays become good films (*The Homecoming*, 1973, dir. Peter Hall from Harold Pinter's 1965 play); some good plays become bad films (*Long Day's Journey into Night*, 1962, dir. Sidney Lumet from Eugene O'Neill's 1941 drama); some bad plays become good films (*Way Down East*, 1920, dir. D. W. Griffith from the 1897 play by Lottie Blair Parker). About the reverse flow—from film to stage—there's much less to say for the obvious reason that, in historical sequence, the theater has been much more of a source for films than vice versa. The few instances I know of the reverse flow have been deplorable: *Sweet Charity* (1966, dir. Bob Fosse from Federico Fellini's *Nights of Cabiria* [1957]), *Sugar* (1972, dir. Gower Champion from Billy Wilder's *Some Like It Hot* [1959]), *Rashomon* (1959, dir. Michael Kanin from Akira Kurosawa's *Rashomon* [1950]), and *A Little Night Music* (1973, dir. Harold Prince from Ingmar Bergman's *Smiles of a Summer Night* [1955]; Prince then adapted his stage version to the screen in 1977). They showed, not surprisingly, that the cinema has its own untranslatable systems of felicities and disguises, that the theater's peculiar strengths can sometimes cripple even a healthy film script. But a trash-detection factor in the theater, analogous to what I've been discussing above, doesn't really apply because I can't think of an original screenplay as poor as the *Equus* film adaptation that has been reworked for the stage.

The aesthetic relations/differences between theater and film aside, a basic duality has increasingly been growing in creative people. Talents coming to maturity these days do not often think of themselves arbitrarily as either playwrights or screenwriters: both arts seem linked, interactive, wonderfully identical, wonderfully different. Even if a writer does choose one or the other, the basic linkage must remain in the twenty-first century. No matter how much a playwright may loathe film, he cannot write for the theater today without awareness of the cinema's effect on vision, rhythm, and realism. No matter how much a screenwriter may disregard the theater, he cannot (if he's serious) disregard what the best modern dramatists have wrought—in strophes of dialogue, surgeries of character, spectrums of imagination. To go back to when this phenomenon began, several decades ago, I can't imagine that Terrence Malick's script for *Badlands* (1973) or Éric Rohmer's scripts for some of his *Moral Tales* (1963–72) would be as they are if Samuel Beckett and the so-called Theater of the Absurd hadn't existed.

So the subject is rosy. And it has really only begun to be cultivated. I describe it here to prevent any misconception about the intent of this piece. I'm not remotely interested in ranking the two arts of drama and cinema. I am interested, and *Equus* brings it up again, in this X-ray detector action of film form on some overrated plays: in showing up the outlines of *papier-mâché* arty décor, in penetrating the surface of superficial realism. The film of *Equus* may have failed at the box office for other reasons, but the adaptation surely showed a lot of people that there is less in the work than met the theater audience's eye.

The Elephant Man: Pomerance and Lynch

The first minute of the film of *The Elephant Man* (1980) is awful. So it's a surprise that the next half hour or so is pretty good. But the rest of the picture is almost as bad as the opening.

That first minute shows us, mistily, John Merrick's mother being frightened by an elephant when she was pregnant. As an explanation of her son's disfigurement—which *he* believes—it's scientifically loony, and, as cinema, it's ludicrous. Then, for a while, the camera of Freddie Francis, guided by the director David Lynch, gives us a "breather": the dank brick of Victorian London is depicted so graphically that we feel rubbed against it. (Francis and Lynch clearly studied Victorian photographs carefully, and the result is that, properly, the whole film is in black and white.)

Through this section, the screenplay by Christopher De Vore, Eric Bergren, and Lynch is laying out its ground vividly enough; but when it wants to swing into action, it doesn't. It repeats and drags, seems only tenuously impelled by an idea, and is written in flabby language. Indeed, the screenplay's dialogue has no flavor at all: it's merely loose or misdirected talk. In the film of *The Elephant Man*, you can hear "contact" used as a verb in 1884. There's also a reference to the "London *Times*"—in London. And the visits of the star actress, Mrs. Kendal, to Merrick, which in the play were at least theatrically effective, are stupid—especially once Anne Bancroft, as Mrs. Kendal, opens her mouth. (Bancroft sounds as if she's just come right off the Bronx subway, and there's no way to explain this except to reveal that her husband, Mel Brooks, was one of the movie's backers.)

The script of Lynch's *Elephant Man* is not based on Bernard Pomerance's now well-known, 1977 play of the same name; both works, however, are derived from the same factual sources: *The Elephant Man and Other Reminiscences* (1923), by Frederick Treves, and *The Elephant Man: A Study in Human Dignity* (1971), by Ashley Montagu. The play of *The Elephant Man*, I continue to think, has merit, despite some patness in arrangement and imbalance in structure. (The real drama is in Treves, the doctor, not in Merrick, who is only a victim without possibilities; but Merrick is so much more eye-catching, especially on screen, that Treves fades.) Some of that merit derives from the playwright's use of deft ellipses and neat irony—for instance, in Merrick's building of a model of the church across the way; and much of Pomerance's dialogue, despite occasional sogginess, is astringent, tart, suggestive.

The play, well or less well, grapples with an immense theme: the arbitrariness of life, its lack of design or reason, posed against what we are capable of expecting. Man's great blessing—or curse—the gift of logic, thus keeps ramming into the illogic of human existence. Lynch's film, nebulously, barely visibly, is about a lesser but good idea: man's fear of that arbitrariness, a fear that can take derisive, "scientific," or sanctimonious form. Treves gets professional status, for example, by discovering and exhibiting Merrick, and Treves's hospital gets renown by sheltering the Elephant Man. Society, even royalty, brings gifts to the patient and feels noble about it. By contrast, the night porter at Merrick's hospital sells places to pub pals to peer at the Elephant Man. (The direction in those scenes is dreadfully heavy-handed.) All these are ways of gaping in fear at a gap in the design of existence. But this theme is not cultivated and harvested. After it's set, it's just reiterated over and over until the fact of iteration obscures it. (And what was the significance of all that smoke issuing from factories and trains and steamers? Is *any* visual motif a valid theme these days? How about Merrick's building of the church model? Why was it left to become just another hobby on his part?)

John Hurt, behind a swollen helmet of makeup, does as well as possible in the title role, though his inflections are a bit subtle for a man who has spoken so little. Pomerance's play deals better with both face and voice. The stage Merrick wears no makeup at all: he contorts his body to suggest disfigurement. Thus we avoid getting used to the horror, and thus, symbolically, we can accept Merrick's supple discourse as being derived from its flip side—intractable grotesqueness. In the film he could not be barefaced: the camera leaves no room for that kind of imagining; yet his lumpy, twisted head soon becomes just one more horror-flick getup, and the drawing-room dialogue issuing from his mouth begins to take on an air of the faintly comic.

What the film of *The Elephant Man* proves, I think, is that this idea really belongs in the theater—where, in fact, it had already found a home.

The Crucible: Miller and Hytner

"At a moment when we are all being 'investigated,' or imagining that we shall be, it is vastly disturbing to see indignant images of investigation on the other side of the footlights" (Miller, *Crucible*: 204). So wrote Eric Bentley in 1953, reviewing Arthur Miller's *The Crucible* in the *New Republic*. Bentley's widely discussed review then commented on the play's implied parallel between the communist witch-hunt in the early 1950s and the Salem witch-hunt in 1692:

> [The parallel] is true in that people today are being persecuted on quite chimerical grounds. It is untrue in that communism is not, to put it mildly, merely a chimera. (Miller, 1996: 205)

The above criticism is still haunting Miller. In a 1996 *New Yorker* article about the writing of *The Crucible*, a moving article generally, he refers to this point (without mentioning Bentley) and replies that the existence of witches, in the seventeenth century, "was never questioned by the loftiest minds in Europe and America" (Frankel, 45). But this is no reply: neither Bentley nor anyone else had questioned that witchcraft was taken seriously in 1692. The real objection was that

McCarthyism, as Miller certifies in his article, was what spurred him to write his play and that the analogy with the Salem witch-hunt was specious.

Paradoxically, this forty-year-old argument was all the more interesting in 1996 because, at that moment, it was irrelevant. (The argument is highly relevant today, in 2021, as the Democratic Party of the United States continues what former President Donald Trump has called its witch-hunt against him and a number of his high-level supporters.) Presented as a film in that year, *The Crucible* was actually helped by the fact that no topical analogy applied. (Diabolist circles don't signify politically.) With no need to weather the political-analogy test, freed too of the gratitude of a 1950s audience hungry for anti-McCarthyism, the play stands on its own and is better for it. I shall now look at it from this 1996 perspective rather than from the vantage point of 2021.

John Proctor is a farmer in the Massachusetts colony; he and his wife, Elizabeth, have two sons. (Reduced, for some reason, from the three sons in the play.) Some months before the start, Elizabeth had discharged their maid, Abigail Williams, because she thought—justly—that something sexual was brewing between her husband and the maid. Now Abigail, living with her clergyman uncle, dances at night in the woods with other girls her age, eighteen or so, more to vent sexual steam than anything else. They are discovered by her uncle, who is enraged. This turmoil leads to brief hysterical paralysis in two of the girls, and this in turn leads to charges that they have been bewitched. Accusations of witchcraft increase.

After a chain of connections, Abigail sees a way, through more accusations of witchcraft, to get rid of Elizabeth so that she can have John. She doesn't see that John, too, will be involved. A cloudburst of panic breaks over the village. (Abigail's uncle presses witchcraft charges against some men because he wants to acquire their land.) A prominent judge is brought in, and trials are held, all of them recorded. Eventually nineteen people are hanged as witches, including Proctor. He is given a chance to clear himself by signing a confession—to acts he did not commit. He signs; then, like Joan of Arc, he tears up his confession and chooses death. (Abigail had arranged for him to escape with her; he refused, and she fled alone.)

Miller says that he saw his way into the historical material, as a playwright, when he read in the record about a gesture of Abigail's toward John, a gesture revealing tenderness. Thus the play became possible for him when he saw sex as a motivation for Abigail's charges, to which he added land-greediness in others. (When Jean-Paul Sartre wrote the first screenplay of *The Crucible* in 1957, called *The Witches of Salem* [dir. Raymond Borderie], he saw the drama baldly as class war.) No one can quarrel with the possible truth of Miller's interpretation, but it's noteworthy that he couldn't envision his play until he saw it in sexual and material terms, which were not at all the supernatural terms in which the colonists and those "loftiest minds" saw the matter.

Besides these mundane reductions of motive, there are other points to consider. Once the characters are arranged in relation to one another, we simply watch the play unfold predictably. Of course this is also true of great tragedy, but *The Crucible*, as it moves along, seems more the fulfilment of an author's pattern than the grinding of an inexorable fate. And in that pattern there is a gap. Abigail, the Iago of the piece, runs away. And Miller does not follow; he merely drops her when he has no further need of her—not exactly a Shakespearean tactic. Still, this is the best Arthur Miller work that I know.

First, the dialogue. In Miller's modern plays, the dialogue sometimes sounds like squeaky shoes, stiff, uncomfortable. His writing seems much more at ease, more easily figurative and less dragooned into poetry, in the formalities of the seventeenth century. (Miller acknowledges the help of a poet friend with the dialogue.) As for the wholeness of *The Crucible*, there's no point in comparing it with such moribundities as *After the Fall* (1964), *Incident at Vichy* (1964), *The Price* (1968), *The American Clock* (1980), or *Broken Glass* (1994). The two comparable works are *A View from the Bridge* (1955) and *Death of a Salesman*. But the former is ultimately a bit of police news decked out with tragic garlands; and the latter does not, as it claims, dramatize the fall of a man, under worldly pressures, into self-delusion. Willy Loman is deluded from the beginning.

Unlike *A View from the Bridge* and *Death of a Salesman*, *The Crucible* has sinew. Despite Miller's compression of the metaphysical theme into sweaty contrivings, this is the play of his that comes closest to naked, ancient drama. Decades after it was written, shorn of contemporary "utility," the play stands a bit taller, especially toward the end (in Act IV), where Proctor must make his gaunt choice. When he rips up his false and cowardly confession, thus choosing the gallows, his wife, weeping, throws herself on him. He looks at the judges and says: "Give them no tear. Show honor now, show a stony heart and sink them with it" (Miller, *Crucible*: 144).

Miller made his own screen adaptation for the 1996 film of *The Crucible*, and, considerably experienced in this work, did it deftly. He has pruned his play for the sake of cinematic movement and expanded it for the same reason. (For instance, to let us see the girls dancing in the woods.) I don't understand why John and Elizabeth have their last private conversation on a beach, with the jailers a hundred yards away, when all they had wanted was to be alone; and I much prefer the way the drama ends, with Elizabeth's closing lines after John leaves ("He have his goodness now. God forbid I take it from him!" [Miller, *Crucible*: 145]), to the film's finish on the gallows. But Miller has clearly had a fresh look at his work and has restructured *The Crucible* as if he had conceived it for the screen; he hasn't been content to saw up his play and re-tack it together.

Nicholas Hytner, the director, is less limber here than he was with the earlier *Madness of King George* (1994). Once in a while he indulges in stage "pictures" rather than film flow; and once in a while he misses the center of the action. Early on, when one of the pseudo-paralyzed girls sits up, she is just discernible at the bottom left corner of the screen. Hytner also "missed" the music, which is characterized by many tympani and therefore much heaviness. The score he commissioned from George Fenton sounds as if the composer had been listening to Leonard Bernstein's score for *On the Waterfront* (1954, Elia Kazan)—another allegorical work about communist witch-hunts.

Miraculously, however, Hytner has evoked something like a performance from Winona Ryder as Abigail. She doesn't reveal a burning talent, but at least here she is not the star of a college show. Daniel Day-Lewis, as Proctor, gets better the less he has to be a believable farmer and the more he becomes the protagonist of a moral drama. Joan Allen, who at the time was Mrs. Nixon in *Nixon* (1995, Oliver Stone), has always been a rather cool actress, so the part of Elizabeth Proctor fits her. Paul Scofield is the senior judge and speaks his lines adequately. Scofield is of course a highly accomplished actor, but in some roles he does little more than burnish his lines carefully and serve them up on the silver salver of his experience: no bother about creating a man behind the lines. That's what Scofield did as the King of France in Kenneth Branagh's *Henry V* (1989), and that's what he does here. He gets away with it; the film itself does better.

Miss Julie: Strindberg and Figgis

It would have been odd to predict good work from Mike Figgis. To wit: in the 1990s, this British director was best known in the United States for *Stormy Monday* (1988), an imitation American gangster flick set in a small English city, and *Leaving Las Vegas* (1995), a contraption in which an alcoholic man and a hooker find sudsy bliss together. Certainly, Figgis is not a man from whom we would have expected a film of August Strindberg's *Miss Julie*—at all. Or that it would turn out to be (even) as good as it is. Surprises are not often pleasant in the film world, yet, in 1999, Figgis served up a double pleasure.

Comment on any production of this play must start with the cast. Either the two principals are excellent, or the enterprise is doomed. Figgis has cast those two roles superbly, with two British actors little-known in the United States. Saffron Burrows is Julie and has precisely the face and temperament that the role needs, a beauty that promises trouble—for herself as well as others. When she sweeps in, the moody, tyrannical, teasing daughter of a nineteenth-century Swedish count, she brings an immediate air of class that is both her weapon and her prison, along with a sexual drive that we can almost hear seething. The best Julie I had previously seen (I think, since I was a teenager at the time) was the Swedish actress Inga Tidblad, who came to New York with the Royal Dramatic Theater of Stockholm in 1962 and scintillated in the role (as directed by Alf Sjöberg), though she was sixty-one at the time. Burrows, in her twenties, as she would have to be on screen, plunges just as daringly into the middle of the storm and swirls through it to the play's catastrophe.

Peter Mullan is the count's valet, Jean. (Strindberg gives this Swedish servant a French name to mark him as a man who is all too well aware of his class and is unquiet in it.) The best Jean I had previously seen was Christopher Walken, in 1973 at the Long Wharf Theatre in New Haven. Mullan, though quite dissimilar in timbre, matches Walken in tacit, smoldering strength and insolent competence. One not-so-minor point: Mullan is shorter than Burrows. Figgis thus deliberately defies the theater-film convention that a man must be taller than the woman who plays opposite him. Yet with a grim blend of reserve and drive, Mullan towers.

The third character, Christine, the cook who has been Jean's lover, is played by Maria Doyle Kennedy, a quite competent actress who doesn't quite fit. Kennedy, fine-featured, looks more like a cousin of Miss Julie than the earthy working-class woman that Strindberg presumably had in mind as contrast to her mistress. But Christine is a lesser role: the excellence of the two chief actors propels the drama.

Strindberg's play, in one long act, was written in 1888. (Why the opening legend moves the film ahead to 1894 is a mystery.) It is set in the large kitchen of the count's country residence on Midsummer Eve, an annual festival of song and dance with a smack in it of pre-Christian fertility rites. In the celebration outside, the twenty-five-year-old Julie has been dancing with the thirty-year-old Jean. Her excitement and heat drive her to follow him into the kitchen, where he has withdrawn to avoid the trouble he senses may come from her. In the first section of the play, the two of them play their class roles, but they also frivol and flirt, and quarrel and reminisce, and thus draw closer to each other. When the servants are heard approaching with song and dance—salacious in tone—Jean takes Julie into his bedroom to avoid the others. There the pair make love. (In the film, the place where it happens is less luxe than a bed.)

After the servants leave the kitchen and the lovers return, the play explodes in lightning ashes of harmony and quarrel, of possibly feeling together abroad, of some disgust in each for the other, of pity, of despair, of perception of the bleak future—at least for Julie. At the end, exhausted, hollowed, she asks Jean to order her what to do. She knows what he will say. With cool, god-like dispensation, he hands her his razor, and she goes to her suicide. Some years ago a theater director who was planning to produce *Miss Julie* told me that his basic underlying design was to have Julie consciously-unconsciously headed for that razor from the moment that she first enters in high spirits. This, of course, is the quintessence of the tragedy.

In his epochal foreword to *Miss Julie*, Strindberg explains his view of characterization in the play: he maintains that contradictions and variations, rather than consistencies, are the core of human behavior. Though he was hardly the first dramatist to perceive it, his use of this truth advances the play through its reality more than its plot. This makes it a groundbreaking work, formally as well as characterologically. Eric Bentley says of *Miss Julie* that Strindberg "destroyed the French 'well-made' play that had been the technical basis of later Ibsenism" (Bentley, 61). Ibsen's *A Doll House* (1879) and *Hedda Gabler* (1890), though revolutionary in idea and intent, are molded in popular theater structures of the day; *Miss Julie* is not. The Strindberg scholar Evert Sprinchorn writes: "Whereas Ibsen's plays are all exposition, *Miss Julie* is all climax and catastrophe" (Sprinchorn, 36). Thus the play's very organism becomes part of what it is about.

What it is about, at its very base, is history. The transgression of class boundaries occurs here as much because of the century in which Julie and Jean live as because of their present actions. Without in the least being mere signet figures, they arise out of a Europe roiling after 1848. And as part of its historical relevance, this pre-Freud play is startling in its sexual insights. (Not incidentally, it is the first play I know of that mentions menstruation.) We hear about Julie's games with a whip that she played with her former fiance, her dream of being atop a pillar, Jean's boyhood escape from the count's garden through an outhouse, his childhood sense of filth in relation to Julie's purity, his revenge for his pollution—which is what we witness. All these elements can be found in the Freudian index.

Helen Cooper, who wrote the screen adaptation of *Miss Julie* from a translation that she had done for theater production, obviously understands all these matters. She has tried to sustain them, but by her rearrangement and condensation—for cinematic fluency, as she saw it—she has hobbled them somewhat. (I remember being bothered by Sjöberg's 1951 film of the play, as well.) Cooper's version moves the action outside once in a while; further, she—or Figgis—includes a number of fades to black, apparently to denote brief passages of time. But this is precisely what Strindberg did not want—time-lapses or shifts of locale to divert the play from its dynamics. *Miss Julie* takes place, except for the offstage sex, in one room and in real time: interruptions and rearrangements interfere with its almost Sophoclean wholeness.

The very existence of this film involves a collision of two arts, much more jarring than with most films of great plays. The difference is as much phenomenological as aesthetic. In the theater, part of the play's power is that it happens in the real time that passes for us, too, as we are sitting there. This not only gives the play a temporal shape, it heightens the *agon* of Jean and Julie, for we see them going through it minute by minute. But any film, we know, is made over a period of time. Even if Figgis's picture was done in weeks, instead of the usual months, on screen it was still performed in distended time; and the fade-outs only increase our awareness of this fact. To see a good performance of the play is, in an almost literal sense, to endure it—for an hour and a half. This experience is intrinsically impossible with a film because we know that it is composed of scenes shot over many days. And this fact detracts, too, from the effect of the acting, as compared with theatrical performance. At the finish of a stage production of *Miss Julie*, the actors seem almost heroic for having passed through the fire—continuously—before our eyes. This precise effect is not achievable in a film.

Figgis does all he can do, and it is a lot, to controvert this ineluctable fact. With the lithe and darting camera of Benoit Delhomme, he keeps close to his people, pressing us against them so often and so intensely that we seem to feel their bodies and breath. (Figgis did some of the shooting himself, and he did all the music [which is apt and helpful] for *Miss Julie*—even as he has composed the score for some of his previous films.) Throughout, we sense that Figgis wants to beat his film's innate handicap, to give it a victory over its sensory difference from the theater. Yet for all his fervour, for all the fine acting he has evoked, when the picture is done, we miss the arc, the trajectory, of the play. It would have been pretty lame to nail the camera down and perform Strindberg's whole drama in front of it, but a cinematic adaptation of this particular work seems like the old sci-fi device of trying to transfer a soul from one body to another.

The Cherry Orchard: Chekhov and Cacoyannis

All great plays suffer in some measure when adapted for film, because they are great plays, but Anton Chekhov's plays suffer more than most. Of all great dramatists, Chekhov is one of the least amenable to screen adaptation. He often seems to be one of the easiest: he seems so modern, in many ways so immediate. But in terms of form and concept, he is more distant from cinema than many other dramatists, even some earlier ones.

Michael Cacoyannis undertook the Chekhovian transfer with *The Cherry Orchard* in 1999. This Greek director had been absent from the screen and the American stage for many years, but long ago he did much honorable work: films in Greece (*Stella* [1955], *A Girl in Black* [1956]), Greek classics Off-Broadway, the movie of *Zorba the Greek* (1964), ancient Greek adaptations (*Electra* [1962], *The Trojan Women* [1971], *Iphigenia* [1977]), and more. One might think that if a Chekhov play was to be filmed, Cacoyannis (in his seventies at the time) was as likely an adapter-director as could be. But Chekhov resists, simply by being what he is—a unique dramatist.

The largest difficulty with *The Cherry Orchard* (1904) is that, like all this dramatist's major plays, it was conceived in four acts. Such an arrangement is not, for Chekhov, a typographical matter or a theater convenience: it is absolutely integral to his work. Most plays are written in acts that the author uses as building blocks; only a few playwrights conceive those acts doubly—as building blocks, certainly, but also as entities in themselves, burnished and whole, even though they are parts of a larger work. For Chekhov, to whom form is not constraint but beauty, the theater presented the chance to create a work in separate yet cumulative entities. For such authors—Chekhov prime among them—the acts of a play are like movements of a symphony, whole in themselves yet cumulative. *The Cherry Orchard* is not divided into four acts: it is an organism built of four related organisms. "The structure of each act," says Francis Fergusson, "is based upon a more or less ceremonious social occasion" (Fergusson, 177). Each of those occasions is the armature of the act, separate from but preceding or following other social occasions.

A film cannot solve this four-act problem merely by inserting three intermissions along the way, because the film adapters usually feel there must be rearrangements of the material and interpolations. The result, as in this *Cherry Orchard*, is like playing a symphony with its four movements intermingled a bit and with some riffs added. For me, the only truly successful film of a Chekhov play is Louis Malle's *Vanya on 42nd Street* (1994). This is not only because Malle filmed a theater production of *Uncle Vanya* (1898) that André Gregory and his ensemble had been working on for the previous five years—yes, five years—but because Malle's film is not an adaptation. It is Gregory's theater production dexterously photographed, with the play's architecture emphasized by brief intermissions. Free of the stilting that theater-on-film often entails, Chekhov's play, as a play, courses through a film channel; and the result is transfiguring.

Malle's comprehension of form gives his film of *Vanya* a rare depth: it enters the most profound mystery of Chekhov, which is open to good theater production of his plays but eludes most films of them. Three elements compose this mystery. First, there is what we see and hear, the action—life as it flows before us, in all its currents and colors. This flow discloses the subtext beneath the action, the large theme or themes of the play. And beyond that subtext, we come to a stillness, absolute stillness. The text and the subtext, as sculpted in four sections by the author, ultimately lead to a quiet at the center of the whirlpool, a halting of breath, an immobile purity, a fixing of melancholy, a whisper of mortality. Without the shape of the play as Chekhov shaped it, this stillness is out of reach.

In *The Cherry Orchard*, he used a unique device to emphasize this stillness. In Act II, most of the characters are lounging in a meadow at the edge of the orchard. They fall comfortably silent. Here is Chekhov's next stage direction, in Ann Dunnigan's translation: "All sit lost in thought.... Suddenly a distant sound is heard, as if from the sky, like the sound of a snapped string mournfully dying away" (Chekhov, 1739). They all wonder what that sound was: several of them guess at it. (Cacoyannis doesn't use a snapped string: he puts in a distant rumble like a jet plane high above, so the various guesses don't remotely apply.) For me, that distant sound, never really explained, is Chekhov's means of underscoring the play's central stillness—not the momentary silence of these characters but the play's crystalline core. Since Cacoyannis's film is never near this core, that mysterious sound underscores nothing and is irrelevant.

Quite in disregard of Chekhov's design, this adaptation of *The Cherry Orchard* frequently bows to the supposed gods of screen adaptation. In the first instance, though the play is utterly Russian—about the sale of an estate in Russia and the complex meanings of that sale—the film begins in Paris. Anya, the daughter of Madame Ranyevskaya, the estate's owner, has gone there to bring her extravagant mother home. In Act I of the play itself, all of which takes place on the estate, Anya tells us that she made this trip; but Cacoyannis "opens up" the play by beginning in Paris. This attempted flexing into cinematic form breaches the enclosure of place, of specific place, that Chekhov intended. (Theatrically speaking, it also injures Ranyevskaya's entrance. In the film we see her sitting in her Paris attic, amid friends, placid. In the play we first see her returning to her home after a five-year absence, savoring her return both truthfully and histrionically.) Such an alteration also ignores a basic aesthetic difference between film and theater. Film ventures forth, finding and following action. In the theater, the action arrives: the theater does not go looking for it. For Chekhov, this theater principle is essential.

Here's another instance of ill adaptation in the film of *The Cherry Orchard*. In Act III, as Chekhov planned it, Madame Ranyevskaya is giving a party that she can ill afford, at the same time that elsewhere her estate is being put up at auction. Again Cacoyannis cannot resist the temptation to cinematize: he intercuts these simultaneous events. Thus the quasi-suicidal bustle of the party is interrupted, and when the affluent peasant Lopahin breaks into the party to announce that he has bought the place, the impact of his announcement is diminished.

A paradox, an additional pity, clings to Cacoyannis's film: most of the actors are exceptionally good. Charlotte Rampling, at the time blossoming in mid-career, decks Ranyevskaya with nobility and with a profligacy that belongs to the past. Alan Bates, another actor who kept growing, plays Gayev, her lazy, endearing brother, dispensing elegance and kindly imperception. Katrin Cartlidge, as Ranyevskaya's adopted daughter Varya, gives tacit pain to a frustrated marriage. As the student Trofimov, who came to the estate to tutor Ranyevskaya's son and stays around after the boy's death, Andrew Howard amply provides the fire with which his character sees the future. Owen Teale is Lopahin, the peasant who was not even allowed in the kitchen when he was a boy and who now owns the place. The tearful-joyful outburst in which he announces his purchase is one of the pinnacles of dramatic literature; Teale almost attains it. (My measure of Lopahin is James Earl Jones, who was superb in an all-black production of the play [also directed by Jones] in New York in 1972.) Of the capable others, I note only Michael Gough, who, after being the valet in *Batman* (1989, Tim Burton), turns up here as another valet, doddering old Feers, who is forgotten at the end when everyone else moves on.

With this cast and even with this adaptation, Cacoyannis could have done better. Chekhov called *The Cherry Orchard* a comedy—in my view, he insisted on this point because, fearing the slow and mournful tempo he knew Stanislavsky (the director of the premiere) would try to achieve, he wanted to prod him to keep things moving. With Cacoyannis, the phrase "slow and mournful" is almost vivacious. The pauses, the slow pick-up of cues, are examples of what is often assumed to be Chekhovian style but is only a facile dolor that hurts the work's true gravity. I must add, as a postscript, that the difficulties mentioned above apply only to Chekhov's plays. His stories, for formal reasons, are much more congenial to the screen. One of the most beautiful films that I know is Josef Heifitz's adaptation of *The Lady with the Dog*, made in the Soviet Union in 1959. I should say that "I knew," though I obviously can still see Heifitz's film today on a television screen, even on a digital, wide-screen, high-definition TV. I don't think, however, that the likes of such a film (adaptation though it may be) will appear again in anybody's neighborhood, university, or art-house cinema any time soon. For cinephilia as we once knew it, during the Golden Age of Cinema, began decaying in the late 1990s (and may now in fact be dead)—precisely when *The Cherry Orchard*, about decay and death of another kind, was made.

Works Cited

Bentley, Eric. *The Playwright as Thinker*. 1946. Minneapolis: University of Minnesota Press, 2010.

Chekhov, Anton. *The Cherry Orchard*. In *Understanding Literature: An Introduction to Reading and Writing*. Ed. Walter Kalaidjian, Judith Roof, & Stephen Watt. Boston: Houghton, Mifflin, 2004. 1717–1760.

Ferguson, Otis. "The Screen Presents—Hollywood's Gift to Broadway." *Theater Arts Monthly*, 20 (Feb. 1936): 136–43.

Fergusson, Francis. *The Idea of a Theater: A Study of Ten Plays*. Garden City, NY: Doubleday, 1949.

Frankel, Benjamin. *History in Dispute: The Red Scare after 1945*. Detroit: St. James Press, 2004.

Genet, Jean. *The Balcony*. Trans. Bernard Frechtman. 1958. New York: Grove Press, 1966.

Miller, Arthur. *The Crucible*: Text and Criticism. Ed. Gerald Weales. New York: Penguin, 1996. AND: "Why I Wrote *The Crucible*." *New Yorker* (Oct. 21 & 28, 1996): 158–160, 162–164.

Sprinchorn, Evert. *Strindberg as Dramatist*. New Haven, Conn.: Yale University Press, 1982.

5 Comparison and Contrast

This section consists of short model, or sample, essays on the comparison and contrast of two plays similar in style, structure, or meaning. Treated here are a modern adaptation of Sophocles' *Antigone*, a Chinese take on the theater of Bertolt Brecht, a twentieth-century updating of Ben Jonson's comedy of humours, the relationship between the dream play and a Strindbergian tragedy, and the difference between radio drama and staged plays. The following plays have been chosen for their representativeness, modernity, variety, and quality:

1. August Strindberg's *Miss Julie*
2. Fernand Crommelynck's *Golden Guts*
3. David Hare's *Fanshen* and Bertolt Brecht
4. Luis Rafael Sánchez's *Passion of Antígona Pérez* and Antigone
5. Dylan Thomas's *Under Milk Wood* and Thornton Wilder's *Our Town*

For reading and learning purposes, the "Key Analytical Question" below can be applied to any of the above plays or all of them.

Key Analytical Question: "Concerning two plays similar in style, structure, or meaning, what are the differences in their sociohistorical contexts (if there are any), and which thematic threads do they share?"

"Strindberg's *Miss Julie* and the Dream Play"

August Strindberg's playwriting can effectively be divided into two major stages: the naturalist works from the late 1880s to the early 1890s, and the predominantly expressionist dramas that date from 1898 onwards. These later plays display a preoccupation with distorted inner states of mind—a preoccupation that understandably derived from his "inferno crisis." The fragmentation of character so characteristic of Strindberg's expressionism first appears in *To Damascus* (Part I, 1898), a play with Biblical overtones but simultaneously a projection of the problems of the dramatist's second marriage. The fullblown expressionism that followed is chiefly represented by *A Dream Play* (1901)—which did so much to free the stage from the time- and space-bound assumptions of naturalism—and is also seen in the earlier *Dance of Death* (1900). Parallelling and enlarging on many of the discoveries made around the same time in the fields of psychology and psychoanalysis (as in Freud's first important study of the unconscious, *The Interpretation of Dreams* [1900]), these non-realistic plays depend not on the (neo)classical unities but instead on the individual, subjective mind for their overall shape, with the erratic structure of dreams playing a prominent part in their creation.

As Strindberg himself explained in his note to *A Dream Play*, he was attempting to reproduce "the disconnected but apparently logical form of a dream." Because this drama is a dream, "Anything is apt to happen, anything seems possible and probable.... The personalities split, take on duality, multiply, vanish, intensify, diffuse and disperse, and are brought into focus. There is, however, one single-minded consciousness that exercises a dominance over the characters: the dreamer's" (171). The dreamer, of course, was the playwright himself, and the disconnected events of the play vividly project his melancholic vision of the human landscape, where "men are pitiable creatures" beset by an assortment of miseries. Posing exceptional problems for any producer, *A Dream Play* was successfully staged at the 161-seat Intimate Theater in Stockholm, which Strindberg helped to found in 1907 and which brought the independent theater movement to Sweden.

The naturalistic *Miss Julie* (1888) itself is not normally thought of as a dream play, written as it was when Strindberg was under the influence of such hardheaded masculine mentors as Charles Darwin, Émile Zola, and Friedrich Nietzsche. The dramatist wrote a brash, confident preface to the play in which he congratulated himself for adhering to the most strenuous authenticity and objectivity in its composition: the three unities of time, place, and action are religiously adhered to; throughout we deal primarily with the two characters of Jean and Julie—each of whom acts out of a "multiplicity of motives" or confluence of biological as well as social circumstances—and only to a lesser extent with a third, Christine; the action never strays from the kitchen, and the time-span required for the drama to run its course onstage corresponds roughly to what it would have taken in real life.

Moreover, the one-act form of *Miss Julie* eliminates all intermissions, and the set for the play is to be diagonally arranged, so that, as they would in real life, "the actors have to play face on or in half profile when they are seated opposite each other at the table" (*Miss Julie*, 66). The action itself is set in a kitchen that really functions, for the play begins with Christine frying a piece of kidney on the stove, and it reaches a climax with Jean's beheading of Julie's greenfinch on the kitchen chopping block. In all these respects, Strindberg carried naturalistic theater further than any of his contemporaries—extending it to its logical and psychological limits.

Despite Strindberg's pose as a literary scientist, however, he was incapable of remaining detached from his material, especially since *Miss Julie*, like *The Father* (1887), was inspired by his embattled relations with his first wife, not to speak of his artistic battles with Henrik Ibsen over the depiction of women in particular and the social classes in general. (Indeed, Strindberg wrote *The Father*, in which a calculating woman drives her husband into madness, in direct response to Ibsen's "sick" play *A Doll House* [1879].) And *Miss Julie*, besides featuring such normally non-naturalistic elements as ballet or dancing, pantomime, and a musical interlude (additions, thought Strindberg, that would allow the audience a momentary rest from the intensity of the play's performance without sacrificing the illusion of reality that the dramatic action has created), includes the narration of two dreams in which Strindberg, anticipating Freud, locates the very life drives of his central characters.

The dreams are concerned with rising and falling. Jean, a valet who aspires to the nobility, recurrently dreams about lying on the ground beneath a great tree, determined to pull himself up from the dirt to a golden nest above. Julie, an aristocrat who likes to mix with the servants, dreams about looking down from the height of a great pillar, drawn to the earth below though she is fearful that the fall will mean her death. These dreams are insinuated into the dramatic design of the play, shaped by Strindberg like two intersecting lines. Jean, a young man of robust working-class origin, reaches up and Julie, a representative of the refined but decadent upper classes, falls down, both meeting on equal ground only at the moment of seduction, in the arms of that great equalizer, sex.

Strindberg's sympathies toward these rising and falling characters are divided rather than neutral. Like Tennessee Williams—whose *A Streetcar Named Desire* (1947) recapitulates *Miss Julie* in contemporary terms—he is attracted by the superior social graces of his heroine, and also by the brutal animal magnetism of his hero. (Thus did Strindberg's Darwinism, with its emphasis on natural selection and the survival of the fittest, meet his recently acquired Nietzschean ideology of a superior race.) Jean triumphs over Julie sexually, but she commits a noble sacrificial act of which he is incapable, by taking her own life at the end of the play. As she walks resolutely to her death at sunrise, razor in hand, and Jean cowers abjectly near the boots of Julie's father, the Count, the split loyalties of the author are clarified. She has remained an aristocrat and died, Jean has remained a servant and lived, while their dreams have been played out in a reality that suggests the great sexual and social conflicts of our time.

The fairy-tale quality that creeps into this play about a valet and the daughter of a count—a princess and an ass, if you will—may seem out of place in a naturalistic work, but Strindberg has infused *Miss Julie* with just such a dreamlike aura, just as Shakespeare infused *A Midsummer Night's Dream* (1595–96), which is set on the same day. (*Miss Julie* takes place on the eve of St. John's Day, which is also Midsummer Eve—traditionally a holiday of festive release, of all-night merrymaking, when lovers reveal themselves to each other and almost anything can magically happen.) No small part of that aura consists of the signs of Julie's father. Throughout the play the Count's absent presence weighs ominously on the scene (like General Gabler's in Ibsen's *Hedda Gabler* [1890]), a disembodied reminder of the social realities governing the action, personified as he is by the speaking tube and his elegant, polishing riding boots replete with spurs. A dreamlike—even nightmarish—presence, indeed.

Works Cited

Strindberg, August. Preface to *A Dream Play*. Trans. Arvid Paulson. In *A Treasury of the Theater*. Ed. John Gassner & Bernard F. Dukore. Vol. 2. 4th ed. New York: Simon & Schuster, 1970. 171.

——. *Miss Julie* and Other Plays. Trans. Michael Robinson. New York: Oxford University Press, 1998.

"Crommelynck's *Golden Guts* and the Comedy of Humours"

As D. Heyward Bock points out in *A Ben Jonson Companion*, "although Chapman's *An Humourous Day's Mirth* (1597) was the first humours play, Jonson was the first playwright to develop a theory of comedy derived from the theory of humours and to use humours characters to portray various types of irrational and immoral behavior" (129). Or, as John Enck puts it in his *Jonson and the Comic Truth*, "human neuroses have found their ideal dramatic transpositions in the humours of Ben Jonson's farcical characters" (46). According to the theory of humours, a person's physiological and psychological health depends exclusively on the balance among the humours, the four liquids that, corresponding to the four primary elements of earth, air, fire, and water, control the human body: blood, phlegm, yellow bile or choler, and black bile or melancholy. Ideally, these four liquids exist in harmony, thus producing perfect physical and mental health. Whenever one of the humours becomes dominant, however, there is a corresponding imbalance in the temperament of the individual—that is, a sickness of the mind as well as of the body. In his "Induction" to *Every Man Out of His Humour* (1600), Jonson translated this (in his day) medical theory into dramatic terms:

> As when some one peculiar quality
> Doth so possess a man, that it doth draw
> All his affects, his spirits, and his powers,
> In their confluctions, all to run one way,
> This may be truly said to be a Humour. (62)

In a famous essay on Jonson, T. S. Eliot himself concluded that "the Humour . . . is not a type . . . but a simplified and somewhat distorted individual with a typical mania" (18).

In Fernand Crommelynck's *Golden Guts* (1925), Pierre-Auguste perfectly fits Jonson's definition of a humours character. His "irrational and immoral" behavior can be explained in terms of an excess of yellow bile in the liver, which triggers his antics, his anger, and his irritability. The condition of Pierre-Auguste's mental health—and thus indirectly of his belly—deteriorates precisely as a result of the impairment of his glands. Accordingly, he begs Barbulesque, the veterinarian who has acted as his quack doctor throughout the play, to graft new ones for him. According to the humoural theory, writes Henry Snuggs, "one's temperament could change under great stress of emotion or circumstance into another temperament" (118). This is exactly what happens to Pierre-Auguste. In *Golden Guts*, the shock of the inheritance on Pierre-Auguste is so great, or so grand, that he loses consciousness and is even feared to be dying. But such a change in this character's behavior or condition is possible only because of his physiological, humoural predisposition; external factors serve simply to tilt a precarious internal balance. In John Enck's words, "where humours dominate, no other psychology prevails" (45).

Unlike Harpagon (in Molière's *The Miser* [1668]), whose jealousy constantly needs the servant La Flèche's prompting, Pierre-Auguste is his own La Flèche: his humoural self-motivation alone moves the plot along and brings it to a resolution. And his humoural predisposition predates the play in which he stars. We discover during *Golden Guts* that before he inherited the fortune of his uncle, Pierre-Auguste used to work overtime as an accountant and save his earnings in preparation for his future marriage to one Azelle. But he always postponed the wedding under the pretext that the sum of money he had gathered—in the form of gold, which he kept hidden in a small leather purse around his neck—was still not enough to ensure their happiness. Conversely,

Pierre-Auguste never really stops being what he used to be, that is, a generous being. Except that his charitableness is more and more overwhelmed by overflowing yellow bile, a product of the glandular fever from which he suffers, and this internal conflict slowly destroys him.

Crommelynck's humours, then, work psychologically as well as physiologically, and this close relation between the mind and the body is clearly alluded to in Act II of *Golden Guts* in a hilarious converstaion between Pierre-Auguste and Barbulesque:

> *Barbulesque*: When you sleep, what part of your person is asleep?
> *Pierre-Auguste*: My body.
> *Barbulesque*: Not at all. Your blood is circulating, your heart is beating, your lungs are whistling, and, if you have the scabies, you scratch. Oh, yes!
> *Pierre-Auguste*: Then, it's my mind.
> *Barbulesque*: Not at all. Your mind is wandering. You dream that you're discovering a treasure, you're stroking it, you're kissing it, you're wallowing in it, and you wake up disappointed. Oh, yes!
> *Pierre-Auguste*: Does it mean, then, that my body and my mind sleep apart?
> *Barbulesque*: Not at all. If you have flatulences, you'll have a windy dream; if you have a blister on your heel, you'll have a pesdestrian dream. If your mind makes a nightmare full of death, crime, and ruin, your skin will release its sweat and your eyes all their water.
> (75–76; my translation)

To treat Pierre-Auguste's glandular fever, Barbulesque orders him to eat his gold in the hope that it will dissolve his body's malignant yellow bile by some strange alchemy. But this remedy can only prove inefficient against what is a kind of gold fever in the first place: the gold just feeds Pierre-Auguste's infection and thus constitutes a striking visualization or externalization of his ailing humour. In fact, Pierre-Auguste is not to be cured. His illness prompts him to make over his entire environment to fit his humour, as the physical change in his character and the setting of *Golden Guts* itself attests. This protagonist then becomes violent in the extreme to preserve his newly creatred "order" until the bitter end.

It follows that any purely psychological approach to *Golden Guts*, besides being doomed to fail, would be reductive of Crommelynck's metaphorical, universal art. "Some critics consider me a psychological playwright," Crommelynck said in a conversation reported by his friend René Gimpel, "and they are wrong. Ah! That was Marcel

Proust's big mistake: the critics told him so often he was a psychological writer that he lost his magnitude" (277; my trans.). Moreover, Pierre-Auguste's painful self-consciousness mirrors that of a century that had just gone through, in its second decade, the shattering experience of World War I. Through this character, Crommelynck ruthlessly caricatures the behavior of his contemporaries in their futile quest for the absolute, their desperate search for answers during a troubled era that had seen the elegant sureties of its *Belle Époque* destroyed by the First World War. Crommelynck stigmatizes this hunger for absolutes through his portrait of the miser ridiculously eating his gold in order to secure undeniable possession of it. In this *Golden Guts* shows some affinities to the major avant-garde movements of the first quarter of the twentieth century, especially Dada and late expressionism, which condemned the hopeless quest for moral and metaphysical certainties in a chaotic world by assuming a particularly cynical, even destructive stance.

Despite its tragic undertones, the situation presented in *Golden Guts* is far too grotesque, far too excessive, to be accepted within the framework of tragedy. Performed as a tragedy, the play soon moves beyond the spectator's ken and loses its credibility. The vision of Pierre-Auguste sitting atop his potable potty throne can only be accepted within the logic of a humoural design. The absurdity of Pierre Auguste's behavior jolts the spectator and makes it impossible for him to identify with this protagonist in the usual tragic manner.

To study the great dramatic archetype of the miser, Crommelynck thus puts it under the magnifying lens of humoural comedy, where even the most appalling human vices can be ridiculed and where death itself loses its grimness, for it is considered the logical, necessary, indeed natural conclusion of a life of gross excess. Pierre-Auguste's avarice is an irrational response, and the genius of Crommelynck lay in his choice of such a rational dramatic form in which to portray it—one that makes an impossible situation seem to be totally probable.

Works Cited

Bock, D. Heyward. *A Ben Jonson Companion*. Bloomington: Indiana University Press, 1983.

Crommelynck, Fernand. "Fernand Crommelynck Interviewed by Jacques Philippet." I.N.R. (Belgian radio), Feb. 26, 1956.

———. *Tripes d'or* [*Golden Guts*]. In *Théâtre 2*. Paris: Gallimard, 1968.

Eliot, T. S. "Ben Jonson" (1920). In *Ben Jonson: A Collection of Critical Essays*. Ed. Jonas A. Barish. Englewood Cliffs, NJ: Prentice-Hall, 1963.

Enck, John J. *Jonson and the Comic Truth*. Madison: University of Wisconsin Press, 1966.

Gimpel, René. *Journal d'un collectionneur marchand de tableaux.* Paris: Calmann-Lévy, 1963.

Jonson, Ben. "Induction." *Every Man Out of His Humour.* In *Ben Jonson's Plays.* Vol. 1. Ed. Felix E. Schelling. 1910. London: J. M. Dent, 1956.

Snuggs, Henry L. "The Comic Humours: A New Interpretation." *PMLA*, 42.1 (March 1947): 114–122.

"Hare's *Fanshen* and Brecht"

In an influential review, Michael Coveney once described David Hare's *Fanshen* (1975) as a "marvellous play that, in my opinion, is the nearest any English contemporary writer has come to emulating Brecht" (31). *Fanshen* does indeed resemble such *Lehrstücke* (learning plays) of Bertolt Brecht's as *He Who Says Yes* (1930), *He Who Says No* (1930), and *The Measures Taken* (1930). As in Brecht's "plays for learning," as in *Fanshen*, there is, according to David Bathrick,

> an emphasis upon the open, tentative, and heuristic presentation of ideas; upon learning through involvement, through active, critical, testing participation. The quintessence of the "play for learning" . . . is the very opposite of "didactic," for it requires that the audience not accept action and characters as finished products, but rather as unhewn attitudes and behaviors which must be tested; as models for critical experimentation. (213)

Bathrick is right to point out that the *Lehrstück* exists "to a lesser or greater degree in all of Brecht's political plays, whether in the works he specifically referred to as *Lehrstücke* or in the 'epic' *Schaustücke* (*Mother Courage, Galileo,* etc.) of the later years" (214). It is equally true that the concept of character Brecht employed in plays such as *Mother Courage and Her Children* (1941) and *Life of Galileo* (1939), which treat "main characters" or single protagonists and their victimization or alteration by society, is the same one he employed in the *Lehrstücke*, which emphasize the *group* and the individual's role in strengthening or improving it. This is the concept of character that David Hare employs in *Fanshen* as well.

About Brecht's own concept of character," Walter Sokel has written that

> . . . from the beginning Brecht was unable to accept the concept of dramatic character as the ultimate, absolute, and fate-determining quality which it had been for the traditional European drama, "the

drama of Renaissance and classicism," as Peter Szondi called it. He had to reject it because that concept is rooted in the religious and metaphysical idea of an indivisible and eternal soul. (177)

Brecht had to reject such a concept because it is also rooted in the idea of an unchangeable world. The drama of Renaissance and classicism accepts the world as it is, and the focus of this drama becomes a person's suffering because of inherent flaws, because of "human nature." People may change at the end of the great Western tragedies in the sense that they learn something significant about themselves. But, as previously noted, the character's knowledge almost always comes too late, since the character gets it in dying or in experiencing some other form of great misfortune. And it is generally not the kind of knowledge from which audience members can profit, though they may have been purged emotionally by watching the protagonist's journey from darkness to light. The likelihood is that they themselves will have to go through a similar experience in order to learn similarly.

Brecht wanted, according to Sokel, to portray "permanent changeability in place of unity and consistency of characters. [His] characters are 'without qualities,' or rather, are equipped with changeable, exchangeable, and mutually contradictory traits" (178). The dramatist wanted to portray permanently or fundamentally changeable characters whose change came about less through some internal process, from what is called "tragic recognition," than from some change in their environment or circumstances. He wished to take the focus away from the internal person in an unchanging world and place it on the external person, the one of observable actions rather than hidden motivations, in a world changed by this individual and others.

This shift of focus, Brecht thought, was the only way in which the world, specifically the capitalist- and imperialist-dominated one, could be changed: by showing that people are not tragically isolated from an unchangeable and insensate society, but rather are products of the societal conditions under which they live. A change in them for the better, according to Brecht, should lead to a change for the better in so-called immutable human nature, an improvement in the relations of human beings with one another. A change for the worse, or no change at all in already bad conditions, as in *A Man's a Man* (1926), can lead only to further deterioration in the relations among people. Unless, that is, *a person* takes action. What is important for Brecht is that people themselves must make the changes in the social system that are going to improve their lives. They will not occur miraculously.

People themselves do make the changes in *Fanshen*. To summarize the play's action: after World War II, Long Bow, located 400 miles southwest of Beijing, is turned by its one-thousand inhabitants from a village exploited by feudal landlords into one run on a rudimentary model of Chinese communism: land and goods are distributed to all as equally as possible, and decisions are made collectively. The change for the better in the social system leads to a change for the better in the nature of the citizens: a beggar becomes a leader of a women's organization; a quiet, shy man learns that he can be an eloquent and persuasive speaker; and the brutal, greedy, wanton Yu-lai—super-ficially, the most conventional figure in the play, the villain, and therefore the one least susceptible to productive reform, as opposed to gallows repentance, in Western drama—is broken and eventually reformed.

Yu-lai, for one, is not a villain *by nature*. He is the villainous product of once feudal social conditions in Long Bow, and he has remained so out of bad habit. Conditions have changed, and Yu-lai can change with them if he is given a chance and the proper guidance. Even as the social and economic structure of the village has been transformed, so too must its delinquent citizens be. Not to transform them—and place them back in the community as models of rehabilitation to other miscreants—is itself to foster delinquency. The message is that human beings must not only make the changes in the social system, as the Communists did in Long Bow and throughout China; they must also help their fellows to change in harmony with an improved environment. Yet we never see Yu-lai himself as a changed, finished product. For *Fanshen* ends openly, "in process," like Brecht's *Lehrstücke*. The implication is that, once reformed, Yu-lai, like his fellow villagers, will continue to change in response to a dynamic society.

Works Cited

Bathrick, David. "Brecht's Marxism and America." In *Essays on Brecht: Theater and Politics*. Ed. Siegfried Mews & Herbert Knust. Chapel Hill: University of North Carolina Press, 1974. 209–225.

Coveney, Michael. "*Fanshen*: Criticism." *Plays and Players*, 22.9 (June 1975): 31.

Hare, David. *Fanshen*. London: Faber and Faber, 1976.

Sokel, Walter. "Brecht's Concept of Character." *Comparative Drama*, 5.3 (Fall 1971): 177–192.

"Sánchez's *Passion of Antígona Pérez* and Antigone"

At the time of the writing of *The Passion of Antígona Pérez* (1968), Luis Rafael Sánchez (born 1936) was the most promising young writer contributing to the renaissance in literature and drama taking place in Puerto Rico over the previous two decades. Like older and more celebrated authors such as René Marqués and Francisco Arriví, he explored the cultural impact of Puerto Rico's relationship to the United States, whose commonwealth or territory it is. Sánchez's focus, however, is distinct, for his work illustrates not only the imposing specter of U.S. political domination, but also Puerto Rico's equally strong cultural ties with Spanish-speaking America.

In this drama, a modern or even contemporary Antigone is inspired by the life of Olga Viscal Garriga (1929–95), a member of the Puerto Rican Nationalist Party. Held captive in the palace of Generalísimo Creón Molina, Antígona Pérez is a political prisoner awaiting death. She stole and buried the bodies of two friends who attempted to assassinate Creón and accepts her sentence by refusing to disclose the location of the graves. The conflict in this play involves more than Antígona's defiance of Creón, however, for these two characters symbolize contrasting elements of Latin American political life. Antígona expresses the desire for self-determination and freedom from economic as well as political exploitation, while Creón represents the domination of military dictatorship and foreign influence. addresses her "Homeland, America," exhorting the following: "America, don't give up; America, don't die; America, don't suffer; America, don't lose; America, awake; America; be calm; America, watch out" (Sánchez, Act II, scene 2). When the play is performed in the United States, the plea of the protagonist, Antígona Pérez, often receives uneven responses from confused audience members. Is Antígona sending a message to the United States to intervene in her Latin American homeland? Is she boldly rejecting the assumed right of the United States to characterize itself as America? Or is she warning U.S. citizens that what is happening in the fictional country of Molina may also happen in their own nation?

Thus the notion that Antígona might be calling for U.S. intervention with her "America" lines is textually erroneous. Lines delivered throughout the drama by a chorus of "yellow" journalists establish that the United States already supports the military regime that Antígona opposes. Moreover, the U.S. ambassador "defends the military governments of Latin America by declaring that they are totally distinct from those of the days of Trujillo, Batista, and Porfirio Díaz"; and the Secretary of State declares that "the United States will continue to intervene unilaterally whenever necessary to defend the Western Hemisphere from Communism (Sánchez, Act I, scene 1). Antígona reveals that it is actually the ruler Creón Molina who seeks foreign intervention: "A perfect set-up for the landing of 2,000 United States Marines" (Act I, scene 3). Enormous political placards described by the playwright as part of the scenic background—"YANKIS GO HOME," "THE CANAL BELONGS TO PANAMA," "BOLIVIAN MINES FOR THE BOLIVIAN PEOPLE" (Sánchez Act I, scene 1; Sánchez, Act II, scene 2)—further establish the play's perspective on the interference/intervention of the United States in Latin America. Therefore, the confusion of audience members at Antígona's "America" lines seems to derive not from the text itself, but from their own unfamiliarity with events shaping the modern political history of Latin America and their tendency—strongly reinforced in nearly every aspect of U.S. society—to think of America exclusively as the United States.

Although Antígona's "America" does not directly include the United States, the play assumes additional thematic qualities when performed for North American audiences. What we in the United States egotistically consider America is refined in Sánchez's drama, and Antígona Pérez calls on the people of all nations in the Western Hemisphere—all American countries—to examine themselves in terms of the "passion" being performed before their eyes. Her exhortation also implies that our culture can no longer afford to ignore or suppress important social, political, and artistic developments in other countries of the Western Hemisphere. In this way, the play provides a Latin American view of the United States; but, beyond that, its representation of the small and isolated nation of Molina illuminates the political process in the United States as well, for Sánchez juxtaposes different concepts of the nature of human existence in general. One is based on social order and political expediency above all else, whereas the other addresses personal dignity, individual freedom, and self-determination. The conflict between these two views of humanity, or society, remains one of the most pressing concerns of all modern nations, including the United States.

In *The Passion of Antígona Pérez*, Sánchez modifies the *Antigone* of Sophocles by thus bringing the conflict between Créon and Antigone into the sphere of modern political history—of the *Americas*, not just the United States of America. The result is a dialectical drama in which the classical struggle between individual rights and the laws of the state is re-enacted. As the play begins, the imprisoned Antígona declares, "I am twenty-five years old and I am going to die tomorrow." The subsequent action bears out her statement, revealing the circumstances that make her death necessary within the context of the drama. The plot itself is nearly scientific in the analytical sense of the word, for it places emphasis on the reasoned explanation of political actions rather than on the actions or events themselves; on the explication of theme rather than on the dramatic incitement of further action. The change from action to idea, from suspense to analysis, does not, however, diminish the play's appeal. Its apparent didacticism is neither dull nor propagandistic, for the play illuminates the familiar story in a new, inclusive, and meaningful way.

In Sánchez's version, Antígona is the daughter of Créon's half-brother, Colonel Pérez y Santisteban, who was executed for insurrection. Her mother, now nearly destitute, is the first prison visitor who attempts to persuade her to confess. Sophocles' Ismene becomes Irene, a friend who sheltered Antígona after she was forced by Créon to leave her mother's home. Haemon is effectively translated through the unseen character of Fernando Curet, a young officer in Créon's army. Antígona loves Fernando, so to expedite her confession he is promoted by Créon to supervise her incarceration. Antígona's crime, unlike that of Sophocles' Antigone, includes placing a bomb in a library as well as stealing and burying the bodies of the two would-be assassins, Héctor and Mario Tavárez. The Tavárez brothers were Antígona's comrades-in-arms and attempted an almost-certain-to-fail assassination of Generalísimo Créon Molina, the self-styled dictator, in the hope of precipitating a crisis that would attract international attention.

Sentenced to death for her crime, Antígona can presumably have her sentence reduced or voided by confessing to Créon where the bodies are buried. Indeed, the attempt to persuade Antígona to confess is the unifying action of the play. The burial of the Taváres brothers, along with Antígona's capture and sentencing, are secondary and have already taken place as the drama gets under way. Her real crime is the embarrassment of Créon, who had publicly displayed the men's bodies as a gruesome warning to other subversives. Antígona's refusal to capitulate poses the same threat to Créon as the aborted assassination, for the Generalísimo's authority cannot be challenged without undermining his absolute rule.

Antígona's conflict with Créon is personal as well as ideological. He is powerful, shrewd, imposing, and nearly magnificent in his political machinations. Yet, Créon is also insecure and haunted by the erratic history of other Latin American rulers. He fears being labeled a dictator, sponsors an opposition political party, and supports general elections. His character is complex, for he operates out of a well-developed sense of right and wrong, law and justice. Moreover, Créon is a staunch Roman Catholic, intensely anti-communist, and firm in his belief that his regime protects the citizens of Molina. His wife, Pilar

Varga, further complicates his character, as her charm, ambition, and lust for power are additional forces influencing Créon. Both characters are composites drawn from the attributes of a variety of Latin American rulers, but they each transcend classification as stereotypes. The principles they uphold are often consistent, their methods well-honed, and their personal appeal undeniable.

Other characters reflect the power and magnetism of Créon. Monsignor Bernardo Escudero, for example, represents the complicity of the Church with the rule of State. He visits the imprisoned Antígona and uses his spiritual influence in an attempt to persuade her to confess and be saved. Two choruses are used throughout to further amplify the play's political ambience. The five Journalists demonstrate the role of the "yellow" press in upholding Créon's regime, whereas the Multitude—a crowd of six men and six women—evince a psychology of fear and repression, supporting Créon at the same time as they resist him, encouraging Antígona but also renouncing her.

In relating her "passion," Antígona's focus is on the audience more than any of the other characters. She narrates and interprets the details of her "crime," and her role as witness-commentator-participant provides the spectator with multiple perspectives on her relationship to the people around her. Commenting on Molina, Créon, Pilar, the Monsignor, and her own actions and imprisonment, Antígona simultaneously reveals an objectivity, a cynicism, and an anguish that help her to build a rapport with the audience. The action itself serves to verify her narration, and it is here that Sánchez's indebtedness to Bertolt Brecht is most evident. Though the plot's progression is linear, the scenes themselves are short and self-contained, and each one provides new insight into the reasons for Antígona's impending execution. Furthermore, each character supplies the actor or actress with the opportunity for sociopolitical commentary as well realistic portrayal.

In keeping with Brechtian staging, the *mise-en-scène* described by the dramatist is versatile and mobile. Antígona's cell, for instance, can also be the palace bedchamber, a reception hall, or the streets of Molina. Huge murals resembling political placards and billboard advertisements themselves may serve as the constantly changing backdrop for the action. The quasi-documentary environment established by the playwright is further enhanced by his emphasis on the function of lighting, which should be clean, exposed, and expository in order to create the ideal dramatic atmosphere and complement the multi-level theatrical space.

In sum, Luis Rafael Sánchez's *Passion of Antígona Pérez* is not significantly different from the *Antigone* of Brecht (1947), Walter

Hasenclever (1917), or Jean Anouilh (1944). Each modern version attempts to bring the conflicts of idealism versus practicality, of humane values as opposed to human order, and of individual rights versus the rights of the state—conflicts first explored by Sophocles' drama (441 BC)—into the common experience of its twentieth-century audience. The importance of the Sánchez adaptation is that in radically departing from the original Greek play, he is nevertheless able to re-create its immediacy for audiences in contemporary America, where each nation of the Americas, South or Central, continues to play out its internal political and economic struggles as well as its external ones—with Latin neighbors as well as with North America in the person of the United States.

Work Cited
Sánchez, Luis Rafael. *La pasión según Antígona Pérez* [*The Passion of Antígona Pérez*]. Hato Rey, P.R.: Ediciones Lugar, 1968. (All translations by James R. Russo.)

"Thomas's *Under Milk Wood* and Wilder's *Our Town*"

If there is any work that resembles Thornton Wilder's otherwise *sui generis* drama *Our Town* (1938) in form as well as content, it is oddly enough Dylan Thomas's "play for voices" written for British radio, *Under Milk Wood* (1954). There is no evidence of which I am aware that the poet Thomas knew the American *Our Town*, let alone consciously modeled his only drama—if in fact *Under Milk Wood* can be called one—after it. Nonetheless, not only are the resemblances there, but Thomas's play, like Wilder's, may also be his best-known work. It is the purpose of this essay to explore the resemblances between *Under Milk Wood* and Wilder's play: to read Thomas's play, as it were, through the lens of the earlier *Our Town*.

Along with his lilting poems about childhood like "Fern Hill" and his story "A Child's Christmas in Wales" (which has come to rival Dickens' *Christmas Carol* [1843]), *Under Milk Wood* helped Dylan Thomas to become a popular, selling author late in his relatively short life through its attempt in poetic, alliterative prose to imagine a world that is completely good, to recapture the enchantment of original innocence. So much so that he has been called the J. M. Barrie of our time—a description that should lead us to reconsider Thomas's work as a whole, whose bracing romantic modernism has come to be overshadowed by this Welshman's reputation for fatally heavy drinking.

Thomas's *Under Milk Wood* is the portrait of a small Welsh, seaside village named Llareggub (Laugharne in reality), whose inhabitants are heard in vocal self-revelation during the course of a single day, from early morning to the dark of night, and in the process evoke a magical, golden age of Celtic peasantry expressing themselves in lyrical cadences. Like *Our Town, Under Milk Wood* contains no dramatic conflict, no development of character or even encounters between characters, no action in the usual theatrical sense of that word. There is, however, a surprising amount of "movement," from one part of the village to another; from character to character among the play's cast of around seventy "voices," for whom Thomas provides rich verbal textures or colors for the ear; and, as in the case of Wilder's piece, there is movement from the present to the past and back again.

Moreover, like the Stage Manager of *Our Town*, the "First Voice" of *Under Milk Wood* serves as a kind of narrator or choral figure (assisted by the "Second Voice"), a vocal guide who opens, accompanies, and closes the "action" and so seemingly fulfills the idea from which the work sprang in Thomas's mind in 1939: that of a mad village visited by a kindly inspector from the outside, certified by him as collectively insane, and sealed off so as not to infect the rest of the world. In the end, however, the village of Llareggub turns out to be the only sane and happy place surviving in a mad, mad world that had given us, during the genesis and gestation of *Under Milk Wood*, the Second World War, the neutron bomb, the Holocaust, and the long Cold War to come between the Soviet Union and the United States.

In its retreat to the idyllic rusticity of the Welsh seaside, *Under Milk Wood* thus resembles *Our Town* with its look back in protectionist nostalgia to one of the many small towns bedecking the vast landscape of pre-World War I America. The difference, however, is that Thomas's wistfully compassionate vision is leavened by a rollicking sense of humor, a fair sprinkling of songs, poems, and ballads, and a joyful expression of bawdy (e.g., the name of the Welsh village, which should be read backwards), not to say realized in brilliantly imagistic-atmospheric language that is sometimes self-consciously poetic in the same way that Wilder's language is self-consciously unpoetic, even pedestrian or homely. The difference also is that Thomas's almost expressionist technique of mental projection in his radio play—with its cheerful blend of romance, sentiment (if not sentimentality), saltiness, and comedy—owes something to the "Circe" episode in *Ulysses* (1922), whereas the Wilder of *Our Town* (and of *The Skin of Our Teeth* as well, whose cosmic point of view suffers from a certain cuteness) seems able to absorb only the universal dimension or generalizing function from Joyce's work. Moreover, the characters of *Under Milk Wood* are a bunch of eccentrics who vigorously express their individuality and freedom—a town full of accommodated Simon Stimsons, as it were—in contrast to the stick figures of *Our Town* who (excepting Stimson) conform in every way to their era's notions of normality and decency.

The very title of the play poetically suggests the uniqueness of the village of Llareggub, not the idea that it belongs to us or is at one with us. The wood, named as "Milk Wood" only briefly during the play, is of no special significance to the "action." It is a haunt of courting couples and it probably is filled with milkwood trees: more than that we cannot say of the wood, yet Thomas takes his title from it, a title that first went through several prosaic incarnations from *The Town that Was Mad* to *Quite Early One Morning* to *Llareggub, a Piece for Radio Perhaps*. The poetry of the title *Under Milk Wood* is in its juxtaposition of two such incongruous nouns, wood and milk, whose contrast between solidity and fluidity evokes the selfsame contrast between the solidity or fleshliness of the play's characters, whom we nonetheless do not see, and the fluidity or the mellifluousness of their voices, which is all that we hear. The poetry is additionally in the wordplay of the title, which suggests a connection with milkwood trees, known to secrete latex. The implication—since the wood is a trysting place—is that Thomas was making a private joke about (defective or counterproductive) condoms, for the "milk" could also be semen.

In the end, *Under Milk Wood* try to memorialize the little Welsh town by the sea, Laugharne, where Dylan Thomas spent his happiest and most fruitful times, and of whose communal life he therefore had intimate knowledge. This perhaps spells the real difference between Thomas's play and Wilder's *Our Town*: that the one springs from deeply felt, affectionate experience, whereas the other derives from Wilder's *idea* of what life in an American small town (Grover's Corners itself is an imaginary place) was like. It is his version of pastoral, as it were, for this was a man who grew up in China, graduated from both Yale and Princeton, and studied archeology in Rome. For a more credible rendering of small-town life in the United States in the first two decades of the twentieth century, one would do better to turn to the stories of Sherwood Anderson's *Winesburg, Ohio* (1919)—whose own recurrent figure, the young newspaper reporter George Willard, in the end rejects the town and sets out in search of the freedom and vitality that such a place can but dimly offer—or even to the poetry of Edgar Lee Masters' *Spoon River Anthology* (1915), whose free-verse epitaphs by citizens buried in an Illinois cemetery can compete with anything the deceased inhabitants of Grover's Corners say in Act III of *Our Town*.

Like Masters' work, *Under Milk Wood* could itself be called a kind of narrative poem, whose narrative "Voices" for this reason seem less obtrusive, artificial, or spuriously folksy, in their existence on the page, than does Wilder's Stage Manager (as those "Voices" do in staged readings as well as on the radio for which the play was designed, where they are invisible like everyone or everything else). Moreover, even as George Willard abandoned Winesburg for the wide world, Dylan Thomas tragically left Laugharne for the fame and funding of London and New York. Thornton Wilder, for his part, never departed from Grover's Corners—because he had never been there in the first place.

Works Cited

Anderson, Sherwood. *Winesburg, Ohio*. New York: B. W. Huebsch, 1919.
Dickens, Charles. *A Christmas Carol*. London: Chapman and Hall, 1843.
Joyce, James. *Ulysses*. Paris: Sylvia Beach, 1922.
Masters, Edgar Lee. *Spoon River Anthology*. New York: Macmillan, 1915.
Thomas, Dylan. "Fern Hill." In his *Deaths and Entrances*. London: J. M. Dent, 1946.
———. "A Child's Christmas in Wales." 1952. Norfolk, Connecticut: New Directions, 1954.
———. *"Under Milk Wood": A Play for Voices*. London: J. M. Dent, 1954.
Wilder, Thornton. *Our Town*. New York: Coward McCann, 1938.
———. *The Skin of Our Teeth*. New York: Harper & Brothers, 1942.

6 Names and Titles

This section consists of short model, or sample, essays on the subject of the thematic or symbolic significance of a play's title, the name of one of its characters, or the name of its setting. Treated here are the *pièce à clef*, or "play with a key"; the Faust character in dramatic literature; the use of bad (but pointed) French; and such mundane terms as "mouse" and "slag." The following plays have been chosen for their representativeness, modernity, variety, and quality:

1. Ben Hecht and Charles MacArthur's *The Front Page*
2. Gertrude Stein's *Doctor Faustus Lights the Lights*
3. Tennessee Williams' *A Streetcar Named Desire*
4. David Hare's *Slag* and Brackenhurst
5. John Steinbeck's *Of Mice and Men*

MODEL ESSAYS

For reading and learning purposes, the "Key Analytical Question" below can be applied to any of the above plays or all of them.

Key Analytical Question: "Of what symbolic or thematic significance is the title of a play, the name of one of its characters, or the name of its setting?"

"Hecht and MacArthur's *The Front Page* as *pièce à clef*"
Most people do not know that Ben Hecht and Charles MacArthur's play *The Front Page* (1928) is a *pièce à clef*. Not only is its whole flavor actually that of a frantic and long-vanished age of American journalism, but some of the names of characters and institutions, some situations, even some bits of dialogue, were taken from real life, even though the co-authors felt that they had to tone down what they knew to be the truth. For one thing, the language of the streets was diluted, to be restored to something like its original vulgarity only in Billy Wilder's 1974 film version (the third movie adaptation). Still, the famous curtain-closer of cunning editor Walter Burns ("The son of a butch stole my *watch*!" [183]) created a stir, much more than the sprinkling of goddamns and such in the rest of the play. Indeed, the New York police wanted to arrest the cast; and even in the first movie version, released in 1931, a well-placed clatter from a typewriter obscured the coarsest part of the closing line. As late as 1970, when the second Broadway revival was adapted for television, one critic felt obliged to comment that "this particular production marks a break-through for TV profanity because the play's classic last line, which is the essence of the character of Walter Burns, is intact."

To address now the real-life counterparts of the characters in *The Front Page*, Earl Williams, the condemned prisoner, is a composite of various radicals, but his escape from the Cook County Jail derives from the case of Terrible Tommy O'Connor, a thirty-five-year-old Irish immigrant convicted in 1921 of killing a night watchman during the robbery of the Illinois Central Railroad's downtown station. He broke out days before he was sentenced to hang but, unlike Williams, was never recaptured; one rumor had it that he returned to Ireland and perished fighting the British. For decades, the gallows in Chicago remained intact in the event he should ever be caught. The year before *The Front Page* appeared, Hecht had used the O'Connor escape in his script for Josef von Sternberg's *Underworld* (1927)—which was the first of the Hollywood gangster films.

Where the reporters are concerned, the Canadian writer Vincent

131

Starrett, who knew Hecht and MacArthur when he worked on the Chicago dailies, recalled years later, "There was no newspaper slave in Chicago but swore he recognized every figure on the boards" (254). Certainly the most obvious of the shanghai victims is the ace reporter Hildy Johnson. He's based on a Swedish immigrant named Hilding Johnson, who once broke into a jury room with a deadline pressing, learned of the verdict by going through old ballots in the waste-paper basket, then left phony evidence for a competitor he knew would be breaking in later. "Poor Hildy!" wrote Starrett. "He died a few years after the play was produced (in 1931, at age forty-five)—I saw him laughing in his box opening night—and it was said that his determined effort to approximate his reckless counterpart on the stage had hastened his untimely end" (254).

In fact, the eccentricity of *The Front Page*'s characters was considerably de-emphasized in the paste-pot process by which Hecht and MacArthur fashioned their finished product. As Hecht was said to have remarked, no one in the audience would have believed the real thing. The character of Walter Burns is a case in point. It was based on Walter Crawford Howey, for whom MacArthur had worked on both the *Tribune* and the *Herald-Examiner* and who possessed one of the most robust personal legends in Chicago journalism. One of his early triumphs was a series of muckraking articles that drove Mayor Fred Busse (according to notes in *The Front Page* script, the original owner of Bensinger's rolltop desk) out of office. As city editor of the *Tribune*, Howey became notorious for a style of news-gathering that included intimidating witnesses and blackmailing municipal, county, and state authorities, whose signed but undated resignations he kept in his desk for use in emergencies. He and a few of his rivals came to symbolize daily journalism in the 1920s, a time when each big story was a melodrama.

In 1910, Howey blew up at the owners of the *Tribune* and transferred his allegiance to Hearst's *Herald-Examiner*, the "Madhouse on Madison Street" (Murray). Dion O'Banion, the notorious gangster later shot down in his flower shop by Al Capone's henchmen, was the *Her-Ex* circulation manager. His job (not unlike Diamond Louie's in the play) was to persuade vendors to carry the Hearst paper in preference to the *Tribune*. Soon full-blown circulation wars developed. Howey had only one eye, and some said he lost the other one fighting in such wars. Others contended that he lost it by falling on a copy spike while sitting drunkenly at his desk. Whatever the case, Hecht remarked that he could tell the glass eye from the natural one: the glass eye, he said, had warmth. The *Herald-Examiner* folded in 1939, and thereafter

Howey's career declined steadily. He died in 1955 at age seventy-three. In a last tribute to his old boss, MacArthur visited him in the hospital during his final illness and gave him a watch engraved "To the Best Newspaperman I Know"—just like the one in *The Front Page*.

Works Cited

Hecht, Ben, & Charles MacArthur. *The Front Page*. New York: Covici-Friede, 1928.

Murray, George. *The Madhouse on Madison Street*. Chicago: Follett Publishing Co., 1965.

Starrett, Vincent. *Books Alive: A Profane Chronicle of Literary Endeavor and Literary Misdemeanor*. New York: Random House, 1940.

"Marguerite Ida-Helena Annabel in Stein's *Doctor Faustus Lights the Lights*"

The Faust legend is something of a retelling of the Biblical myth of the Garden of Eden as it appears in Genesis 2–3. There Eve is tempted by the devil, in the form of a serpent, to taste fruit from the tree of knowledge and to share that fruit with Adam—an action that banishes all humanity from paradise. Similarly, the Faust of legend is tempted to sell his soul to the devil (and, consequently, his right to a place in the paradise of heaven—the only Eden humankind can ever know) in exchange for omniscience, even omnipotence. Throughout Gertrude Stein's play *Doctor Faustus Lights the Lights* (1938), major characters themselves usurp or reject power typically associated with God. Faustus claims the power to create light, as does Marguerite Ida-Helena Annabel, although she seems less interested in this power than Faust.

This female character's dual names and fluctuating identity mark her as a kind of conflated womankind. (Marguerite Ida-Helena Annabel's names themselves derive from various recountings or dramatizations of the Faust legend by Christopher Marlowe [1588], Karl von Holtei [1829], George Sand [1869], Ida Hahn-Hahn [1840], and Stephen Vincent Benét [1937].) And womankind, as represented by Marguerite Ida-Helena Annabel, in the end rejects all deities, turning her back on both the sun (which could be interpreted as a natural god) and the electric light (the new technological god).

Unlike the Biblical Eve—who is only tempted or figuratively "bitten" by a serpent—Marguerite Ida-Helena Annabel is literally bitten by a viper. Initially, however, Marguerite Ida-Helena Annabel appears to triumph over the bite. Faustus cures her, despite his repeated assertions that he cannot see her, and thereafter Marguerite

Ida-Helena Annabel becomes immune to the viper's poison. As Stein's Chorus intones, "See the viper there, / Cannot hurt her" (106). At first glance, this seems to be a triumph of science over God, but Marguerite Ida-Helena Annabel rejects not only the natural light of the sun but also the science of Faust. And for the first time in the play she gains a unity of identity: "With her back to the sun / One sun / And she is one / Marguerite Ida and Helena Annabel as well" (107).

With both unity and duality thus present in her main female character, Stein focuses attention on the multiple identities of women. Like the Dadaists, who expressed skepticism about the unity of character in any dramatic or theatrical presentation (let alone life itself), Stein creates a character who, in name alone, evokes both the good and evil depictions of women in history and literature. Half of the four-part name, Marguerite Ida, contains positive connotations of motherhood—Margaret the faithful wife and mother of multiple Faust legends, and Ida the mother of the gods—while the second half, Helena Annabel, suggests images of sexual temptation and demonic, anti-familial sentiment, aside from its possible (ironic?) reference to the mother of the Virgin Mary. (Annabel suggests the name Hannah, which in Hebrew refers to the Anna Perenna of Italian tradition and also to the mother of the Virgin Mary.) In creating such a fractured, complex identity for this figure, Stein is contradicting one-dimensional representations of women and illuminating the absurdity of the long-standing Madonna-Whore dichotomy. A reader or viewer must constantly reconcile the manifold nature of Marguerite Ida-Helena Annabel with the singular pronoun "she." The stubbornness of Stein's technique, moreover, is evident in criticism of the play, where scholars almost always shorten the character's name to "Marguerite Ida" or her initials, MIHA, rather than confuse their own readers' sense of grammar and logic.

The duality of Marguerite Ida-Helena Annabel's character is visible not only in her name, but also in the events that surround her. She is at once an agent of action and the passive victim or recipient of others' actions. She survives the bite of the snake, to become as powerful as Doctor Faustus in her ability to create light—candlelight in this case. Nevertheless, she still succumbs to "the man from the sea" (107), who appears as an embodiment of the same viper she had earlier encountered and seduces her, exclaiming that "I am the only he and you are the only she and we are the only we" (108). His language, of course, recalls Adam and Eve, the first he and she. But through Marguerite Ida-Helena Annabel, Stein inverts the story of Adam and Eve in the Garden of Eden. For this Eve not only is not responsible for her own temptation (she is unwittingly bitten by the serpent and even fails to realize it was a serpent that was responsible for the bite), she is also relieved of responsibility for the fall of humanity—something Faustus himself accomplishes, by selling his soul for electric light before the play even begins.

Work Cited
Stein, Gertrude. *Doctor Faustus Lights the Lights*. In her *Last Operas and Plays*. New York: Rinehart and Co., 1949.

"'Belle Reve' in Williams' *A Streetcar Named Desire*"

To my knowledge, no one has ever questioned or accounted for the grammatical incorrectness of the French name for the DuBois family plantation in Tennessee Williams' *A Streetcar Named Desire* (1947). "Belle Reve" (Beautiful Dream) may sound better in English pronunciation than "Beau Rêve" (the correct French), but its feminine adjective disagrees with its masculine noun. Assuming that Williams knew this, since he was able to get his French right in Scenes 5 (84) and 6 (88) of the play, and gets his French wrong exactly in the same way in Scene 3 (54–55), why did he persist in his use of the grammatically incorrect "Belle Reve"?

It is possible that Williams erred in construing "rêve" as feminine, confusing this noun with "rive," which is in fact feminine and whose French pronunciation (with a long "e") is more or less the English pronunciation of "Reve" (which should be pronounced with a short "e," as it is in French). It's also possible that Williams *wanted* the reader or spectator to think of both "rêve" and "rive" when that person read or heard the name "Belle Reve," since "rive" can mean "skirt of woods" and thus associates the name of the DuBois plantation with the DuBois name itself ("bois" signifies a "woods" or "forest"). "Rive's" first meaning, however, is "river bank," as in "rive gauche" (the Left Bank of the Seine), which Blanche conjures in Scene 6 (88) as a substitute for both the amusement park at Lake Pontchartrain and the street named Elysian Fields that runs alongside the Mississippi River, and which "rive" suggests not only her predilection for bohemian or unconventional manners and mores but also her addiction to water (3, 37, 48, 83, 97, 101–102, 105, 109–110, 122–124, 132–133, 136).

There are additional reasons why Williams may have intentionally juxtaposed the feminine "Belle" with the masculine "Reve." Blanche is, after all, a (faded) Southern *belle* who once attracted her share of *beaux*, and whose dream was to fall ideally in love with one of them and live the rest of life in plantation-style luxury. (Moreover, "Belle" was the name of the woman on whom Williams based the character of Blanche: his free-spirited, hysterically eloquent Aunt Belle [Gussow, 21].) But the DuBois men—Blanche's grandfathers and father and uncles and brothers—"over hundreds of years . . . piece by piece . . . improvident[ly] exchanged the land for their epic fornications" (43), so that finally there was no plantation left on which Blanche could settle down. The coarse masculine element of the DuBois family, that is, had eroded the beauty of its feminine ideal. Belle Reve was lost to creditors, or what was left of it fell into their mercantile hands: the house itself and twenty acres, including a graveyard, to which the remaining DuBoises, all women and all alone, had beaten a steady retreat.

In marrying, at a young age, the beautiful, even poetic Allan Grey—a man who, like the name "Belle Reve," could be said to combine or contain the masculine and the feminine in one form or expression—Blanche was perhaps consciously trying to repudiate the meanness and incontinence of her male relatives. Conversely, in indulging her desire in the wake of Allan's suicide, in seeking out "intimacies with strangers . . . to fill [her] empty heart with" (118), Blanche was unwittingly emulating the promiscuous behavior of the DuBois men at their masculine worst. (Hence the blurring of sexuality in Blanche's full name [translated as "white woods"], the confusion of gender between her given name and her surname—which in French should be "Blanc Bois" or "Blanc du Bois," not "Blanche DuBois.") In other words, she was allowing the grossness of their mannish spectacle to cloud over the fineness of her feminine vision.

In ultimately fleeing the tender, boundless dream of Belle Reve for the grim reality of New Orleans' Vieux Carré (with a stopover along the way at the Hotel Flamingo, or Tarantula Arms, as Blanche sarcastically describes it to Mitch in Scene 9), the Old or French Quarter with its squared-off city streets, streetcar routes, box-like apartments, and bordering train tracks, Blanche would again adopt the role of demure, chaste Southern belle, this time to combat the crudeness and lasciviousness of her sister Stella's husband, Stanley Kowalski. Stanley nevertheless lends his masculine coloration to Blanche's life, to her illusions—at one point actually laying his clumsy hands on her love letters from Allan Grey, at another taking into his possession the mortgage papers which are all that remains of Belle Reve, at still another point violating his sister-in-law's person as well as her spirit through rape. The result is that Blanche's beautiful dream of uniting with the seemingly sensitive Mitch is shattered, together with her sanity. Despite her fondest wishes, Blanche DuBois's Belle Reve will not have been resurrected or sanctified—made whole and holy—by any bold man's *beau geste*.

Works Cited
Gussow, Mel. "Elusive Playwright." Review of *Tennessee Williams: Everyone Else Is an Audience*, by Ronald Hayman. *The New York Times Book Review* (27 February 1994): 21.
Williams, Tennessee. *A Streetcar Named Desire*. New York: New American Library, 1951.

"Hare's *Slag* and Brackenhurst"
In David Hare's *Slag* (1971), three women run an upper-class boarding school for girls with a name that sounds refined, imposing, and staid: Brackenhurst. The trouble is, the school has a declining enrollment—there are only eight students at the start of the play, and by the end there are none. Moreover, the admitting of boys is out of the question, as the following vow—made in Scene 1 by the school's leaders, Joanne, Elise, and Ann—makes clear:

> I do solemnly promise to abstain from all forms and varieties of sexual intercourse; to keep my body intact in order to register my protest against the way our society is run by men for men whose aim is the subjugation of the female and the enslavement of the working woman. (11)

Joanne wants to make Brackenhurst an all-female society that will be a model of socialism for the world, and whose ultimate goal will be the abolition of men from the planet. When Elise asks her how women will reproduce without men, Joanne simply says, "Some other method" (62). Elise and Ann seem to take the above vow more because they like Joanne than because they agree with her sexual politics. For her part, Elise loves sex and likes men; and Ann herself detests socialism. Unlike Joanne, neither of these two is from, or identifies with, the working class. Yet both of them seem as imprisoned by Joanne's dream of a feminist society as Joanne is. Indeed, at the end of *Slag*, after the last student has left, all three raise their arms to repeat the vow they made in Scene 1.

The title of this play and the name of the boarding school are comments on the dramatic action. "Slag" is defined in *Webster's New World Dictionary* as "the fused refuse of dross separated from a metal in the process of smelting." Brackenhurst, then—as an upper-class boarding school in a country where the aristocracy has long since been eclipsed—is a kind of slag. In the creation or "smelting" of modern England, the dross of Brackenhurst has been separated from a society that no longer has a need for it: the school has few students, only three troubled teachers, and a location that is unspecified. Brackenhurst seems to be nowhere, even as schools like it once were everywhere in England. To enhance this idea of placelessness, Hare writes few descriptions of scenery and no description of the surrounding town and countryside. And to underline Brackenhurst's loss of function, he gives the school at least one teacher who wants to prepare its students not to take their place in "polite" society, but to join working women under the banner of socialism.

As for the name Brackenhurst itself, "bracken" is defined in *Webster's New World Dictionary* as "any of a genus of large, coarse, weedy ferns . . . occurring . . . especially in wastelands." A wasteland itself, of course, is (1) "land that is uncultivated, barren, or without vegetation"; or (2) "a neglected, improperly managed, or intellectually unproductive activity, endeavor, etc." A "hurst" was once "a grove or wooded hillock," but the word now occurs almost exclusively in place names such as Brackenhurst. Brackenhurst the boarding school can therefore be described, figuratively speaking, as a wasteland where groves and greenery once flourished, but where now only large, coarse, weedy ferns are able to survive.

Brackenhurst is barren in two senses: as previously noted, it has been steadily losing its students and by the end of the play has lost all of them; and its teachers make a vow never again to have sex with men. It does appear for much of *Slag* that Ann has broken her vow by carrying on an affair with Haskins, the butcher, but she finally reveals the following to Elise: "I never knew Haskins. I pretended. Think I'd sleep with a tradesman? I've got some pride left. I just wanted to annoy [Joanne]" (74). Elise herself becomes mysteriously pregnant after Scene 4, but in the sixth and last scene her pregnancy disappears as mysteriously as it had arrived. She leaves the stage pregnant at one point during Scene 6, then returns moments later and declares, "[*Her stomach is quite flat.*] It's gone. There was a great wet fart and it has gone" (77).

Aside from being barren, Brackenhurst is certainly a wasteland in the sense that it is improperly managed. Its teachers neglect their duties because they are bored or because their students are unresponsive. Joanne, for one—when she does teach—leads intellectually unproductive activity, teaching her girls to masturbate, to love socialism, and to despise Ann and discount Elise.

The title *Slag*, then, characterizes Brackenhurst school in general terms, while the name "Brackenhurst" specifically describes the school.

In short, Brackenhurst is a waste: it exists in no fruitful relationship to modern English society or its school-aged girls, and its three female teachers engage in no fruitful relationships with men.

Works Cited

Hare, David. *Slag*. London: Faber and Faber, 1971.

Webster's New World Dictionary: 2nd College Edition. New York: Simon & Schuster, 1982.

"The Mouse in Steinbeck's *Of Mice and Men*"

One of the ways in which the character of George Milton in *Of Mice Men* (1937) is elevated, or magnified, is through John Steinbeck's thorough weaving of the seemingly throwaway, sentimental symbol of the mouse into the fabric of the play's action. We see that symbol first in the play's title, which Steinbeck took from the Robert Burns poem ("To a Mouse") containing the lines "The best laid schemes o' mice an' men / Gang aft agley [go often astray]" (96). It is clear why the dramatist borrowed the phrase "of mice and men," for George and Lennie Small's plan to get a small place of their own goes astray once Lennie kills Curley's Wife. But there is another, less immediately apparent reason, for Steinbeck uses the dead mouse to symbolize the past and to foreshadow the future. To wit, Lennie always killed the mice that his Aunt Clara gave him to play with by pinching their heads; he could have killed the girl in Weed when he tried to feel her dress as if she were a mouse, and she strongly resisted. He and George were chased out of the town of Weed because of this incident, and, at the start of the play, they are on their way to a ranch job in the Salinas Valley when they stop for the night in a small clearing. George throws into the brush the dead mouse that Lennie has been secretly petting during their journey, but Lennie retrieves it when he goes for firewood. Then George takes it from him again and tosses it as far away as he can.

George's action is symbolic, for he is removing from his sight an omen of the future. After they go to work, Lennie kills first the puppy Slim gives him, by handling it too often and too roughly; then he kills Curley's Wife by accidentally breaking her neck when she tries to stop him from stroking her hair so hard. He flees the ranch and returns to the small clearing to wait for George, who has told him to go there if he gets into trouble. Lennie returns, that is, to the place where his past and his future converged in the symbol of the mouse, and where he, as a kind of pet to George, will await at George's hands the fate of the mice, the puppy, and Curley's Wife: death.

MODEL ESSAYS

The play is thus the story of two men and the symbolic mice that surround them and contribute to their doom—a doom whose seed lay, in the first place, in the very nature of their relationship: Lennie's dimwitted "mouse" to George's mindful man. Even as Lennie "loved" the mice, the puppy, and Curley's Wife so much that he inadvertently killed them, so too did George love Lennie so much that he wound up having to kill him. He wanted to remain with Lennie and lead a normal life eventually on a small farm, whereas the best place for his friend would have been in a home or hospital or even in the wild. Precisely at the moment that they are able to get the farm with the help of Candy's money, the inevitable happens when Lennie kills Curley's Wife. George then shoots Lennie as one would an animal, since he does not want him to suffer a savage death at Curley's hands, or, if he escaped death, to waste away in jail. It is no accident, then, that in the opening scene of *Of Mice and Men* Lennie is naturalistically likened to an animal: George angrily proclaims that he should be in a cage with lots of mice, where they can pet *him*, and Lennie retaliates by saying that perhaps he would be better off alone, living in the hills or in a cave.

Works Cited

Burns, Robert. "To a Mouse" (1785). In *The Canongate Burns: The Complete Poems and Song of Robert Burns*. Ed. Andrew Noble & Patrick Scott Hogg. Edinburgh, UK: Canongate Books, 2003. 96.

Steinbeck, John. *Of Mice and Men*: A Play in Three Acts. New York: Covici-Friede, 1937.

7 Nature, Landscape, and Setting

This section consists of short model, or sample, essays on the use of nature, landscape, and setting in drama: that is, how settings in general and the natural world in particular are deployed to create meaning in traditional as well as experimental drama. The following plays have been chosen for their representativeness, (post)modernity, variety, and quality:

1. Arthur Miller's *Death of a Salesman*
2. Thornton Wilder's *Our Town*
3. Hélène Cixous's *Portrait of Dora*, Tadeusz Kantor's *The Dead Class*, Heiner Müller's *Explosion of a Memory/Description of a Picture*, and Martha Clarke & Charles Mee's *Vienna: Lusthaus*
4. Harold Pinter's *The Homecoming*

5. John Steinbeck's *Of Mice and Men*
6. J. M. Synge's *Riders to the Sea*

For reading and learning purposes, the "Key Analytical Question" below can be applied to any of the above plays or all of them.

Key Analytical Question: "How would you distinguish the use of nature, landscape, and setting in a particular play from that of other plays?"

"Nature and Miller's *Death of a Salesman*"

Since the rise of Ibsenian realism and Strindbergian naturalism subsequent to European romanticism, alienation or divorce from nature—that is, the loss of natural paradise—has become a theme in Western drama. An early, famous example of such a play from the German theater is the Georg Büchner's *Woyzeck*, from 1836. Why did Western drama take up the theme of alienation or divorce from nature? Because, along with its realism and naturalism—as influenced by the seminal writings of Sigmund Freud, Charles Darwin, Émile Zola, Auguste Comte, Karl Marx, and Friedrich Nietzsche—inevitably came psychology, sociology, economics, and biology and with them our sturdy, scientific, secularist belief that all problems can eventually be solved, that humans can change or improve any aspect of their condition, including the natural environment in which they live. We put ourselves above nature, in other words—not to speak of God or religion—instead of inside it or alongside it. Ominously, we retreated into the mind and placed our ultimate faith in the superiority of human intelligence, rather than projecting human consciousness onto the natural world and embracing our humble position in it.

The loss of such natural paradise is not at first apparent in such twentieth-century American plays as Lynn Riggs's *Green Grow the Lilacs* (1931), Erskine Caldwell's *Tobacco Road* (1933), and John Steinbeck's *Of Mice and Men* (1937)—whose very title bespeaks a kind of union between man and nature—but that is because drama about the land and those who till it was fast becoming an anachronism by the 1930s. Nonetheless, these dramas touched on some deep American themes: the great myth of the road and male companionship, as well as men's hunger for hearth-and-home together with "brotherhood"—a hunger enhanced by the seeming loneliness, if not homelessness, of many Americans during the Great Depression. Perhaps because of this apparent loneliness and fraternal longing, the 1930s were years when the theater, along with the other arts, looked outward and rediscovered America: its vastness, its regions, and its distinct populations.

By the time we get to probably the most famous character in all of American drama—Willy Loman from Arthur Miller's 1949 play *Death of a Salesman*—we find a friendless man divorced from nature and out of touch with reality. A man who has sold things without making them, who has paid for other things without really owning them, who is an insulted extrusion of commercial society battling for some sliver of authenticity before he slips into the dark, Loman is a survivor of that early tradition of "drummers" in the United States.

These were men—including the signal characters Stanley Kowalski from Tennessee Williams' *A Streetcar Named Desire* (1947) and Theodore Hickman from Eugene O'Neill's *The Iceman Cometh* (1946)—who sold products on the road, figuratively drumming up business from door to door or store to store. Viewing their personality, not their product, as their chief ware, drummers liked to claim that they could sell anything. Except that Willy himself could not sell anything: that is the pathos of his drama. He was never a great salesman, not even during America's huge postwar economic boom, and he compounded his "failure," if it actually was a failure, by dying for money. He kills himself for it, to give his older son, Biff, a life insurance benefit as a stake for possible future business dealings, and because this aging, jobless father confuses materialistic success with a worthiness to be loved.

From the perspective of this essay, however, the interest in Willy's story is less its connection with jobs and business, or selling and commerce, than with nature. And *Death of a Salesman* does have such a connection, in common with both O'Neill's *The Hairy Ape* (1921) and Williams' *The Glass Menagerie* (1944). Willy Loman, like the "hairy ape," Yank Smith, is divorced from nature, yet, like Laura Wingfield if not her glass menagerie, he yearns to unite with it once again. We find evidence for this in Willy's comment that, while driving to a business appointment in New England—the very New England, the oldest part of the United States, featured in Thornton Wilder's *Our Town* (1938)—he was "observing the scenery. You can imagine, me looking at scenery, on the road every week of my life. But it's so beautiful up there . . . the trees are so thick, and the sun is warm. I opened the windshield and just let the warm air bathe over me" (3).

We also find evidence for Willy's desire to reunite with nature in his nostalgic reflections about his wagon travels across America, as a boy, with his flute-carving father:

> Father was a very wild-hearted man. We would start in Boston, and he'd toss the whole family into the wagon, and then he'd drive the team [of horses] right across the country; through Ohio, and Indiana, Michigan, Illinois, and all the Western states. And we'd stop in the towns and sell the flutes that he'd made on the way. (34)

As opposed to the life of a traveling salesman, spent in cars and hotel rooms, living in, and traveling by, horse-drawn wagons necessarily means living on or near the land, and it is the land to which Willy wishes to return: through tools and seeds, building and planting. Early in Act II of *Death of a Salesman*, for instance, he talks to his wife about getting "a little place out in the country, and I'll raise some vegetables, a couple of chickens . . . I'd build a little guest house. 'Cause I've got so many fine tools, all I'd need would be a little lumber and some peace of mind" (53). And toward the end of the play, shortly before his suicide, we find Willy seeking that peace of mind in the little garden outside his home in Brooklyn, New York, where he digs up the earth with his hoe and plants carrots, lettuce, and beets.

Willy's problem, in fact, is that he never fully realizes that the natural life is a genuine alternative to the business ethos of capitalism, which is to sell and consume as much as possible without regard for the welfare of one's fellow human beings, in towns and cities, or for the welfare of one's fellow living creatures, in the environment. Again, Willy dies for money—or at least he *thinks* he does, since his insurance company may not pay off on a suicide. Willy also dies an unnatural death, by his own hand, in a car crash. It is left to his son Biff to figure out what his father never consciously could: that the natural life, in the outdoors, is a viable alternative to object, conspicuous consumption and empty-headed, palpable wastefulness.

Here is what Biff Loman, recalling the farmland and ranch-hands of Steinbeck's *Of Mice and Men*, has to say about this subject:

> In Nebraska when I herded cattle, and the Dakotas, and Arizona, and now in Texas. . . . This farm I worked on, it's spring there now, see? And they've got about fifteen new colts. There's nothing more inspiring or—beautiful than the sight of a mare and a new colt. . . . Why am I trying to become what I don't want to be? What am I doing in an office, making a contemptuous, begging fool of myself, when all I want is out there, waiting for me the minute I say I know who I am! (11, 132)

Biff is the exception in modern American drama, though, not the rule, and it is no accident that he will not act on his recognition or perception until *after* the drama of *Death of Salesman*, until after the death of his father. This is because drama is built on conflict—external conflict with others, on the one hand, and internal conflict, or self-division, on the other. And once you find your paradise in nature, in union with the natural world, as Biff plans to do, there can be no conflict: which is to say, all has become one, and one is all, in harmony and peace.

To be sure, nature plays a relatively slight direct role in drama in general and modern or contemporary drama in particular—as seen in the case of *Death of a Salesman*. The reason, of course, is that drama deals essentially with the relationship between *people*, whereas cinema deals with the relationship of people not only to other people, but also to things and places—including nature. But one could say that the problem, finally, is less the drama's than the world's. That is, given the extent to which humanity has despoiled nature over the last few centuries, the need to depict such defilement or defoliation through art is now more acute than ever (and is a need perhaps best met on film, by the nature documentary). Yet traditional drama can for the most part only lament (not delineate) this sad state of affairs by portraying, in action as well as words, its characters' cognitive estrangement or dissociation from nature: witness Willy Loman.

Work Cited
Miller, Arthur. *Death of a Salesman.* New York: Viking/Penguin, 1949.

"Wilder's *Our Town* and Isolationism"

Thornton Wilder's *Our Town* was first published and produced in 1938 for a Depression-weary and war-wary American public; thus it seems to me no accident that the play looks back to an earlier, almost innocent or idyllic era, before the events of 1914–1938 changed forever the way Americans would regard the world and each other. (By 1938 the New Deal was over, and the Roosevelt administration was turning its attention from domestic reform to the gathering storm in Europe and the Far East.) In this sense, the play is not simply a nostalgic tribute to the "good old days" of the late nineteenth and early twentieth centuries, a generalized instance of the American tendency to idealize the past, as Francis Fergusson (52–53), George D. Stephens (262, 264), and Thomas E. Porter (219) maintain. Rather, *Our Town* is in fact nearly a piece of isolationist propaganda that promotes the virtues of a simple, unhurried, unthreatened life in the isolated small towns of America—where for one place the virtues of such a life need no such promoting, despite Emily's criticisms of her fellow townspeople and to the detriment of the play's artistic wholeness or thematic unity.

It may seem folksy, for example, that Dr. Gibbs would rather remain at home in Grover's Corners than visit so cosmopolitan a city as Paris, France, but Mrs. Gibbs's explanation of her husband's desire to stay put rings of isolationism-cum-chauvinism:

> No, he said, it might make him discontented with Grover's Corners to go traipsin' about Europe; better to let well enough alone, he says. Every two years he makes a trip to the battlefields of the Civil War [on which Dr. Gibbs is an expert] and that's enough treat for anybody, he says. (20)

In apparent contradistinction to her husband, it occurs to Mrs. Gibbs "that once in your life before you die you ought to see a country where they don't talk in English and *don't even want to*" (20; emphasis mine). Emily Webb might have responded, based on her speech to her classmates about the Louisiana Purchase (27, 29–30), that with the addition of this Southern state Mrs. Gibbs already had a little bit of France in America. (Recall that Emily's alternate speech topic was the Monroe Doctrine [27], which tellingly proclaimed that the United States would not brook any political or economic interference in the Western hemisphere by European powers.)

Like the Gibbses' remarks and Emily's American history assignment, the following, seemingly innocuous lines by the Stage Manager in Act I also smack of isolationism-cum-chauvinism. He implies here that America's participation in World War I—which ended in the winter of 1919 with the signing of five treaties, one of them in the Parisian suburb of Versailles—served no purpose whatsoever; and that the first nonstop, solo airplane flight from New York to Paris, made by Charles Lindbergh in 1927, was and is no more important than the daily life of any small, New England town:

> [Joe Crowell] got a scholarship to Massachusetts Tech. Graduated head of his class there [. . .] Goin' to be a great engineer, Joe was. But the war broke out and he died in France.—*All that education for nothing.* (10, emphasis mine; see the Stage Manager's opposite remark, in Act III, about Union soldiers from New Hampshire who died during the Civil War [80–81])

> I'm going to have a copy of this play put in the cornerstone [together with a Bible and the Constitution of the United States, so that] people

a thousand years from now'll know a few simple facts about us—*more than the Treaty of Versailles and the Lindbergh flight.* (32; emphasis mine)

Among those few simple facts about what the Stage Manager calls "the *real* life of the people [. . .] in the provinces north of New York at the beginning of the twentieth century" (32), by which he means the quotidian activities of citizens as opposed to the public pronouncements and pursuits of princes or their martial equivalents, one should not ignore our country's internal isolationism of two kinds. First, there is the comic regionalism, indeed "state-ism," championed by the Stage Manager when he remarks that "the Cartwright interests have just begun building a new bank in Grover's Corners—had to go to Vermont for the marble, sorry to say" (31–32); by Emily when she declares that "Grover's Corners isn't a very important place when you think of all—New Hampshire; but I think it's a very nice town" (66); then by George when he responds to her later in the same conversation, "I guess new people aren't any better than old ones. [. . .] I don't need to go [away to State Agriculture College] and meet the people in other towns" (67); and finally by Sam Craig when he reveals, upon returning to Grover's Corners for Emily's funeral, that he's now in business out West—which is where Buffalo, New York, is located as far as he is concerned (82).

Second, and most important, there is our internal isolationism of a tragic kind: that is, the segregation of American towns according to race and ethnicity, which we began to remedy only after World War II, when veterans from minority groups demanded equal treatment in housing along with other areas of civilian life in return for their military service to the nation. The pre-Great War world of the Gibbses and the Webbs, then, is decidedly *not* "an anti-elitist vision of human existence," as David Castronovo believes (93). In Grover's Corners, for instance, "Polish Town's across the tracks, [along with] some Canuck families" (6), and the "Catholic Church is over beyond the tracks" (6) as well. Such segregation, of course, was the result as well as the cause of what the Belligerent Man in *Our Town* calls "social injustice" and "industrial inequality" (24).

When asked by this "belligerent" man what the citizens of Grover's Corners are going to do about poverty and discrimination in their town, Mr. Webb lamely—and peremptorily—responds,

> Well, I dunno. . . . I guess we're all hunting like everybody else for a way the diligent and sensible can rise to the top and the lazy and quarrelsome can sink to the bottom. But it ain't easy to find. Meanwhile, we

do all we can to help those that can't help themselves and those that can we leave alone.—Are there any other questions? (25)

Mr. Webb's statement that "we do all we can to help those that can't help themselves" may appear to be charitable, but in fact it is obfuscatory, for it assumes that the racially and ethnically segregated are *unable to* help themselves as opposed to being *prevented from* doing so. Similarly, when he declares that "we're all hunting [. . .] for a way the diligent and sensible can rise to the top and the lazy and quarrelsome can sink to the bottom," Mr. Webb seems to be in favor of equal treatment for everybody, but in reality he is playing to his audience's prejudice that blacks and newly-arrived European immigrants belong at the bottom of the socioeconomic ladder.

That prejudice is confirmed early in the play by Dr. Gibbs's report that he is returning home from the birth of "*just* some twins [. . .] over in Polish Town" (9; emphasis mine); by the Stage Manager's remark that "the earliest tombstones in the cemetery [belong to] Grovers and Cartwrights and Gibbses and Herseys—*same names as are around here now*" [with the exception, that is, of those belongings to Poles and "Canucks"] (7; emphasis mine); and by the Stage Manger's ominous interruption of Professor Willard's anthropological survey of Grover's Corners—a survey that itself avoids mention of the program of genocide we conducted against the Indians—at the moment this "rural savant" comes to the Slavic and Mediterranean migration to America:

> *Professor Willard*: Yes . . . anthropological data: Early Amerindian stock. Cotahatchee tribes . . . no evidence before the tenth century of this era . . . hm . . . now entirely disappeared . . . possible traces in three families. Migration toward the end of the seventeenth century of English brachiocephalic blue-eyed stock . . . for the most part. Since then some Slav and Mediterranean—
> *Stage Manager*: And the population, Professor Willard? (22)

This same ethnic prejudice is confirmed later in the play by Constable Warren's report that he has been out "rescuin' a party; darn near froze to death, down by Polish town thar. Got drunk and lay out in the snowdrifts" (94). When Mr. Webb tells the constable that "We must get [this story] in the paper" (96), Warren quickly avers, "'Twan't much" (96). And that's the end of the matter, because the drunk is naturally a "dumb Polack," one of the ten per cent of the town's illiterate laborers (23), not a member of the Anglo-Saxon Protestant majority.

This fellow must not be as dumb as the women of Grover's Corners, however, for at least he got to vote if he was twenty-one (and a citizen), whereas "women vote indirect" (23), which is to say only by influencing their husbands' votes. The women of the United States did not gain suffrage until 1920. Nor, of course, did they achieve equal educational or professional opportunity until quite some time after that, as *Our Town* inadvertently makes clear when it portrays Emily Webb as "naturally bright" (28), indeed "the brightest girl in school" (15), and in any event brighter than the dimwitted if kindhearted George Gibbs (whom she must help with his math homework in Act I); yet Wilder makes *George* President of the high-school Senior Class to Emily's Secretary-Treasurer, and gives him the chance to go away to college but not her. Young Joe Crowell, Jr., sums up the thinking in Grover's Corners on the status of women when, in response to Dr. Gibbs's question, "How do you boys feel about [the upcoming marriage of your schoolteacher, Miss Foster]?" he innocently but revealingly declares that "if a person starts out to be a teacher, she ought to stay one" (9). In other words, women cannot or should not combine family with career; and Miss Foster's choices, or the limitations thereon, are clear: either remain the teacher she was trained to be and become a spinster, or give up teaching for the life of a wife and mother. Moreover, as a mother she should teach her own daughter not to waste taxpayers' money on a higher education that in the end she will not use!

I have gone to the trouble in the preceding paragraphs of documenting the historicity of *Our Town* because this historicity works against the play's universalizing tendency. *Our Town* would be a play for all people of all time—in deliberate contrast to the drama of sociopolitical consciousness, even left-wing propaganda, produced by such writers as Clifford Odets, John Howard Lawson, and Elmer Rice during the 1930s—but in its own time it is not even a play for all the ethnic and racial groups of Grover's Corners, let alone all the nationalities of the world. The Stage Manager relates Grover's Corners to the past civilizations of Greece and Rome as well as to future ones, to the surrounding countryside and to evolution (21–22, 32, 71, 80); Wilder eliminates scenery almost completely in order to avoid the suggestion that the meaning of the play's action relates only to Grover's Corners, New Hampshire; and Rebecca Gibbs connects the individual to town, county, state, country, world, universe, and God when she quotes the address on Jane Crofut's letter in Act I (45). Yet for all these attempts to link the Grover's Corners of 1901–1913 to the great world beyond as well as to other historical periods—perhaps partly as a *result* of these attempts—*Our Town* remains time- and place-bound. It is the conservative record or dramatic preservation of a conservative, even reactionary, attitude toward life.

Works Cited
Castronovo, David. *Thornton Wilder*. New York: Ungar, 1986.
Fergusson, Francis. "Three Allegorists: Brecht, Wilder, and Eliot." In his *The Human Image in Dramatic Literature*. New York: Doubleday, 1957. 41–71.
Porter, Thomas E. "A Green Corner of the Universe: *Our Town*." In his *Myth and Modern American Drama*. Detroit: Wayne State University Press, 1969. 200–224.
Stephens, George D. "*Our Town*—Great American Tragedy?" *Modern Drama* 1.4 (Feb. 1959): 258–264.
Wilder, Thornton. *Our Town*. 1938. New York: HarperCollins, 1985.

"Landscape and the Avant-Garde in Cixous's *Portrait of Dora*, Kantor's *The Dead Class*, Müller's *Explosion of a Memory/Description of a Picture*, and Clarke and Mee's *Vienna: Lusthaus*"

Post-1950, ahistorical, nonlinear avant-garde practitioners have continued to engage in a dialogue with the theories of the earlier, established, European-centered historical avant-garde—one reflected, for example, in Robert Wilson's spatio-temporal experiments inspired by Gertrude Stein's landscape theory. However, the post-1950, pluralistic avant-garde, operating under the postmodern assumptions of simultaneity and fluidity of forms, structures, and ideas rather than their centrality and stability, have shifted from the predominance of the playwright as primary creator to the increased role of other theater artists in creating theater practice, as seen in the work of Wilson, Peter Brook, and Tadeusz Kantor, as well as the collaborative projects of groups such as the Open Theater and the Wooster Group.

In both *The Death of Character* (1996) and *Land/Scape/Theater* (2002), Elinor Fuchs distinguishes between two aspects of Stein-like landscape on stage: representational and perceptual. Representational landscape refers to productions in which the spatial elements use simultaneous actions but deliberately avoid a single focal point. By using multiple focal points and weighting them equally, the performances encourage the audience to view the entire stage at once. Objects from different places and temporal zones occupy the stage at the same time, forcing the audience to absorb odd juxtapositions and seeming inconsistencies into a new vision of the theatrical world. Perceptual landscapes, however, form in the spectator's mind rather than eye. The landscape is not visible at any one moment but is created over the course of the performance: by layering repeated and revised actions rather than forwarding a plot, the performance allows spectators to accumulate similar events and images in their minds. Whereas in representational landscape the audience sees a variety of times and places compressed into one stage space and time, in perceptual landscape spectators apprehend a multilayered image as it builds in their own minds over time. The two aspects of landscape can even overlap, to the extent that each approach—whether representational or perceptual, in the eye or in the mind—appears somehow embedded in the other.

Viewing theater as landscape permits spectators to focus on the interplay between the "land" or space and human adaptations to, and indeed *of*, it. In this way, landscape foregrounds the points of view of the artists who created it. The arrangement of key elements on stage communicates a point of view or perspective through contrasts and juxtapositions, though the central elements will vary depending upon the formal concerns of the individual artist. Stein herself discovered in such works a new kind of dramaturgy in which the stage itself could be the ground on which landscapes of *words* could be arranged and put in motion. These arrangements communicate ideas in a nonlinear way, allowing audience members to experience the totality of a theatrical-cum-verbal event, rather than simply to follow a plotted action through time.

In works like Kantor's *The Dead Class* (1975), Hélène Cixous's *Portrait of Dora* (1976), Heiner Müller's *Explosion of a Memory/Description of a Picture* (1985), and Martha Clarke and Charles Mee's *Vienna: Lusthaus* (1986), one sees just an effort to capture the fluidity of the human mind's process of association. At the turn of the nineteenth century, symbolist playwrights began to explore ways in which theater could express internal psychic landscapes; beginning in the 1930s, surrealists explored the melding of dreams and reality. Many such "landscape" works extend this concept by rejecting different aspects of traditional dramaturgy, playing with space and time and alternating our idea of inner (mind) and outer (body) space to shatter any sense of linear or logical progression. In the works of Kantor and Clarke and Mee in particular, the artists embrace multiple models of collaboration, using the group dynamic to create the shifting patterns of a single thought process.

Indeed, the strong voices of several types of collaborative teams—choreographer and writer (Clarke and Mee in *Vienna: Lusthaus*), writer and director (Müller and Robert Wilson in his *Explosion of a*

Memory/Description of a Picture), *auteur* and ensemble (Kantor and the original cast of *The Dead Class*)—add to the layers of competing production elements that create the landscape effect. Landscape plays require spectators to absorb and process a great deal of complex and often contradictory information, much of which can be fully realized in rehearsal but some of which cannot come to life completely until performed before a live audience. Hence, landscape lives on the border between text and performance, indeed, sometimes on the border between what can and cannot be seen in nature—a world of cryptic yet evocative objects, signs, and symbols. Landscapes not seen in nature in fact link the works of Cixous, Müller, Kantor, and Mee and Clarke. These artists all share an impulse to explore, through writing and staging, dream sequences, memory processes, and webs of fantasy. Such landscapes of the mind capture the free-flowing, associative habit of human consciousness and reflect the effect of fragmented, "traumatized" memory on perception.

In *Picture of Dora,* which is based on Sigmund Freud's famous case study of female hysteria in his patient Dora, Cixous focuses primarily on memory, time, and the human mind. Though the play is more clearly articulated on the page than many avant-garde plays of this period—perhaps because Cixous is, first and foremost, a writer, and at the time had yet to collaborate with Ariane Mnouchkine—her use of simultaneity of time distinguishes *Dora* from more traditional efforts to explore human psychology. Simultaneity has been a prominent tool in the avant-garde arsenal since the Italian futurists began to play with simultaneous action in their *sintesi*; Wilson uses this technique regularly as well. Through the use of voiceovers, which come across as thoughts rather than visions, Cixous creates a labyrinth of the memories, dreams, and fantasies of Freud's Dora; by thus making the convoluted mind of Dora the engine of the play, Cixous undermines Freud's rational attempts to analyze and contain his patient.

Drawing his inspiration from Dada collages as well as John Cage's and Allan Kaprow's "happenings," the Polish director Kantor himself creates his "partyturas," or collections of overlapping and fragmentary texts, concepts, and memories, which are similar in construction to Tadeusz Różewicz's *Birth Rate* (1968). Unlike Różewicz, however, Kantor retains control of his productions both in rehearsal and performance, taking on the role of director and performer by often placing himself in the middle of the performance. Through this technique, Kantor literally inhabits the landscape of the mind, an ever-present reminder to audience members of their invited presence in his mind, dreams, and associations.

The Dead Class explores his mind or memory through the interplay between the living and the dead: the Old People in black, carrying life-sized, wax figures of children, embody an image of the dead carrying the memory of their childhood. As the journey into the world of the dead continues, the line between life and death becomes less discernible: human characters (the Old People) appear to inhabit the world of the dead, but inanimate objects (life-sized mannequins) seem to embrace the world of the living. By employing objects such as wax figures of children and schoolroom benches as tools to retrieve memory, Kantor transforms a flat, still memory into a multidimensional spatial fold—of landscape theater. When the theatrical act of retrieving and reliving the past breaks down, the memories of the Old People turn into dreams or nightmares or they just disappear. As Kantor inhabits the theatrical space of the production, the audience feels his palpable role as author and director, a theater "conductor" conceiving and guiding the characters' journeys—and the audience's passage—through the spatial labyrinths of memory.

Whereas Kantor's productions map a personal landscape of his memory, Müller's texts evoke post-apocalyptic images drawn from individual and collective memory and reflect multiple, sometimes parallel, states of consciousness. In *Explosion of a Memory/Description of a Picture*, Müller's theatrical world attempts to break down all boundaries between internal and external space, or between human consciousness and the physical world. Müller and Wilson collaborated on the first production, which was produced as a prologue to Wilson's 1986 production of Euripides' *Alcestis* (438 BC) at the American Repertory Theater in Cambridge, Massachusetts. Scholars frequently regard these two artists as diametrically opposed, outside their collaborative works: Wilson, a visual stage artist, preoccupied with vision and time at the expense of politics; Müller, an East German who came of age during World War II, obsessed with politics and the socialism of his day. As the critic Laurence Shyer suggests, despite their profound cultural differences, Wilson discovered in Müller a "writer who seemed to share the same visual impulse, someone whose language translates not into rhetoric or narrative but pictures of the mind" (119–120). Thus, two minds—one more visual, one more verbal—came together on several occasions to create visual dramaturgy that combines text and vision into a dissociative theatrical event.

Müller's own aesthetic defies any dramatic or theatrical principles that are even remotely plot-based and character-centered. *Explosion of a Memory/Description of a Picture*, which embraces the imagery of civil war among various species, is a kind of scenic poem whose poetic quality is embedded in a flow of associative spaces that make up a complex and somewhat incongruous picture. In Müller's plays, the erasure of borders between humans and inanimate objects, the dissolution-cum-unification of multiple identities, and the collapse of temporal structure result in a vivid picture of nonetheless indeterminate meaning. Spectators must perceive and interpret the images for themselves; by accepting the dissolution of character and the absence of a relationship among time, logic, and space, audience members are compelled to create landscapes in their minds and thus accept responsibility as co-authors of this particular theatrical journey.

Mee's text for *Vienna: Lusthaus* returns to Freud as a subject for speculation about, and exploration of, dream states. Though Freud's theories had been the subject of strenuous criticism among psychologists in the twentieth century, his status as the "father" of modern psychology continued to serve as a lightning rod for theatrical consideration. In this play, the creative process started with Clarke's work. Mee, inspired by images of Vienna as though constructed by a subconscious mind, created the text to support Clarke's vision—which already involved simultaneous physical actions—evoking a sense of a cinematic "dissolve" between and among dreams. Thus, although the product shares much in common with the other "landscape" works, the creative process was inverted, with the vision and movement of physicalized dream states leading to the creation of a text. Ultimately, the audience members must resolve the tensions among simultaneous times, images, and places, bridging the temporal and spatial gaps for themselves each in his or her own way.

Clarke and Mee's collaboration evokes a late nineteenth-century Vienna permeated with intoxication, disease, hallucination, and sexual fantasy. This world is a multilayered dreamscape, a compilation of dreams woven together and influenced by different sources, including Freud's *Five Lectures on Psycho-Analysis* (1909). In this terrain of subconscious, surrealist imagery, the connection to Freud may be inevitable but the play repeatedly undermines Freud's authority as an interpreter of dreams, just as Cixous did in *Portrait of Dora*. Mee's spoken text, which consists of short, seemingly unrelated fragments unified by recurrent perceptions and oneiric imagery, opens a myriad of interpretive possibilities for visual translation in Clarke's choreography, thus fusing perceptual and representative landscapes. The incomplete and fragmentary nature of Mee's "perceptual" text, along with Richard Peaslee's music, complements the boundless web of visual compositions created by the dancers' bodies on the bare white setting that Robert Israel designed for the original production.

It was Gertrude Stein, it must be repeated, who first applied the term "landscape" to a style of avant-garde theater in a series of lectures written for her 1934 tour of the United States, maintaining that landscape drama lives in a continuous present where events from different temporal zones exist in the same space without relative weight or focus. The notion of theater-as-landscape resists the traditional use of time and space found in realistic narratives. Events are no longer structured according to a causal, horizontal or linear chronology; instead, actions accumulate vertically through accretion and juxtaposition. Story and character slip from the foreground, and realistic, representational space is sacrificed in favor of the simultaneous depiction of events from more than one time in a single space—the landscape.

Works Cited
Cixous, Hélène. *Portrait of Dora*. 1976. In *Selected Plays of Hélène Cixous*. Trans. Ann Liddle et al. London: Routledge, 2004.
Clarke, Martha, & Mee, Charles L. *Vienna: Lusthaus*. The Drama Review (TDR), 31.3 (Autumn 1987): 42–58.
Fuchs, Elinor. *The Death of Character: Perspectives on Theater after Modernism*. Bloomington: Indiana University Press, 1996.
——, & Una Chaudhuri, eds. *Land/Scape/Theater*. Ann Arbor: University of Michigan Press, 2002.
Kantor, Tadeusz. *The Dead Class*. 1975. In "Special Double Polish Theater Issue" of *Gambit*, 9.33–34. Trans. Karol Jakubowicz. London: John Calder, 1979.
Müller, Heiner. *Description of a Picture/Explosion of a Memory*. Trans. Carl Weber. *Performing Arts Journal*, 10.1 (1986): 106–110.
Shyer, Laurence. *Robert Wilson and His Collaborators*. New York: Theater Communications Group, 1989.
Stein, Gertrude. *Writings and Lectures, 1911–1945*. Ed. Patricia Meyerowitz. London: Peter Owen, 1967.

"Water and Weather in Pinter's *The Homecoming*"
Whatever one might think of Ruth's leaving her husband to become the mother-whore of his father and two brothers in Harold Pinter's *Homecoming* (1965), she clearly chooses one way of life over another: the life of a prostitute in England over that of a philosophy professor's wife in America. Pinter underlines the stark contrast between the two ways of life by comparing the former to wetness and cold and the latter to dryness and heat.

Ruth has been living in America with her husband Teddy for six years prior to the start of the play. She describes her home: "It's all rock. And sand. It stretches . . . so far . . . everywhere you look. And there's lots of insects there" (53). One can guess from this description that she, Teddy, and their three sons have been living in a university town in the Southwest. To judge by their behavior toward each other when they arrive at the family home in North London and by Ruth's eventual decision to remain with Max, Lenny, and Joey, Ruth and Teddy were having marriage problems back in the States. Therefore Teddy decided a week's vacation in Venice would do them good before the start of the fall term: he takes his wife from the desert of the American Southwest to the Lagoon of Venice, from sand to water. The decadence that is associated with the city of Venice prefigures the decadence that will surround Ruth's life as a prostitute. (This may be Pinter's little joke since, unlike us, he does not judge Ruth or anyone else in the play.)

Ruth and Teddy arrive at the family home at night, wearing light raincoats. In the 1973 film of the play (directed by Peter Hall, director of *The Homecoming*'s world premiere in London), the camera went outside the house to let us know that it had been raining. Teddy offers Ruth something hot to drink; she refuses. Lenny later offers her a glass of water, which she accepts. When he tries to take the glass from her, she resists:

> *Ruth*: I haven't quite finished.
> *Lenny*: You've consumed quite enough, in my opinion.
> *Ruth*: No, I haven't. (33)

Then Ruth taunts Lenny with the glass:

> (*She picks up the glass and lifts it towards him.*)
> *Ruth*: Have a sip. Go on. Have a sip from my glass. (*He is still.*) Sit on my lap. Take a long cool sip. (*She pats her lap. Pause. She stands, moves to him with the glass.*) Put your head back and open your mouth. (34)

Finally, Ruth "laughs shortly, drains the glass," saying, "Oh, I was thirsty" (34–35). Water seems to be her lifeblood.

In Act II, Lenny asks Ruth if she wants her drink "on the rocks? Or as it comes?" (61) She replies, "Rocks? What do you know about rocks?" The images of cold and heat conjoin: Lenny speaks of rocks of ice, while Ruth refers to the rocks of the desert. Also in Act II, Ruth describes an outdoor modeling job (a call girl's assignment?) she took several times in the English countryside. She had to pass by train "a large white water tower" (57) to get to the place where she would be working. Once there, she found trees and a lake; in the house, drinks were served and there was a cold buffet. Before leaving for America, Ruth visited this house in the country where she had modeled and, standing outside it, found all its lights on, found it "very light" (58)—the lightness here prefigures her life in the American Southwest, which will be suffused with, and oppressed by, sunlight.

Pinter does not imply that the "wetness and cold" of Ruth's life as a prostitute are superior to the "dryness and heat" of her life as wife and mother. He chooses these contrasting images because it is impossible to judge one as preferable to the other. He does not judge Ruth's choice; indeed, he suggests that Ruth will be as much mother to Max, Lenny, and Joey as whore (while working as a prostitute to supplement the family's earnings). Teddy prefers the cleanness and sunniness of the American Southwest, Ruth the coldness and darkness of London.

Shortly after a conversation between Ruth and Teddy about the cleanness of the Southwest versus the dirtiness of North London, Ruth and Lenny exchange these words:

Lenny: Well, the evenings are drawing in.
Ruth: Yes, it's getting dark. (*Pause*.)
Lenny: Winter'll soon be upon us.... 56)

Ruth and Teddy must part: the image-structure of the play as well as their behavior toward each other tells us this. Ruth comes home to London, and Teddy goes back home to America.

Work Cited
Pinter, Harold. *The Homecoming*. New York: Grove Press, 1967.

"Steinbeck's *Of Mice and Men* and the Natural World"

Somewhat like Lynn Riggs's *Green Grow the Lilacs* (1931), Erskine Caldwell's *Tobacco Road* (1933), Paul Osborn's *Morning's at Seven* (1939), and even Arthur Miller's *Death of a Salesman* (1949), John Steinbeck's play *Of Mice and Men* (1937) is an instance of nature-drama—or the decline thereof in the first half of the twentieth century.

Of Mice and Men, unlike the many big-city plays—and big-city sound films—from the 1930s, for its part concentrates on the unemployed of the farmlands, the itinerants and ranch workers, while it alludes to the bus drivers and truckers whose travels through the country permitted them to observe the state of the American nation in its broad horizon. Thus there is a strong residue of nineteenth-century feeling for the land in *Of Mice and Men*—that working on the land is the basic good, while owning some of it is salvation. With the possible exception in 1976 of Sam Shepard's *Curse of the Starving Class* (and, peripherally, Eugene O'Neill's *Long Day's Journey into Night* [1942, 1956], in its depiction of the itinerant actor and Irish immigrant James Tyrone's obsession with land ownership), it is difficult to pinpoint another successful American drama since the 1930s with such a feeling for the land, or even one centered on rural work.

Steinbeck genuinely understood Americans' erstwhile longing for a home on the range, not a mere feeding place. And in *Of Mice and Men* he suggests, with something akin to an austere, tragic sorrow, as opposed to the radical, activist politics of thirties dramatists like John Howard Lawson and Clifford Odets—or the politics of Steinbeck's own 1939 novel *The Grapes of Wrath*—that many of America's underprivileged will never reach the home *they* crave even if they arrive at greater social consciousness. As Crooks, the black character in *Of Mice and Men*, himself says of the ranch workers in the drama:

> I seen hundreds of men come by on the road and on the ranches, bindles on their back and that same damn thing in their head. Hundreds of 'em. They come and they quit and they go on. And every damn one of 'em has got a little piece of land in his head. And never a god-damn one of 'em gets it. (126)

Tragically, George Milton and Lennie Small, the two main characters in Steinbeck's play, do not get their land, their home, either. One of them loses his life in the attempt to get it, while the other is condemned to live out his life, in loneliness and regret, on the road. Indeed, Steinbeck uses the symbol of a dead mouse in order to unite such men and beasts, in nature, in mutual suffering—a suffering evoked by the following lines from a 1785 Robert Burns poem, spoken to a mouse:

> I'm truly sorry Man's dominion
> Has broken Nature's social union,
> An' justifies that ill opinion,
>   Which makes thee startle,
> At me, thy poor, earth-born companion,
>   An' fellow-mortal! (96)

Because of what has happened since it was written—the rapid decline of family farming, the relentless burgeoning of mechanized agribusiness, the despoiling of more and more of the nation's (let alone the world's) land, the increasing homelessness of women and children as well as single men—*Of Mice and Men* has come to be a play about the end not only of George and Lennie, but also of something in America, in American drama, and in the American Dream. No one in the United States thinks or writes anymore, really, about owning land—acres of land, not just a place to put your house or summer cottage—living on that land, tilling it, and belonging to it as do the animals. Everyone thinks instead about making *money*, as much money as possible, as if paper and metal and material gain were safeguards in the end against spiritual emptiness, psychic loss, and simple human mortality.

Works Cited
Burns, Robert. "To a Mouse" (1785). In *The Canongate Burns: The Complete Poems and Songs of Robert Burns*. Ed. Andrew Noble & Patrick Scott Hogg. Edinburgh, UK: Canongate, 2001. 96.
Steinbeck, John. *Of Mice and Men*: A Play in Three Acts. New York: Covici-Friede, 1937.

"Image and Inevitability in Synge's *Riders to the Sea*"

Often called one of the finest one-act dramas, if not the finest, ever written in English, John Millington Synge's *Riders to the Sea* (1904) exhibits, more than Synge's other plays, the influence of the Aran Islands on his art. Yet this short work also furnishes the best evidence that, in spite of his Rousseauist love of nature, its author was not a naïve worshipper and champion of the primitive. He sensed the tragic possibilities inherent in natural inexorability and, indeed, *Riders* may be the only one-act play in dramatic history that can be called a tragedy in the fullest sense. In its economy of form and simplicity or baldness of passion, it nonetheless resembles Hermann Heijerman's *The Good Hope* (1900), bears comparison with García Lorca's *Blood Wedding* (1933), and influenced Bertolt Brecht's *Señora Carrar's Rifles* (1937) as well as Derek Walcott's *The Sea at Dauphin* (1954). Furthermore, like these plays, *Riders* is naturalistic in conception, with a protagonist from a lower social rung who is to a large extent the victim of economic necessity. Hers is a society where it is so difficult to make a living that the menfolk are compelled to take what often prove to be fatal risks as they fish or transport their livestock to market on the roughest of seas.

The central character of *Riders to the Sea* is Maurya, an old Aran-Islander woman who has lost her husband, father-in-law, and five sons to the treacherous sea. *Riders* opens as Maurya's two chorus-voiced daughters, Cathleen and Nora, receive clothing from the body of a drowned man and identify him as their fifth brother, Michael, who has been missing for nine days. Meanwhile, Bartley, Maurya's last and youngest son, prepares for a journey to a horse fair on the mainland, setting off despite his mother's entreaties and even her withholding of her blessing. Then, in a prophetic vision of death at a spring well, Maurya claims to have seen Bartley riding down to the sea on a red mare, with her son Michael behind him on a gray pony. The terrible vision is presently fulfilled when the old woman learns not only that Michael's body has been identified, but also that Bartley has been knocked into the sea by the gray pony and drowned.

The rhythmic, imagistic language of Synge's play, while not in verse, adds to its overall effect—which can be seen as the effect of marrying richness to austerity, prodigality of imagination to poverty of means, peasant colloquialism to princely feeling. Technically, Aran Islanders speak both Gaelic and English, but partly as a result of being cast in the "foreign" syntax of Gaelic (as in "There's someone after crying out by the seashore" [21]), their second language of English is marked by a very expressive and idiosyncratic flavor.

That language is also is also marked by the quality of inevitability: since death is almost a way of life among the islanders, their language cannot help but be affected by its presence. At one point, for example, Nora says, "And it's destroyed he'll [Bartley] be going till dark night, and he after eating nothing since the sun went up" (11). "Destroyed" means in this context "fatigued" or "exhausted," but it also carries the meaning of "killed," so that the ending of the play is suggested by Nora's line. A little later Cathleen says, "Let you [Maurya] go down now to the spring well and give him [Bartley] this bread and he passing" (13), and we get the same effect. "Passing" means "passing by," but it can also mean "dying or passing away." Trying to open the bundle of clothes the priest gave to Nora, Cathleen says to her sister, "Give me a knife . . . the string's perished with the salt water, and there's a black knot on it you wouldn't loosen in a week" (15). "Perished" here means "contracted and hardened," but again, even though it refers to the string and not to Bartley himself, "perished" contributes to the death imagery that moves us forward to the end of the play. It is as if the islanders speak the language of death in recognition of death's looming and ineradicable presence in their lives—almost in defiance of such presence.

MODEL ESSAYS

This recognition carries over into the islanders' use of adjectives as well as verbs. Note in the above examples the phrases "dark night" and "black knot." "Dark night" is preceded by Maurya's "black night" (11), but the word "night" clearly implies darkness or blackness, so there is no real need to preface it with the adjective "dark" or "black." Yet the islanders do, and in the context of *Riders to the Sea* these adjectives forebode something bad or harmful. The family's pig has "black feet" (9); Michael's body is found in the sea near "the black cliffs of the north" (15), where "black hags" (17) fly about; and there is a "black [exceedingly hard to undo] knot" (15) in the string that ties Michael's bundle of clothes. The word "black" thus becomes a kind of leitmotif in the dialogue, preparing us subliminally for the death of Bartley that we know must come at the end of the play. We see this "black" even in the gray pony of death that knocks Bartley from the red mare of life into the sea.

Although *Riders to the Sea* may depict the sufferings of a superstitious peasant woman, it contains the same kind of intense drama found in ancient Greek tragedies. In fact, the play moves with an intensity that can only be achieved by poetic means; and, although *Riders* is not technically poetic drama as were the tragedies of Aeschylus, Sophocles, and Euripides, it is one of the finest twentieth-century examples of poetry *of* the theater. (Such poetry is to be distinguished, in Cocteau's terms, from poetry *in* the theater, as discussed in the preface to his 1921 play *The Wedding on the Eiffel Tower*.) Like Greek tragedy, moreover, *Riders* is permeated by a feeling of fatality or impending doom—a feeling embodied in its heightened language, austere setting, and telescoped action.

Works Cited

Cocteau, Jean. "Preface: 1922" to *The Wedding on the Eiffel Tower*. Trans. Michael Benedikt. In *Modern French Theater: the Avant-Garde, Dada, and Surrealism*. Ed. Michael Benedikt & George E. Wellwarth. New York: E. P. Dutton, 1966. 96–97.

Synge, J. M. *Riders to the Sea*. In his *Plays: Book I*. Ed. Ann Saddlemyer. Vol. 3 of *J. M. Synge: Collected Works*. Gen. ed. Robin Skelton. London: Oxford University Press, 1968. 1–27.

8 Form and Structure

This section consists of short model, or sample, essays on the subject of dramatic structure, or how a play is formed or put together. Treated here are the memory play, climactic drama, Epic Theater, avant-garde form, and anti-realism in general. The following plays have been chosen for their representativeness, modernity, variety, and quality:

1. Thornton Wilder's *Our Town*
2. Harold Pinter's *The Homecoming*
3. Tennessee Williams' *The Glass Menagerie*
4. Griselda Gambaro's *Stripped*, Reza Abdoh's *The Hip-Hop Waltz of Eurydice*, and Caryl Churchill's *Far Away*
5. David Hare's *Fanshen*
6. Alfred Jarry's *Ubu Roi*

For reading and learning purposes, the "Key Analytical Question" below can be applied to any of the above plays or all of them.

Key Analytical Question: "What type of structure does a particular play have, and how does this structure help to express the dramatist's meaning?"

"Wilder's *Our Town* and Avant-Garde Form"

Thornton Wilder's *Our Town* (1938) hides behind what appears to be radical, self-searching dramaturgy but is in fact little more than contrived, self-serving theatricalism. To wit, on the surface *Our Town* has the trappings of an avant-garde play, or of such a play as influenced by the anti-illusionistic conventions of the Asian theater (Sang-Kyong, 288–299): a narrator, the Stage Manager, who disrupts the illusion of present-tense reality and attempts to work against the rule of sentiment onstage; "No curtain [to conceal the 'fourth wall']. No scenery" (5), no props to speak of, which necessitates the miming of actions such as eating and drinking, as well as delivering milk or newspapers; characters who address the audience (like Professor Willard, Editor Webb, and Mrs. Webb) and acknowledge the existence of the Stage Manager, as well as dead characters who speak in the last act; an episodic dramatic form stretching over twelve years (Act I takes place in 1901, Act II in 1904, and Act II in 1913) that allows for flashbacks (the courtship of George and Emily in Act II, Emily's twelfth birthday in Act III) and flash-forwards (the Stage Manager's foretelling, in Act I, of the invention of the automobile and the deaths of Dr. Gibbs, Mrs. Gibbs, and Joe Crowell), and that necessitates the building, dismantling, and rebuilding of the town in various configurations upon the same site, such that there is the sensation of movement through time and space within a framework that is ultimately static, in the manner of a cubist collage; and a lyric mood rather than a dramatic conflict in the conventional sense of protagonist-versus-antagonist.

In fact, each time there is the possibility of dramatic conflict in *Our Town*, it quickly dissolves into the clean and clear New Hampshire air. For instance, when Dr. Gibbs confronts his son with failing to perform the chore of chopping wood for Mrs. Gibbs's kitchen stove, George offers no excuse for his behavior; indeed, he sheds tears instead of uttering angry words of self-justification and tacitly agrees to give his mother all the help she needs in the future (36). When Constable Warren and Editor Webb encounter the drunken Simon Stimson on the street at night in Act I, the one man looks the other way, the other says "Good evening" twice, while Simon himself "pauses a moment and stares . . . [then] continues on his way without a word and disappears at the right" (43). And when Emily criticizes George's "conceited and stuck-up" behavior during their courtship scene, George offers no defense of himself whatsoever; instead he embraces her remarks with the following words: "I'm glad you said it, Emily. I never thought that such a thing was happening to me. I guess it's hard for a fella not to have faults creep into his character" (63). Moreover, despite the fact that Emily and George both get cold feet immediately before they are to be married (George declares "All I want to do is to be [single] fella—" [74], while Emily cries out, "I *hate* [George]. . . . I don't want to get married" [75]), nothing comes of their panic and aversion. Instead of having an argument and canceling the wedding, they quickly come to their senses and unite, as planned, in holy matrimony.

Characters like these are typed or familiar, however—the town malcontent, the folksy sheriff, the steady milkman, the knowing newspaper editor, the boy-and-girl next door, all flat figures from the primitive world of folk art—not psychologically complex or "conflicted," let alone inscrutable, and they certainly are not figures who call into question the whole idea of unified character or integrated personality, like those of Pirandello. Indeed, when Editor Webb fields questions from the audience in Act I, he neither drops out of character nor steps out from the play, in character, in order to do so: instead he answers "plants" in the audience—not real audience members asking improvised questions—whose queries manage to keep him firmly within the world of *Our Town*. And nothing is made, either by Wilder or the citizens of Grover's Corners, of the fact that the Stage Manager plays or metamorphoses into multiple roles in *Our Town*: Mrs. Forrest, an old lady into whom George bumps while playing baseball on Main Street (27); Mr. Morgan, the owner of the local drugstore and soda fountain (64); the minister presiding at George and Emily's wedding (71); the literal manager of the stage who belongs to the "real" world of the theater, about which he immediately tells us: "This play is called 'Our Town.' It was written by Thornton Wilder; produced and directed by A. . . . In it you will see Miss C. . . . ; Miss D. . . . ; Miss E. . . .; and Mr. F. . . .; Mr. G. . . .; Mr. H. . . .; and many others" (5); as well as the town's native son, natural leader, and documentary biographer, historical chronicler, or choral spokesman, who speaks of "our" town (5–7) in the same accent as every other citizen of Grover's Corners—every other white Anglo-Saxon citizen, that is (e.g., "holla'" for "holler" or "hollow" [6], "'twan't" for "it wasn't" [72], "hull" for "whole" [6]).

Just as Wilder's *dramatis personae* are not designed either to plumb the depths of character, on the one hand, or to deconstruct it, on the other, neither is his interruption of the linear progression of time designed to probe the nature of time—to suggest its relativistic quality—or to question the principle of inexorable, deterministic causality. Rather, *Our Town* flashes back from 1938 to 1901–1913, then from 1913 to 1899 (the year of Emily's twelfth birthday), for the purpose of chauvinistic nostalgia, even as it flashes forward for the sake of cosmic wonder (although, tellingly, it never really goes beyond the present of 1938); and it does so through the offices of an omniscient, omnipotent, and omnipresent Stage Manager who creates the play's lyric atmosphere, not because he wishes to emphasize the subjectivity of his own voice or to stress the essential "plotlessness" of human existence, but rather out of a desire to banish all dramatic confrontation to the wings, which is to say subsume it within his own quiescent oneness.

In this he is, of course, a godlike figure, if not a spokesman for God himself in such speeches as the following, which more than suggest that human beings are created in the image of the divine and are thus superior to the rest of creation:

> The real hero of this scene [George and Emily's wedding] isn't on stage at all, and you know who that is. It's like what one of those European fellas said: every child born into the world is nature's attempt to make a perfect human being. Well, we've seen nature pushing and contriving for some time now. We all know that nature's interested in quantity; but I think she's interested in quality, too—that's why I'm in the ministry. (71)

> We all know that *something* is eternal. And it ain't houses and it ain't names, and it ain't earth, and it ain't even the stars . . . everybody knows

in their bones that *something* is eternal, and that something has to do with human beings. All the greatest people ever lived have been telling us that for five thousand years and yet you'd be surprised how people are always losing hold of it. There's something way down deep that's eternal about every human being. (*Pause.*) You know as well as I do that the dead [like Emily] don't stay interested in us living people for very long. [. . .] They're waitin'. They're waitin' for something that they feel is coming'. Something important, and great. Aren't they waitin' for the eternal part in them to come out clear? (81–82)

Yes, it's clearing up. There are the stars—doing their old, old crisscross journeys in the sky. Scholars haven't settled the matter yet, but they seem to think there are no living beings up there. Just chalk . . . or fire. Only this one is straining away, straining away all the time to make something of itself. (103)

In the second speech above, the Stage Manager is clearly referring to the immortality of the human soul, but he—or Wilder—does so without the realization that in modern, not to speak of avant-garde, drama, the patriarchal relationship between God and the individual soul has been replaced by the adversarial relationship between man and his own psychology, his will to comprehend himself, even as the patriarchal relationship between ruler and subject has been replaced by the adversarial relationship between man and society, in the form of society's drive to marginalize all those that it cannot or will not homogenize.

In the third speech, quoted from the very end of the play, the Stage Manager seems to want to vanquish any uncertainty the audience might have about the significant of the human species in God's eye. He seems also to anticipate, as well as to relieve, the nationwide panic created by Orson Welles's pseudo-documentary radio broadcast based on H. G. Wells's science-fiction tale of an invasion from Mars, *The War of the Worlds* (1898), which aired on CBS on Halloween night in 1938, about nine months after *Our Town*'s New York opening. In peremptorily concluding that there are no living beings "up there," the Stage Manager sounds rather like the would-be debunkers of Copernicus and Galileo in the sixteenth and seventeenth centuries (even later, of course, especially where Catholic dogma is concerned). These charlatans insisted that the sun revolved around the earth, for to accept the reverse findings of the two scientists—and, likewise, the theory that intelligent life can be found in outer space—was to admit that our planet and its human inhabitants were not at the center of a divinely ordered universe.

MODEL ESSAYS

The moon naturally does revolve around the earth, and Wilder does not miss the chance to underline the stability of its orbit or the competence of those who keep a watchful eye on it, as the following exchange reveals:

> *Rebecca*: George, ... I think maybe the moon's getting nearer and nearer and there'll be a big 'splosion.
> *George*: Rebecca, you don't know anything. If the moon were getting nearer, the guys that sit up all night with telescopes would see it first and they'd tell about it, and it'd be in all the newspapers. (41–42)

The reliable "guys that sit up all night with telescopes" are ironically the same ones who, a few centuries back, incontrovertibly relegated the planet earth to third position in order from the sun, which they now understood to be the central body of the solar system. Along with thinkers like Montaigne and Machiavelli, and later Marx, Freud, Darwin, Comte, Nietzsche, and Einstein—whose theory of relativity itself is questioned by "A Man From Among the Dead" in Act III (102)—they thus initiated the slow death of God in literature as well as life, or at the very least the idea that, if there is a God, He did and does not conceive of lowly man as the greatest, noblest, or worthiest of all His creations.

Our Town to the contrary, the fundamental subject matter of almost all serious plays of the nineteenth and twentieth centuries is the attempt to resurrect fundamental ethical or philosophical certainties *without* resurrecting the fundamental spiritual certainty of a judgmental or mindful God—the very God Mrs. Gibbs appears to invoke when she advises the deceased Emily to "think only of what's ahead, and be ready for what's ahead" (92). Contrary to the evidence I have already adduced from the play showing average human beings who are perfectly aware of the Platonic essence or eternal dimension of reality, as well as contrary to the evidence from Wilder's own non-fiction of his belief that human beings can find their relationship to God or the transcendental in a conscious appreciation of the natural life around them (*American Characteristics*, 207–208; *Journals*, 125), the Stage Manager implies that it is only this God who, in the person of "saints and poets" (like the Stage Manager, whom Wilder himself once played?), can realize the wonder of life while it is being lived or appreciate the extraordinary beauty of ordinary, unremarkable human existence (100). He thereby implies that this God is the providential designer or moral center of a conventional dramatic triad whose two other components are psychology and causality—a triad that governs the traditional narrative of the eighteenth and nineteenth centuries as well.

Yet modern drama (for my purposes, the realism and naturalism of the social-problem play) banished theology as well as autocracy from its triadic paradigm of human action, as I indicate above, thus deepening the dramatic role played by psychology, sociology, and linearity or linkage, while avant-garde drama (all the –isms that react against realism and naturalism, such as symbolism, expressionism, surrealism, and futurism) demonstrated that a play's movement can be governed by something completely outside the triad that links motive to act, act to logical sequence of events, and logical outcome to divine or regal judgment. For the avant-garde, beginning in the late nineteenth century with Jarry if not earlier with such German visionaries as Tieck, Büchner, and Grabbe, the nature of reality itself becomes the prime subject of plays because of a loss of confidence in the assumed model for dramatizing human behavior and thinking about human existence. Wilder writes as if no such revolution in the writing of drama had occurred, though we know that he was well aware of it (if only through his intimate friendship with, professional admiration for, and professed artistic debt to Gertrude Stein, who, in her rejection of the cogency of plot and idea for the sensuality or pure form of language, gesture, and space, was probably the first thoroughgoing American avant-garde dramatist [Haberman, *Plays*, 37–38, 70; Burns, *Letters*, 175]). Or rather he borrows from that revolution its "designer fashions" while continuing to wear the emperor's old clothes underneath.

Works Cited

Burns, Edward, & Ulla E. Dydo, eds. *The Letters of Gertrude Stein and Thornton Wilder*. New Haven, Conn.: Yale University Press, 1996.

Haberman, Donald. *The Plays of Thornton Wilder*. Middletown, Conn.: Wesleyan University Press, 1967.

Sang-Kyong, Lee. "Zur Rezeption ostasiatischer Theatertradition in Thornton Wilders *Our Town*." *Arcadia* 22.3 (1987): 284–300.

Wilder, Thornton. *Our Town*. 1938. New York: HarperCollins, 1985.

——. *American Characteristics and Other Essays*. Ed. Donald Gallup. New York: Harper & Row, 1979.

——. *The Journals of Thornton Wilder: 1938–1961*. Ed. Donald Gallup. New Haven, Conn.: Yale University Press, 1985.

"Internal Consistency in Pinter's *The Homecoming*"

Harold Pinter's *The Homecoming* (1965) has an internal consistency. Taken on its own terms, this difficult play makes sense: we can understand its action. Taken on its own terms, the play also gives a clue to its meaning.

Teddy gives the following well-known speech in Act II, just after his brothers, Lenny and Joey, have made sexual advances to his wife, Ruth, for the first time:

> You wouldn't understand my works.... It's nothing to do with the question of intelligence. It's a way of being able to look at the world. It's a question of how far you can operate on things and not in things.... To see, to be able to see! I'm the one who can see.... You're just objects. ... [Y]ou're lost in it. You won't get me being ... I won't be lost in it. (61–62)

Teddy says, then, that the members of his family, which will soon include Ruth, are just objects, lost in what they are doing: that is, they are not reflective, not self-critical.

Earlier in Act II, Ruth had made a speech that placed her among the "objects" of Teddy's family before she actually became one:

> Look at me. I ... move my leg. That's all it is. But I wear ... underwear ... which moves with me ... it ... captures your attention. Perhaps you misinterpret. The action is simple. It's a leg ... moving. My lips move. Why don't you restrict ... your observations to that? Perhaps the fact that they move is more significant ... than the words which come through them. You must bear that ... possibility ... in mind. (52–53)

Why don't you restrict your observations to my physical being, Ruth says, instead of trying to find meaning in my words? Shortly Lenny and Joey won't simply be observing Ruth, they'll be touching her and lying with her. All three will be "lost in it," in Teddy's words, while Teddy will take on his cherished role of observer. He looks on calmly as Lenny dances with and kisses Ruth, and as Joey "leans her back [on the sofa] until she lies beneath him" (59). Ruth's actions may be shocking in and of themselves, but she has prepared us for them with the speech that I quote above: they are consistent with what has gone before them. She speaks of herself as an object of desire, then she is treated like one and acts like one. She doesn't ask Teddy if she can dance with and kiss Lenny; she does so. She doesn't question whether she should let Joey get on top of her; she simply lets him.

It is Ruth who asks Teddy if his family has ever read his "critical [-philosophical] works" (61): as if she knows how he'll respond, separating himself from her as well as from his family. Later in the evening, after he has given his speech about his works, and while Ruth is upstairs in bed with Joey, Teddy admits to Lenny that he deliberately ate the latter's cheese-roll. He says, "I saw you put it [in the sideboard]. I was hungry, so I ate it" (64). This is one of two instances in which he acts like everyone else in his family, like an "object," simply taking what he wants without regard for the rights of others. Perhaps he steals the cheese-roll because his brothers have stolen his wife: he thus momentarily reduces himself to their level, or he places his wife on the same level with a cheese-roll as an object to be devoured.

In his speech on his critical works, Teddy separated himself from the "objects" in his family, and now that his wife has joined his father and brothers, he has no alternative but to depart. Like Ruth's sexual response to Lenny and Joey, Teddy's departure is consistent with his pronouncement prior to it. It is less that he relinquishes his wife than that he saves himself. (It is less that Ruth leaves him than that she asserts herself or follows her own desires.) To remain with the family is to become like them: that is perhaps one of the reasons he left for America six years before the play begins. Indeed, Teddy may speak for the audience itself in his critical works speech. The characters onstage *are* "just objects," are "lost in it," while we, like Teddy, observe them. We are able to *see*. Like Teddy, we walk away from the family at the end of the drama: we leave the theater.

Was one of Pinter's purposes in *The Homecoming*, then, *not* to mirror reality, but rather to present us with characters quite unlike ourselves? Did he wish to test their attraction for us? What is the attraction of characters who assert themselves but do not reflect on their actions or are not self-critical? Such characters are in a sense a relief to watch, because they seem to behave without guilt, without conscience. This, in my opinion, is the source of our fascination with Max, Lenny, Joey, and Ruth: we identify with them in part because, in doing so, we are momentarily freed from the constraints of existence in civilized society. We laugh at Max and Lenny in the first scene of the play, for example, because we *enjoy* seeing father and son behave in shocking ways—ways other than those we expect. The behavior of Max, Lenny, Joey, and Ruth is, of course, also a source of consternation for us: despite the improbability of our ever encountering a *family* like Teddy's, it is no secret that there are individuals in this world who live beyond conscience, beyond traditional mores, in far more dangerous ways than the characters in *The Homecoming*. Paradoxically, Pinter domesticates terror in this play, makes it more accessible to us, at the same time that he frees our own anarchic impulse.

Work Cited
Pinter, Harold. *The Homecoming.* New York: Grove Press, 1967.

"The Role of Memory in Williams' *The Glass Menagerie*"

Tom Wingfield's romantic lineage as a lone, visionary quester, as opposed to his realistic-naturalistic role as a clear-sighted, participatory narrator, might have been clearer had Tennessee Williams taken himself at his word in the Production Notes to *The Glass Menagerie* (1944):

> Expressionism and all other unconventional techniques in drama have only one valid aim, and that is a closer approach to truth. When a play employs unconventional techniques, it is not, or certainly shouldn't be, trying to escape its responsibility of dealing with reality, or interpreting experience, but is actually or should be attempting to find a closer approach, a more penetrating and vivid expression of things as they are. ... Everyone should know nowadays the unimportance of the photographic in art: that truth, life, or reality is an organic thing which the poetic imagination can represent or suggest, in essence, only through transformation, through changing into other forms than those which were merely present in appearance.... [A] new, plastic theater ... must take the place of the exhausted theater of realistic conventions if the theater is to resume vitality as a part of our culture. (7)

If the playwright had heeded these words, he would have made his alter ego, Tom Wingfield, a genuine expressionistic protagonist, with American antecedents in Eugene O'Neill's *The Emperor Jones* (1920), Elmer Rice's *The Adding Machine* (1923), and Sophie Treadwell's *Machinal* (1928), together with German precedents stretching from the quintessential expressionist Georg Kaiser all the way back to such late, even ironic romantic relatives of his as Heinrich von Kleist and Georg Büchner. That is, Tom would have become a protagonist whose remembrance of familial things past was truly subjective: distorted, dreamlike or even nightmarish, and totally self-generated, a fantastic journey through the mind's inner reaches as well as the world's outer ones.

As it stands, however, Tom's memories are not expressionistic, but *impressionistic*: they are his impressions of his former domestic life, the veracity or accuracy of which is never placed in doubt by Williams. *The Glass Menagerie* may be a memory play, then, but it does not question the reliability of memory, as do such plays as Pirandello's *Six Characters in Search of an Author* (1921) and Pinter's *Old Times* (1971), and as does a film like Kurosawa's *Rashomon* (1951). Instead, Tom's memories (like those of his Irish "offspring," the young narrator of Brian Friel's *Dancing at Lughnasa* [1990]) are very much in the Hollywood tradition of flashback films, whose flashbacks are set in a representational world we all recognize and accept. (Not by accident, *The Glass Menagerie*'s earlier, 1943 incarnation was a screenplay, titled *The Gentleman Caller* but never produced.)

The opening stage directions of *The Glass Menagerie* suggest just such a flashback when they describe the theatrical equivalent of a cinematic "dissolve":

> At the rise of the curtain, the audience is faced with the dark, grim rear wall of the Wingfield tenement. . . . At the end of Tom's opening commentary, the dark tenement wall slowly becomes transparent and reveals the interior of the ground-floor Wingfield apartment.
>
> Nearest the audience is the living room . . . Just beyond, separated from the living room by a wide arch or second proscenium with transparent faded portieres (or second curtain), is the dining room. . . . The audience hears and sees the opening scene in the dining room through both the transparent fourth wall of the building and the transparent gauze portieres of the dining-room arch. It is during this revealing scene that the fourth wall slowly ascends, out of sight. This transparent exterior wall is not brought down again until the very end of the play, during Tom's final speech. (21–22)

After this, Tom steps onstage and begins his narration—the very kind we would hear in voice-over in a flashback film. He should remain onstage throughout, even when he does not appear in a scene (as he doesn't in Scene 2), as the play's one concession to Tom's "subjective" point of view. (Even as it would be a concession to Tom's choral function, though, unlike the choruses of ancient Greek tragedy, Tom is a chorus of one; and, at the end of *The Glass Menagerie*, the individualistic Tom abandons the stage, or his family, whereas the socially-minded Greek chorus never deserted the stage and its fellow citizens.) But the fact that Williams never indicates in the stage directions that Tom is present at all times suggests that he was really writing what he decries in his Production Notes: a "straight realistic play with its genuine Frigidaire and authentic ice-cubes, its characters who speak exactly as its audience speaks . . ." (7).

What we see onstage may be dimly or poetically lit; a screen device (on which images and titles are projected) may be used as the mind's eye of the narrator; a single recurring tune may "weave in and out of

[a] preoccupied consciousness" (9); and eating and drinking may be mimed instead of literally carried out—in other words, the action may appear to be impressionistic or "non-realistic" (though hardly expressionistic)—but this is realism by any other name. And all the more so because, like undisguised realism and naturalism, *The Glass Menagerie* never questions its own, or its narrator's, objectivity.

Work Cited
Williams, Tennessee. *The Glass Menagerie.* 1945. New York: New Directions, 1966.

"Terror and the Avant-Garde in Gambaro's *Stripped*, Abdoh's *The Hip-Hop Waltz of Eurydice*, and Churchill's *Far Away*"

An avant-garde category that can be described as "Terror" corresponds dramatically with states of mind and politics today and spans the gap between early theatrical experiments with acts of "terror" such as the Theater of Cruelty (originally proposed before 1950 by Artaud and documented by Charles Marowitz's 1966 essay ["Notes on the Theater of Cruelty"]) and the dramatic works of such stylistically diverse writers as Caryl Churchill, Griselda Gambaro, and Reza Abdoh, who explore the consequences of violence and terror on society, psychology, and language. Indeed, throughout the past century and even before it, the theater examined and dramatized political terror as characterized by mass arrests and executions. From Georg Büchner's *Danton's Death* (1835) to Harold Pinter's *The Birthday Party* (1958) and beyond (to Edward Bond, Howard Baker, Sarah Kane, and Martin McDonagh), theater artists have investigated the impact of terror on the human psyche. Indeed, stylistic continuity of a "cruel" kind spans the historical avant-garde, tying the surrealist, nightmarish images in Roger Vitrac's *The Mysteries of Love* (1927) to the irrational violence alluding to the horrors of totalitarianism in the plays of Daniil Kharms and Aleksandr Vvedensky—members of the Soviet Oberiuty (Association for Real Art)—from the late 1920s.

Yet in the wake of the unavoidable association between the concept of "terror" and global terrorism after September 11, 2001, a metanarrative on the latter phenomenon in the arts and society has blurred the borders between imagined and actual terror and heightened the sense of imminent danger (but obscured the source). The avant-garde thus shifted from the shocking, visceral experience proposed by Artaud, as well as the dreamlike, nonsensical violence found in surrealist and Absurdist plays, to dramatizing an overwhelming sense of extreme paranoia, indeterminate danger, and complete powerlessness. Although such works as Gambaro's *Stripped* (1974), Abdoh's *The Hip-Hop Waltz of Eurydice* (1990), and Churchill's *Far Away* (2000) were written before the attacks of September 11th, it is difficult, if not impossible, to read them without reference to a new, closer-to-home understanding of terror in the twenty-first century. Indeed, New York Theater Workshop produced the American premiere of *Far Away* on the first anniversary of 9/11.

As a group, these three plays are most deliberately political, confronting governmental torture, the complicity of silence, and gender and sexuality in reaction to oppressive warfare of all kinds. Writing from a clear sense of his complex identity as a homosexual, HIV-positive Iranian theater artist, Abdoh deploys graphic images and extensive use of multimedia images in *The Hip-Hop Waltz of Eurydice* to batter his audience in an attack reminiscent of Artaud's most passionate calls for a Theater of Cruelty. Abdoh, however, experienced more than the crisis of the spirit perceived by Artaud; his was a crisis of social and political identity that took place on the most personal level imaginable. In *Stripped,* Gambaro herself gets personal by dramatizing her reaction to events in Argentina at a time when the government was publicly staging acts of terrorism in order to threaten and suppress political resistance. As a woman was ritualistically stripped of every shred of her clothing and dignity in this play, the original Argentinean audiences experienced a theatrically stylized but no less terrifying re-creation of their own silent collusion in terror.

In *Far Away,* Churchill, for her part, imagines a child's journey from nightmare to reality in which the child's worst fears about the world are supplanted by a reality in which nations, animals, and people devour each other in an all-encompassing war. Churchill directly theatricalizes silence on stage here through the aunt's request that the child not speak of the torture she has witnessed, whereas Gambaro implicitly imposes the responsibility not to speak—or to speak—on the theater audience. In Gambaro's hands, torture becomes stylized and even absurd, whereas Churchill extends the concept of terror to an all-embracing, and all too tangible, world war. Yet both works address the audience's proximity to terror, challenging spectators to question their lack of resistance to events they otherwise might prefer to forget. If survival requires acknowledging terror, then, all three of these plays—*Far Away, Stripped,* and *The Hip-Hop Waltz of Eurydice*—confront audiences with it viscerally, thereby sharing in Artaud's call to arms with much greater political and social awareness.

Works Cited

Abdoh, Reza. *The Hip-Hop Waltz of Eurydice*. In Mufson, Daniel. *Reza Abdoh*. Baltimore, Md.: Johns Hopkins University Press, 1999. 51–87.

Artaud, Antonin. *The Theater and Its Double*. Trans. Mary Caroline Richards. New York: Grove Press, 1958.

Churchill, Caryl. *Far Away*. London: Nick Hern Books, 2000.

Gambaro, Griselda. *Stripped*. In *Women & Performance*, 11.2 (2000): 97–106.

Marowitz, Charles. "Notes on the Theater of Cruelty." *Tulane Drama Review*, 11.2 (Winter 1966): 152–172.

"Hare's *Fanshen* and Western Drama"

David Hare has said that *Fanshen* (1975) "is a story of change and progress" (Lecture, *Licking Hitler*, 62), "of how the peasants of Long Bow built a new world" (Preface, *Fanshen*, 13). Long Bow is intended to be representative of all the Chinese villages right after World War II that were attempting to "fanshen." Hare writes that "literally [this word] means 'to turn the body' or 'to turn over'. To China's hundreds of millions of landless and land-poor peasants, it meant to stand up, to throw off the landlord yoke, to gain land, stock, implements, and houses" (Preface, *Fanshen*, 13). "Fanshen" meant, in other words, to change one's life for the better.

The play is about the destruction of feudalism in China and the gradual creation of the People's Republic. But in a larger sense, *Fanshen* is about the process of change itself, about how the thinking and behavior of people—both leaders and the led—may be transformed. And in this respect, it is different from traditional Western drama, where the emphasis in tragedy is on characters who cannot change or change too late, who suffer because who they are conflicts with what society is; where the emphasis in sentimental drama is on characters whose change is intended to show, not that people are truly changeable, but that people are only asserting the good nature they have had all along and from which they have temporarily been diverted; and where the emphasis in comedy is on characters whose inability to change makes them objects of ridicule.

Traditional Western drama stresses psychology and fate: who you are tends to determine what you will do in a given situation; it is your unified and fixed personality that is the primary object of interest. By contrast, *Fanshen*, like the plays of Bertolt Brecht—another writer strongly attracted to Chinese history—emphasizes sociology and self-determination: who you are is always in flux and is determined by your interaction with the social situation in which you find yourself. Indeed, society and the individual are inseparable in *Fanshen*. Thus, we cannot speak of main characters, but only of the people of Long Bow and their will to change their society, to change themselves. We cannot speak of the private lives of the villagers, but only of the way in which their individual actions affect the collective life of the village, the welfare of its public.

Since *Fanshen* rejects the notions of character psychology and fate, the play is not dramatic in the conventional sense. In the following passage, Hare contrasts the conventionally dramatic with what he views as its alternative in *Fanshen*:

> There's a comment of Len Deighton's which interests me very much; he says, 'I have no interest in going to a debate—unless I know that the loser of the debate is going to be shot at the end. *That* is dramatic.' I feel the exact opposite. I have no interest in who's going to be shot at the end. I feel that the debate itself is what is interesting. (Bradby, "After *Fanshen*," 298)

In the conventionally dramatic play, then, the emphasis is on the outcome of events: on waiting for the debate to end, so that the loser will be shot. Brecht once described this kind of theater as one in which spectators have their "eyes on the finish," in which the plot is linear ("one scene makes another," or each scene follows naturally out of the one that preceded it and cannot be understood except in the order in which it was written), and in which the spectator is called upon to feel or share the experience of the characters (*Brecht on Theater*, 37).

By contrast, in Hare's idea of the dramatic in *Fanshen*, as well as in Brecht's conception of Epic Theater, the emphasis is on the course of events: on the process of the debate, not its product; on how it is conducted, not on what its result will be. Brecht speaks of "narrative" in such a theater, not plot, and of "each scene [standing] for itself" (*Brecht on Theater*, 37). That is, any scene taken out of sequence would still be intelligible, because it exists not to build tension but to say something of itself, to make its own discrete political point. The German dramatist speaks further of a spectator who stands outside the action, studying it and applying reason—as opposed to emotion—to what he sees.

Let us examine Act I, Section 3, Scene iii of *Fanshen* as a paradigm of Hare's method. At the start of this scene, before the action actually begins, Yu-lai says, "We have seized the wealth from fifteen families. Two hundred and eighty-six acres of land, twenty-six draft animals, four hundred sections of house. And behind the temple doors: everything they own" (31). We are not *shown* the seizing of this wealth in detail—we get only one short scene before this (I, 3.i) in which we see the possessions of Ch'ung-Wang confiscated, and even here the emphasis is less on what is taken and what is done to the initially uncooperative landlord, than on the lengths to which he has gone over the years to hide his money and make himself appear less rich than he actually is. Yu-lai *narrates* the seizing of this man's wealth at the top of I,3.iii, even as he narrates the seizing of another man's wealth in I,3.ii in collaboration with Man-hsi, Cheng-k'uan, and T'ien-ming.

As the following excerpt shows, the four men cooperate to tell the confiscation story in I,3.ii in keeping with the play's focus on the people of Long Bow and their public actions, rather than on a few main characters and their inner natures:

> *Cheng-k'uan*: That evening all the people went to Ching-ho's courtyard to help take over his property. It was very cold. We built bonfires and the flames shot up towards the stars. It was very beautiful.
> *Yu-lai*: We dug up all his money, beating him, digging, finding more. By the time the sun was rising in the sky we had five hundred dollars.
> (30)

Now a playwright in the conventionally dramatic theater would place Ching-ho at the center of the action and make the raid on his courtyard the most exciting scene in the play: it would be graphically depicted, not calmly narrated, as it is here. The unrepentant landlord would meet his downfall at the hands of the dedicated revolutionaries, and the drama would end with their celebration. Ching-ho would thus have become the loser of Len Deighton's debate.

In *Fanshen*, however, the character Ching-ho plays only a small part, disappearing after I,3.ii. According to the concept of "fanshen," the *distribution*, not the confiscation, of his and others' wealth is important to the theme of the play—the gradual change effected in people's lives by the destruction of the feudal system. Like Brecht, Hare even includes slogans at the start of scenes, to be projected on a back wall or displayed on a placard to the side of the stage. The slogan for I,3.iii is "Distribution of Fruits." We are told immediately by this slogan—it appears before Yu-lai announces that the wealth of fifteen families has been seized—*what* will happen in the scene, so that we can concentrate on *how* it happens. Traditional suspense is thereby removed.

The point of I,3.iii is that the peasants of Long Bow do not fight greedily for their share of the appropriated wealth. No one attempts through force to get a large share of the land, implements, and animals;

no one tries to become a landlord himself. The peasants are changing, for the better; no longer dependent on landlords, they must depend on one another. Guided by the village leaders, who themselves are guided by the Communist Party, they cooperate to distribute the goods as evenly as possible at this point. I say "at this point" because their change is part of a process, of the interesting debate Hare speaks of. They do not become flawless Communists overnight—Hare's point is that there is no such thing, that the idea of a flawless Communist living happily ever after is as silly as that of a tragically flawed protagonist going blindly to his or her end.

What is dramatic for this particular playwright, then, is the struggle or tension, the debate, between Communist-Party theory and the practice into which it is put by the people of Long Bow:

> [In] China . . . the dialectic is actually seen to mean something in people's lives. In the play *Fanshen* it is dynamic. Political practice answers to political theory and yet modifies it; the party answers to the people and is modified by it. The fight is for political structures which answer people's needs; and people themselves are changed by living out theoretical ideas. (Lecture, *Licking Hitler*, 62)

That dynamic dialectic is seen at work in I,3.iii, where the village leaders appear to misinterpret Secretary Liu's statement in I,2.i about landlords and laborers: "We have liberated a peach tree heavy with fruit. Who is to be allowed to pick the fruit? Those who have tended and watered the tree? Or those who have sat at the side of the orchard with folded arms?" (25).

That is, the leaders deny the beggar woman Hsueh-chen her fair share of the confiscated goods on the grounds that she "did not speak at meetings, did not speak out [her] grievances at landlords" (32). In their minds, she sat at the side of the orchard with folded arms while they and other peasants tended and watered the tree. Approximately two years later, their understandable mistake is corrected. Little Li, a member of the work team sent to Long Bow to help supervise land reform, tells the village the following in I,7.i:

> Some . . . peasants have only partially fanshened or not fanshened at all. Now finally everyone must fanshen. . . Land and goods are to be redistributed on one basis and one basis only: how much you have now and how many there are in your family. So no longer is it a question of what sort of person you are, of whether you are thought to have helped

or hindered the movement. This time, those with merit will get some, those without merit will get some. (47)

So, according to this new edict, Hsueh-chen will get what she needs to support herself and her daughter.

By II,11.i, moreover—approximately six months after Little Li's address to the village—the remaining landlords in Long Bow are to get what they require to survive, and those middle peasants (neither rich nor poor) from whom goods were taken will have them returned. The Communist Party realizes it itself has made mistakes in (1) establishing absolute equality of the peasantry as the criterion of "fanshen"; (2) confiscating goods from middle peasants in order to achieve that equality and thereby "frightening and alienating many [of them], men who were never exploiters but who have always been allies, and should have been treated as such" (*Fanshen*, 80); and (3) assuming that landlords had to be liquidated instead of reeducated and changed like everyone else. By observing their theories in practice and seeing disenfranchised middle and rich peasants and landlords go over to the side of the enemy (the Kuomintang, engaged in a civil war with the Communists), Party officials have learned that "equality cannot be established by decree" (*Fanshen*, 80). Secretary Ch'en sums up the revision to the policy of "fanshen":

> Even if we could give everyone an equal share, how long would it last? The strong, the ruthless would soon climb to the top; the weak and the sick would sink to the bottom. Only in the future when all land and productive wealth are finally held in common and we produce in great abundance will equality be possible.
>
> So we have been judging fanshen by the wrong principles. . . . Land reform can have only one standard and it is not equality. It is the abolition of the feudal system. And that we have achieved. (80)

David Hare has thus mirrored in *Fanshen* the Communist-Party view that a People's Republic in which everyone is equal *can* be achieved, but only through an arduous process and not by decree. He has not written, on the one hand, about the ideal Communist state; he has not willed it into existence through his imagination. He has not written, on the other hand, about the failure of Communism; he has not imagined a state where the absolute equality of its citizens was never achieved and never will be achieved. Hare has depicted the *pursuit* of the ideal Communist state, the attempt to build a "new world" through the act of "fanshen"; and at the end of *Fanshen*, that ideal new world is still in the process of being attained. The action stops in 1948, as work-team members return to Long Bow and call a meeting—to discuss correcting the Party's mistakes.

Works Cited

Bradby, David, James, Louis, & Bernard Sharratt. "After *Fanshen*: A Discussion." In *Performance and Politics in Popular Drama: Aspects of Popular Entertainment in Theater, Film, and Television, 1800–1976.* Ed. David Bradby, Louis James, & Bernard Sharratt. Cambridge, UK: Cambridge University Press, 1980. 297–314.

Brecht, Bertolt. *Brecht on Theater.* Ed. & trans. John Willett. London: Methuen, 1964.

Hare, David. *Fanshen.* London: Faber and Faber, 1976.

———. "A Lecture Given at King's College, Cambridge, March 5, 1978." Printed as an appendix to *Licking Hitler: A Film for Television.* London: Faber and Faber, 1978. 57–71.

"Jarry's *Ubu Roi* and the Modern Theater"

A vicious satire of Alfred Jarry's despised high-school physics teacher, Félix-Frédéric Hébert, *Ubu Roi* (*Ubu the King*, 1896) parodied in the process not only Shakespearean tragedy, most evidently *Macbeth* (1606), but also all the turn-of-the-century thematic and stylistic expectations of serious drama. This was parody that went beyond the literary, however, for *Ubu Roi* is a disparaging attack against the fundamental concepts of Western civilization, specifically as they are embodied in bourgeois aims, attitudes, and practices. The grossly fat and loathsome Ubu himself is the ugly personification of the baser instincts and anti-social qualities—rapacity, cruelty, stupidity, gluttony, cowardice, conceit, vulgarity, treachery, and ingratitude—all of which he inspires as well in the people who surround him, particularly those who are esteemed as honorable, heroic, altruistic, patriotic, idealistic, or simply socially conventional.

Thus Ubu, who at his wife's urging murders the unsuspecting Wenceslas, king of an imaginary Poland, reduces kingship to gorging on sausages and wearing an immense hat; economic competition to a kicking, struggling race; social reform to slaughter motivated solely by envious cupidity; the waging of war to boastful brawling; and religious faith to fearful superstition, manipulated by the unscrupulous for their own benefit. In other words, a figure symbolizing all that bourgeois morality condemns is accepted as the representative and mainstay of bourgeois society, which then stands condemned by its own principles. The creation of such a character as the apocalyptic twentieth century was dawning—a character spawned, in essence, by the bourgeoisie—was gruesomely prophetic, particularly since the Ubus survive the Polish revolt (led by both the Russian czar and the only surviving son of King Wenceslas) and sail off at the end to comfortable exile in France. Ubu's tyrannical savagery, which was seen by many as the creation of a deranged mind—that of Jarry himself—seems tame indeed when compared with the massacres, genocides, holocausts, and terrorisms of subsequent generations.

Dramatically speaking, *Ubu Roi* stands at a turning point in the evolution of the modern theater. In an age in which the traditional distinction between poetry and prose was breaking down (with the invention of *vers libre*, or free verse) and painting was taking its first steps in the direction of abstraction, it was only natural that the theater should attempt to follow a similar path of self-examination and redefinition. Jarry himself was in the forefront of such developments (all the more so as he was fully abreast of similar movements in the fields of poetry and painting and had close personal links with many of those responsible for them): his work in the theater sets out to revolutionize that art with regard to its language, to its forms of expression, and to the underlying purpose and function of the theater itself.

The starting point for Jarry and for a host of subsequent playwrights was an effort to break once and for all with the principles and traditions of the realist-cum-naturalist theater, with its attempt to create on the stage an illusion of the "real" world (or what its practitioners took to be the "real" world) outside the theater. The first significant feature of this new drama lies therefore in the effort to create, in opposition to such conventions, a theater based on the principles of deliberate stylization and simplification, and on the adoption of purely "schematic" modes of representation. Jarry's endeavors in this domain were echoed to some extent by those of the symbolist theater, and by the ideas of theatrical reformers and visionaries of his own time and of the early years of the twentieth century, such as Adolphe Appia and Gordon Craig. Today, of course, an element of simplification and stylization is an accepted part of production methods in the modern theater, even in relation to plays written in a traditional realist or naturalist mode. But the real revolution in our time has been the widespread, total abandonment of this mode by a string of major playwrights, who see the true force of the theater as lying in the adoption of conventions diametrically opposed to those of representationalism.

The second feature of the drama of his time rejected by Jarry, in which he can again be seen as a precursor, is its essentially narrative and psychological function. The theater, he argues, is not the proper place for "telling a story" or for the portrayal and analysis of psychological conflicts, which belong more properly to the novel. Nor is it the place for dealing with social issues or problems. Whether there is a necessary relationship in the theater between social issues or problems and their depiction in the representational mode, the fact remains that historically the two have been closely linked. The inevitable, antithetical corollary is the desire to create a theater that will be concerned with a portrayal of "situations" and "types," or more exactly archetypes, and with the expression of the universal and eternal rather than with historically limited societal subjects and themes. Jarry thus implicitly looks forward to the call of Antonin Artaud for a metaphysical theater that will be concerned with the portrayal of aspects of an unchanging human condition, a conception later fully realized in the work of playwrights such as Samuel Beckett, Eugène Ionesco, or (in his early plays) Arthur Adamov. Jarry also implicitly anticipates Artaud's call for a theater of myth, in the sense of the creation of universal, archetypal images. What after all is Ubu but a "myth" in this sense, an archetypal image of humankind as seen by his creator?

The creation of such a theater has profound implications for the portrayal of character on the stage, and here an additional, third feature of this new drama can be discovered. To reject the portrayal of psychological conflicts is also to reject psychological complexity, and implicitly to advocate a deliberately simplified, schematic presentation of human character—a presentation that, at its most extreme point of development, finds its outward expression in the use of masks or the portrayal of human beings as mere puppets. And this, too, is a central feature not only of the work of Jarry; it has also been a significant (though certainly not universal) trend in the theater of the twentieth century and beyond, most strikingly in evidence in the work of Ionesco, particularly in his early one-act plays or in a highly stylized later work such as *Macbett* (1970).

With this simplification of character goes also, on occasion, an abandonment of psychological coherence and logical motivation (the fourth feature of Jarry's innovative drama), which in turn can have a profound effect upon the plot and action of a play. The unpredictability of Ubu's own behavior—his sudden and unexpected changes from brave resolution to cowardly hesitation, or his apparently gratuitous acts of cruelty—indicates in such instances an absence of unified character and consistent rationale that looks forward in embryonic form to the topsy-turvy world, for example, of the aforementioned early plays of Ionesco. A similar absence of logic in the relationship between events can be found in certain plays of Fernando Arrabal, while discontinuity is a fundamental feature of the theater of Beckett.

Such a portrayal of character points also to the sources of inspiration of the above playwrights and others—sources that indicate another, fifth feature of the theater of Jarry and his successors. In all intended revolutions, whether political or artistic, men tend to turn back, in order to create something radically different from the present or from that which has immediately preceded it, to a more distant past for inspiration. Jarry's attempt to revitalize the theater of his time by a return to the "simpler" and more "naïve" art of the mime and the puppet theater has been echoed by many artists since. Directors and theoreticians such as Craig and Gaston Baty have exalted the expressive possibilities of marionettes, and playwrights like Michel de Ghelderode, Ionesco, and Arrabal have spoken of their childhood delight in the sensational, horrific puppet-drama of the *grand guignol*, which was a source of inspiration in their own work. In the work of Jarry as of these and other playwrights, moreover, the figure of the puppet provides more than simply a source of inspiration: it also takes on a functional significance, providing an image of humanity itself and human beings' situation in the world, and forming an essential part of the playwright's own vision.

"Simplification," in both characterization and themes, does not, however—as Jarry understood it—mean mere simplicity, but rather a condensation or synthesis of complexity. Thus the figure of Ubu is simple only in the sense that he synthesizes and implicitly embodies a multiplicity of different potential meanings. Hence Jarry's invitation to the audience at the premiere of *Ubu Roi* to place its own interpretation upon the play, an invitation that looks forward to the idea of the "openness" of a work of art to multiple responses. Such a concept is an integral feature of Jarry's whole literary aesthetic and underlies his reflections on the possibility of an "abstract" theater, in which the play would constitute no more than a kind of framework onto which the members of audience members would be invited to project their own meaning—thereby participating actively, he maintains, in the process of creation itself through the exercise of the imagination. It is this urge towards abstraction that explains the nature of the setting of *Ubu Roi*— its nowhere/everywhere achieved by a canceling out of mutually contradictory elements—and to which there corresponds a similar imprecision in the work of such playwrights as Ionesco (anonymous but archetypal provincial town), Boris Vian (block of flats in an unnamed town), Arrabal (mythical desert island), or Beckett (deserted country road).

MODEL ESSAYS

A sixth feature of Jarry's new theater, of a quite different nature, can be found in the deliberate provocation of his flouting of the linguistic and theatrical conventions of his time, in his calculated attack upon both the moral and aesthetic susceptibilities of his audience. The original production of *Ubu Roi* provides in this respect an outstanding example of theatrical aggression that has been followed by many directors and playwrights since, from Artaud to Peter Brook and Charles Marowitz, and from the Dadaist and surrealist theater to certain of the works of Romain Weingarten (the first performance of whose *Akara* in 1948 was likened by critics to the opening night of *Ubu Roi*), Jean Genet, Ionesco (whose first play, *The Bald Soprano*, 1950], was provocatively subtitled "Anti-play"), Jean Vauthier, and Arrabal.

Where, however, it was the linguistic and moral aspect of such aggressiveness that had the most impact on Jarry's contemporaries, from our point of view today its most significant feature was its artistic subversiveness: Jarry's creation of forms of deliberate incoherence and logical contradiction that can be seen implicitly to call into question the very nature and existence of the work of art itself. There is, indeed, present in Jarry a dual impulse, a desire to create radically new artistic forms that exists alongside—and simultaneously with—a secret wish to subvert all forms of art from within. The tension resulting from these two conflicting impulses was never resolved in Jarry's work, and can be seen in his theater, in much of his poetry, and in such novels as *Messaline* (1900) and *Le surmâle* (1901), where the apparent reality of the narrative is secretly undermined from inside the narrative itself.

Such a subversive intention is not, however, restricted to Jarry (though he was among the first of modern writers to manifest it); it is shared with a number of modern playwrights and novelists, and is in fact characteristic of the intensely self-conscious and introspective age in which we continue to live. This subversiveness expresses itself at times, as in Jarry, in the inclusion within a work of deliberately contradictory details, and at times also, in the theater, through the presence *within the drama itself* of elements of dialogue or action whose function is to remind us that what we are watching is a "fiction," a "play" in the primary sense of the word. No modern playwright so fully exemplifies this conception of what David Grossvogel has called "the self-conscious stage" as Beckett, in whose plays the affirmation of the essentially "fictional" and "theatrical" nature of what we are watching is a recurrent feature.

Jarry can also be seen as a precursor in his creation and exploitation of a form of humor to which contemporary audiences totally failed to respond (or responded with bewilderment and hostility), but which has become widespread in our own time—humor based on the deliberate exploitation of incongruity or of outright logical contradiction in both action and word, and a form of humor that can legitimately be described as "absurd." The clash of conflicting elements in the set for *Ubu Roi* in 1896, no less than the clock of Ionesco's *The Bald Soprano* (which strikes successively seven, three, zero, five, and two times, then one time in the course of the first scene), or Ubu's declaration that "I'll go and light the fire while we're waiting for him to bring the wood" (113, *Theater of the Avant-Garde*), Ionesco's demonstration in *The Bald Soprano* that when a doorbell rings "sometimes it means that there's someone there and sometimes it means that there's no one there" (104), and Clov's statement in Beckett's *Endgame* (1957) that "If I don't kill that rat, he'll die" (76): all of these provide examples of a form of humor that deliberately flies in the face of the laws of logic or causality. Not only, moreover, is this form of humor widely accepted and exploited in our own age, but it seems to have a particular appeal to those of an intellectual bent, through the provision of a much-needed liberation from the constraints of logic and the processes of reasoning. It is also, finally, a decidedly subversive and destructive form of humor, sweeping all before it in a total derision of rational values, thereby anticipating and responding to Artaud's call for a rediscovery of "laughter's power of physical and anarchic dissociation" (42), which, along with a true sense of the tragic, Western civilization had lost.

Lastly, Jarry in *Ubu Roi* brought to the theater—or more exactly restored to it—the spirit of childhood that had been a part of the medieval stage, but which had been proscribed by the dominant rationalism of the intervening centuries. The vision that presided at the creation of *Ubu Roi*, with its crude exaggeration, its manifest violence, the frequent absence of logical human relationships and coherent motivation for the action, is that of a child's conception of the world; and the character of Ubu himself is nothing more than that of an overgrown child displaying a primeval innocence, but one which is no less terrifying and brutal for all that. It was a vision that Jarry alone among his school fellows had the insight and the artistic sense to preserve, but which looks forward to playwrights such as Ionesco, Vian, and Arrabal, whose work at times either focuses on similarly childlike figures or portrays in other ways an equally terrifying or disturbing innocence. Even more important than this vision itself, however, is the *spirit* that informs Jarry's *Ubu Roi*, and which expresses itself in a spontaneous and innocent love of nonsense, of wordplay and linguistic distortion, and of sheer absurdity. To laugh at such "absurd" forms of humor requires a willingness to suspend the normal habits of rational thinking characteristic of the adult mind, and to enter once again, at least momentarily, into the spirit of childhood. And insofar as we are able to do this today, we are all heirs of Jarry.

In all of these ways, then, Jarry can be seen as a precursor of the modern theater, or at least of one major current in it. That current is a sufficiently important and widespread one to make of Alfred Jarry, as result of the extensive features of his drama outlined above, a major figure in the emergence of modern culture itself, and to make of his King Ubu an archetypal figure for our own time.

Works Cited

Artaud, Antonin. *The Theater and Its Double.* Trans. Mary Caroline Richards. New York: Grove Press, 1958.

Beckett, Samuel. *Endgame* and *Act Without Words I* (1957, 1956). New York: Grove Press, 2009.

Grossvogel, David. *The Self-Conscious Stage in Modern French Drama.* New York: Columbia University Press, 1958.

Ionesco, Eugène. *Plays:* The Lesson; The Chairs; The Bald Prima Donna; Jacques, or Obedience. Trans. Donald Watson. London: John Calder, 1965.

Jarry, Alfred. *The Ubu Plays.* Trans. Cyril Connolly & Simon Watson Taylor. New York: Grove Press, 1969.

——. *King Ubu.* In *Theater of the Avant-Garde, 1890–1950.* Ed. Bert Cardullo & Robert Knopf. New Haven, Conn.: Yale University Press, 2001. 84–122.

GLOSSARY OF DRAMATIC TERMS

Absurdist drama: see "Theater of the Absurd."

Act: traditional segmentation of a play that indicates a change in time, action, or location, and helps to organize a play's dramatic structure. Plays may be composed of acts that, in turn, are composed of scenes.

Action: the physical activity or accomplishment of a character's intentions. Aristotle describes tragedy as "an imitation of an action," meaning that a character's choices are not simply narrated but acted out onstage. Moreover, a play as an "imitation of an action" means that the several events of the play together constitute one large human action; in this sense, action refers to the entire core of meaning of the events depicted onstage.

Agon: literally, a *contest*; an ancient Greek term used to denote the fundamental conflict in any drama, e.g., Hamlet vs. Claudius, or Lear vs. Goneril and Regan.

Alienation Effect: see "Estrangement Effect."

Allegory: an extended metaphor in which characters, objects, and actions represent abstract concepts or principles in a drama that conveys a moral lesson. Allegorical plays were especially popular in medieval England. See "Morality plays."

Anagnorisis: the moment of recognition—of understanding, awareness, comprehension, or enlightenment—that is achieved when the main character discovers his or her true relationship to the incidents in the plot and to the other characters within it, that is, to what has occurred and why. This term was first described by Aristotle in his *Poetics* (330 BC). Perhaps the most famous example in drama is Oedipus's discovery that his wife, Jocasta, is also his mother.

GLOSSARY OF DRAMATIC TERMS

Angry Young Man: the title of an autobiography by the Anglo-Irish writer Leslie Paul, published in 1951. The phrase gained popularity after John Osborne's play *Look Back in Anger* (1956) presented its protagonist, Jimmy Porter, as an angry young man who rebels against the existing social and political order in Britain. The work of a number of British playwrights of the early 1950s—so-called kitchen-sink dramas—was marked by a similar irreverence towards the Establishment and disgust at the survival of class distinctions and privilege.

Antagonist: the person or force that opposes the protagonist or main character in a play. The term derives from the Greek word meaning "opponent" or "rival."

Antihero: a protagonist or central character who lacks the qualities typically associated with heroism—for example, bravery, morality, or good looks—but still manages to earn sympathy from the spectator.

Apollonian and Dionysian: philosophical terms first used by Friedrich Nietzsche in *The Birth of Tragedy* (1872) to demonstrate contrasting elements in ancient Greek mythology and drama. Apollo and Dionysus are both sons of Zeus. Apollo is the god of the sun, of rational thinking and order, and appeals to logic, prudence, and purity or morality. Dionysus (a.k.a. Bacchus) is the god of wine and dance, of irrationality, chaos, and debauchery, and appeals to emotions and instincts.

Aside: a theatrical convention (commonly used in drama prior to the nineteenth century but less often afterwards) in which a character, unnoticed and unheard by the other characters onstage, speaks frankly to the audience.

Avant-garde: originally a military term in French meaning "advance guard," the term was increasingly used to describe unusual and therefore advanced forms of art and theater. The concept of avant-garde art can be applied to numerous theatrical movements aligned in their rejection of social institutions and established artistic conventions, though it is also used to describe artistic experimentation in the interest of pushing the art form forward. Symbolism, futurism, expressionism, Dadaism, and surrealism are all examples of avant-garde movements. See "Theater of the Absurd."

GLOSSARY OF DRAMATIC TERMS

Blank verse: the verse form most like everyday speech; in English, unrhymed iambic pentameter (a line of verse consisting of five metrical feet, each having two syllables, one unaccented and one accented). This is the form in which the great majority of English verse plays, including Shakespeare's, are written, as in the following line from *Hamlet* (1601):
× / × / × / × / × /
To sleep; | perchance | to dream: | ay, there's | the rub.

Box set: a set built behind a proscenium arch to represent three walls of a room. The absent fourth wall on the proscenium line allows spectators to witness the domestic scene. First used in the early nineteenth century. See "Fourth wall."

Burlesque: a satirical play with a strong element of parody (especially of a work by the author's rival). Sheridan's *The Critic* (1779) and Gay's *The Beggar's Opera* (1728) are examples of this type. In late-nineteenth-century America, burlesques incorporating music and elements of fantasy became a popular medium for vaudeville or variety shows featuring bawdy sexual humor.

Catalyst: a character whose function in a play is to introduce a change or disruption into a stable situation and, thus, to initiate the action of the play; the catalyst is often involved in the drama's inciting incident.

Catastasis: Greek word for the crisis or turning point—the height of the action—in a play.

Catastrophe: derived from the Greek, meaning an "overturning" or "overthrowing." See "Dénouement."

Catharsis: the emotional release or sense of relief a spectator may feel at the end of a tragedy. In the *Poetics* (330 BC), Aristotle posits that the proper aim of tragedy is to arouse pity and fear and effectively rid the body of these feelings, and *catharsis* is the term he uses to describe this purging of emotions.

Character: the word for a person in a play and the word for the qualities of mind and spirit which constitute that person. Although techniques of characterization are complex, dramatists typically reveal characters through their speech, dress, manner, and actions. In performance, actors must demonstrate character through *mimesis* or imitation rather than narration.

GLOSSARY OF DRAMATIC TERMS

Chorus: a group of characters in Greek tragedy (and in later forms of drama) who comment on the action of a play without participation in it. Sophocles' *Antigone* (441 BC) and *Oedipus Tyrannos* (430 BC) both contain an explicit chorus that has a leader; Tennessee Williams' *Glass Menagerie* (1944) contains a character who functions like a chorus.

Climactic plot: a plot that has one or more of the following characteristics: begins late in the story, toward the very end of climax; covers a short space of time, perhaps a few hours, or at most a few days; contains a few solid, extended scenes, such as three acts with each act comprising one long scene; occurs in a restricted locale, one room or one house; contains a limited number of characters, usually no more than six to eight; is linear and moves in a single line with few, if any, subplots or counterplots; proceeds in a cause-and-effect chain, with its characters linked in a sequence of logical, almost inevitable development. Ibsen's *Ghosts* (1881) and *Hedda Gabler* (1890) both incorporate climactic plots.

Climax: the moment when the root conflict of the play is resolved. At this point, the root action ceases. The climax is the final, culminating event in the dramatic action, the moment toward which the action of the play has been pointing or moving. The statement of the climax must be narrowed to a single, highly dramatic incident in the script. After this incident there may be clarification, but there is no more conflict. One example is the dueling scene in Act V of *Hamlet* (1601), in which Hamlet dies, along with Laertes, King Claudius, and Queen Gertrude. Sometimes called the "catastrophe," a word derived from the ancient Greek.

Closet dramas: plays initially meant to be performed or recited at small gatherings or read in private. During the first century BC, when the Roman public lost interest in traditional comedies and tragedies, many dramatists, including Seneca, were forced to abandon staged drama and instead wrote closet dramas for recitation at public banquets and other social events. Goethe's *Faust* (1808, 1832) is a later example of a closet drama.

Comedy: from the Greek word *komos*, meaning "band of revelers," comedy is a form of drama that is distinguished by humorous content and endings that are, on balance, "happy" ones. Most comedies attempt to highlight or satirize the absurdities of their society's norms and values. Comedy is concerned with human beings in their social capacity and is therefore heavily dependent on codes of conduct, manners, and morality, which it uses to express or imply a standard against which deviations are measured.

Comedy of manners: a form of comedy that satirizes the foibles of the upper class and the aristocracy by means of witty dialogue and the ridicule of artificial social decorum. The form originated in the late seventeenth century in England, during the Restoration, in the works of William Wycherley, William Congreve, and others. See "Restoration drama."

Comic relief: the use of a comic scene to interrupt a succession of intensely tragic dramatic moments. The comedy of scenes offering comic relief typically parallels the tragic action that the scenes interrupt and puts that action in perspective or "relief." Comic relief is lacking in Greek tragedy, but occurs regularly in Shakespeare's tragedies. One example is the opening scene of Act V of *Hamlet* (1601), in which a gravedigger banters with Hamlet.

Commedia dell'arte: literally "comedy of professional players" in Italian. A genre of Italian theater that emerged at the end of the sixteenth century, continued into the seventeenth and eighteenth centuries, and, from there, spread its influence throughout Europe. Performance relied on the portrayal of stock characters—some of which were derived from Roman comic types—and the improvisation of action and dialogue around a basic (but well-known) plot outline. See "Stock characters."

Complication: any new element that changes the direction of the dramatic action; "discovery" is the substance of most complications.

Confidant: a male character in whom the principal character confides, such as Horatio in *Hamlet* (1601).

Confidante: a female character in whom the principal character confides, such as Nerissa in *The Merchant of Venice* (1596).

Conflict: the central problem in the plot, the obstacle hindering a character from getting what he or she wants. Often, the diverging interests of the protagonist and antagonist create conflict. The rise and fall of conflict is often said to be the indispensable element of any play.

Crisis: the term used in discussion of play structure to designate the point at which the complications of the plot come to a head and, thenceforth, determine the direction of the rest of the play; synonymous with "turning point" or "peripeteia."

Cyclical plot: a plot in which the play ends in much the same way it began, rendering the action of the play more or less static or futile for the characters involved, who remain essentially unchanged. Samuel Beckett's *Waiting for Godot* (1953) has a cyclical or circular plot.

Dadaism: a movement begun in Zurich by Tristan Tzara and others during the Great War (1914–18), as a reaction against the horrors of modern warfare. Dadaism in art signified total freedom from tradition, rules, and ideals, as exemplified in Tzara's *The Gas Heart* (1920).

Danse macabre: the Dance of Death, a reminder of mortality during the Middle Ages, employed dramatically by John Webster, Cyril Tourneur, and, nearly three centuries later, by August Strindberg.

Decorum: literally, *that which is fitting*; applied to action/events thought to be in harmony with the spirit of the play and with conventions governing character presentation—e.g., lofty poetry for noblemen and prose for rustics and common people in Elizabethan drama.

Dénouement: literally, the *untying* (synonymous with the "catastrophe," which itself means "downturn" or "overturning") in a play, the point in which the loose ends or mysteries of a plot are tied up or revealed. The dénouement usually comes with, or shortly after, the climax.

Deus ex machina: literally, "a god emerging from a machine" (Latin). The crane used for special effects in fifth-century Greek theater would suspend an actor in mid-air and propel him over the playing space. Dramatists, especially Euripides, often utilized the device to introduce a god who would appear at the end of the play and miraculously resolve the plot. The term is used in contemporary criticism to describe a sudden and contrived or arbitrary resolution of a difficult situation.

Dialogue: language spoken by the characters in a play, normally in exchange with each other. Dialogue differs from narration because it is delivered in the first person and seeks to imitate human interaction and convey the artistic purpose of the playwright.

Diction: the language of a play; one of the six elements that Aristotle listed as essential to the drama.

Domestic tragedy: a form of drama, popularized at the start of the eighteenth century in England, that deals with the fortunes of middle-class or mercantile characters rather than the upper class or aristocracy, which had been the traditional focus of tragedy. Domestic tragedies have been written in the modern period, for example, by Henrik Ibsen, August Strindberg, Eugene O'Neill, Tennessee Williams, and Arthur Miller.

Dramatic irony: the irony produced when the audience is aware of something that a character or characters in the play do not yet know. It is frequently used to heighten tension or suspense, or to increase our sympathy and understanding—e.g., as in Iago's machinations against Othello, who thinks the former is honest.

Dramatis personae: literally, "people in the drama" (Latin). A character list identifying important characters in the play and their relationships, intended to help the reader or spectator understand the actions and interactions occurring onstage.

Dramaturg: a theatrical professional involved in the development and revival of plays. Dramaturgs are trained in dramatic theory, theater practice, and the history of drama and are thereby equipped to serve in a number of artistic capacities: as a sounding board for directorial concepts, as an extra set of eyes in the rehearsal room, and as a production researcher.

Drame bourgeois: a form of domestic tragedy advocated by the French playwright and critic Denis Diderot (1713–84), which explored social and familial problems of the middle class and departed from the restrictive tenets of neoclassicism. Diderot believed that "middle dramas" such as the *drame bourgeois* and comedies of virtue merited being produced in addition to traditional neoclassical comedies and tragedies.

Epic Theater: Bertolt Brecht's model theater intended to serve as an alternative to Aristotelian theater with its emphasis on continuous plot and tight construction. The Epic Theater addresses human reason rather than feeling, thus discouraging passivity, so that the spectator leaves the theater with a sense that the current social order is alterable and that action is necessary. In this theater, political action precedence over aesthetic wonder. The term "Estrangement (or Alienation) Effect"—*Verfremdungseffekt* in German—refers to an important technique employed by Epic Theater practitioners because it places responsibility on the audience to observe, rather than identify with, the characters. Onstage events are performed in an unfamiliar or unexpected manner, thereby provoking responses of surprise or curiosity on the audience's part and prompting a desire to effect change. See "Estrangement Effect."

Epilogue: a concluding address by an actor or group of actors that is directed toward the audience and sums up the play's action; also an additional scene, following the resolution of a play, intended to comment on the preceding events and offer a final perspective on the part of the dramatist.

Episodic plot: a plot that has one or more of the following characteristics: begins relatively early in the story and moves through a series of episodes; covers a long period of time: weeks, months, and sometimes many years; contains many short, fragmented scenes and sometimes an alternation of short and long scenes; may range over an entire city or even several countries; contains a profusion of characters, sometimes several dozen; frequently marked by several threads of action, such as two parallel plots, or scenes of comic relief in a serious play; contains scenes that are juxtaposed to another, and in which an event may result from several causes or emerge from a network or web of circumstances. Shakespeare's plays generally incorporate episodic plots.

Estrangement Effect: a phrase translated from the German word *Verfremdungseffekt* (sometimes also translated as "alienation effect" or "defamiliarization"), referring to an important tenet of Bertolt Brecht's Epic Theater that asks the audience to examine familiar, everyday events from a critical distance as if they were "strange" or unusual. Brecht describes his theory of estrangement as a rebuttal to the popular Aristotelian perspective that an audience derives pleasure from an empathic connection to the characters and events performed onstage. Instead, Brecht suggests that, in performance, an actor can alter his technique to illustrate ideas of broader historical or social proportions. The actor's self-awareness and awareness of the performative nature of storytelling distances the spectator from an immediate emotional response that, in turn, disrupts identification with the character and

GLOSSARY OF DRAMATIC TERMS

elicits instead a reaction of surprise or curiosity toward an otherwise ordinary or contrived situation. See "Epic Theater."

Exposition: information, often delivered near the beginning of a play, that reveals something essential for the audience's understanding of the world of the play or the story's given circumstances, as well as the basic relationships between characters and events that have taken place offstage or earlier. For an example of exposition, see the opening scene of *Macbeth* (1603), in which the Witches decide to accost him.

Expressionism: a literary and theatrical movement that originated in Europe just before the twentieth century but flourished from 1910 to 1925. Spurred by the overwhelming social and political upheaval of World War I, expressionist playwrights strove to emphasize the moral crisis of the modern, industrial world dominated by machines and masses of people. In its departure from the conventions of realism, expressionist drama features characters who are often nameless and defined solely by their occupations; who use primal gesture (exaggerated, emotive movement); who speak stylized dialogue that emphasizes certain words or expressions; and who inhabit a theatrical world that includes exaggerated or distorted, macabre or dreamlike, images that reinforce the drama's theme. In this way, expressionist plays seek to project onto the stage the emotional perspective or state of mind of the protagonist. Some representative German expressionist plays are Reinhard Sorge's *The Beggar* (1912), Georg Kaiser's *From Morn to Midnight* (1912), and Walter Hasenclever's *The Son* (1914).

Falling action: term used in discussion of dramatic structure to indicate the period in the play after the crisis or turning point has been reached, in which the complications of the rising action are untangled and the action moves to its destined end.

Farce: a genre of fast-paced comedy characterized by rapid stage action, a series of misunderstandings in an otherwise highly improbable plot, ludicrous characterizations, and abundant physical humor.

Flat characters: characters in a play, often but not always minor characters, who are relatively simple; who are presented as having few, though sometimes dominant, traits; and who thus do not change much in the course of a play and, for this reason, are sometimes called "static characters." For example, the selfish son, the pure woman, the lazy child, the dumb blonde, etc. See "Round characters."

Foil: a character whose qualities or traits highlight those of another. In Shakespeare's *Hamlet* (1601), for instance, Laertes serves as a foil to Hamlet because both are put in the position of avenging a murdered father.

Foreshadowing: hints of what is to come in the action of a play. Ibsen's *A Doll House* (1879) includes foreshadowing, as does Synge's *Riders to the Sea* (1904). The use of symbolic imagery is commonly used to foreshadow events, as is the convention of narrative prophecy often employed by classical Greek dramatists.

Fourth wall: theatrical term applied to the realist stage, where actors no longer played directly to the audience but instead focused on each other. In nineteenth-century England, the convention became increasingly popular and stage sets were designed to replicate a traditional room with three walls, the "fourth wall" (that is, the proscenium arch, or front of the stage) being open for observation of the action by the audience.

Futurism: a phenomenon of the early twentieth century, futurist theater rejected an inward-looking art. For Italian futurists such as F. T. Marinetti, Umberto Boccioni, and Francesco Cangiullo, drama should be inspired by the scientific and technological discoveries that had changed man's *physical* environment, and that should correspondingly change human perceptions. Man should, in fact, become like a machine, abandoning the weaknesses and sentimentalities of the past. *Sintesi teatrali* (theatrical syntheses) were futurist works of extreme brevity and concentration, in which the traditional three-act play was replaced by *attimi* (moments) intended to capture the essence and atmosphere of an event or situation as it occurred.

Gesamtkunstwerk: literally, "total work of art" (from the German), a term coined by Richard Wagner in his long essay *Art and Revolution* (1849), which describes his interest in the integration of dramatic literature, music, theatrical performance, and visual elements such as set and lighting design into a new and comprehensive synthesis.

Gesture: the physical movement of a character during a play. Gesture is used to reveal character, and may include facial expressions as well as movements of other parts of an actor's body. Sometimes a playwright will be very explicit about both bodily and facial gestures, providing detailed instructions in the play's stage directions. Shaw's

Arms and the Man (1894) includes such stage directions. See "Stage directions."

Grotesque: The term Theater of the Grotesque refers to an anti-naturalistic school of Italian dramatists, writing in the 1910s and 1920s, who are often seen as precursors of the Theater of the Absurd. Rejecting theatrical and social conventions, Grotesque works are characterized by ironic, macabre, darkly comic, even contradictory elements inspired by life during the World War I era. The Theater of the Grotesque derives its name from Luigi Chiarelli's play *The Mask and the Face* (1913), subtitled "a Grotesque in three acts." The Grotesque's most notable Italian practitioner was Luigi Pirandello, who influenced the work of such later Italian dramatists as Ugo Betti, Carlo Terron, and Diego Fabbri.

Hamartia: the Greek term used by Aristotle to describe a character's intellectual error, mistaken assumption, or internal division that prompts the tragic outcome of his or her actions. Often described as the "tragic flaw" or self-destructive force that triggers the downfall of the hero or heroine.

High (verbal) comedy: comedy that achieves its effect from the depiction of character and the use of language rather than through physical devices; its appeal is therefore primarily to the intellect.

History play: a play that deals with characters, events, and subjects taken from history. Shakespeare wrote a number of plays about English history, including *Richard II* (1595), *Richard III* (1592), and *Henry IV, Parts 1 and 2* (1597, 1600).

Hubris: the tragic flaw of pride, arrogance, over-confidence, or willful ignorance that can lead a hero to make an error in judgment and disregard accepted moral codes or warnings from the gods, prompting his or her own downfall.

Humours comedy: popularized by Ben Jonson in England in the early seventeenth century, this genre of comedy drew upon the classical medical theory that an individual's temperament or psychological disposition was determined by the balance (or imbalance) or four bodily fluids (known as "humours"): black bile, phlegm, blood, and choler or yellow bile. Characters in humours comedies are motivated by their predominant humours.

Impressionism: a term derived from Claude Monet's style of painting, which was concerned not so much with objective reality as with the *impression* it made on the viewer. Impressionism could be said to be the subjective rendering of the visible world, as opposed to expressionism, which is the subjective expression of an inner world, an internal vision. Chekhov's plays are sometimes said to be impressionistic, as is the work of Arthur Schnitzler.

Inciting incident: the "disturbance" that initiates the conflict-resolution process of the play. The inciting incident launches the root action of the drama. It is not necessarily the first action of the play, nor need it be the first event of a broad conflict that may have existed before the dramatic action begins. Rather, the inciting incident is the event of the play that puts the forces of conflict in motion.

Laughing comedy: a term championed by Oliver Goldsmith, who suggested that the popular sentimental comedies of eighteenth-century England were a lesser form of drama. Goldsmith endorsed a more traditional conception of comedy in his "Essay on the Theatre" (1773) by stating that "comedy should excite our laughter by ridiculously exhibiting the follies of the lower part of mankind." Richard Brinsley Sheridan was one of the leading proponents of laughing comedy, in such plays as *The Rivals* (1775) and *The School for Scandal* (1777). See "Sentimental comedy."

Linear plot: a traditional plot sequence in which the incidents in the drama progress chronologically; that is, all of the events build upon one another and there are no jumps, for example, from the present to the past. The Greeks and neoclassicists adopted this structure as the template for creating effective tragedy. See "Climactic plot."

Liturgical drama: a form of medieval European drama that sprang from the elaboration of liturgy, or the act of public worship found in the Latin Mass. As early as 925 BC, antiphonal tropes, or musical passages that incorporated the imitation of religious figures in a call-and-response dialogue, served as interpolations in religious services. These tropes, credited as the first mimetic performances in the Church, were initially part of Easter Mass, and then were added to services held on other holy days; they also became more dramaturgically complex over time. Typically, liturgical plays explore the mysteries and miracles depicted in the Bible and in the lives of saints.

Low (physical) comedy: as opposed to high comedy, low comedy gains its effect, which is usually hearty laughter, from the use of slapstick and broad comic devices instead of character and dialogue.

Major dramatic question: the question the play exists to answer; the major dramatic question may change as the play progresses. Often phrasing the dramatic question will illuminate the play in such a way that the root conflict and root action emerge clearly. In *Oedipus Tyrannos* (430 BC) the major dramatic question might be as follows: Will Oedipus discover the murderer of Laius, as directed by the gods, and lift the plague from Thebes?

Melodrama: a serious play that does not attain the heights of tragedy or have the same purpose as comedy; originally, a drama in which music is used to heighten emotion (the Greek *melos* means "song"). As it was popularized during the nineteenth century in France, Britain, and the United States, this genre grew to be characterized by stories of adventure and intrigue calculated to provoke audiences' heightened emotional response. Melodrama offers sensational plots (rather than subtle ideas or character development) that exaggerate the moral qualities of good and evil, focus on outer struggle (rather than the inner struggle of tragedy), and emphasize virtue triumphant.

Metatheater: a term coined by the critic Lionel Abel in 1963 to describe the self-conscious examination of the nature of theater itself, primarily the relationship between reality and theatrical illusion. Conscious displays of theatricality and role-playing are two prominent conventions in such drama. Luigi Pirandello and Jean Genet are known for the use of metatheatrical, self-referential techniques in their plays.

Mimesis: the Greek word for imitation that is used to describe the artistic practice of representing reality (or creating theater). In the *Republic* (380 BC), Plato argues that the mimetic arts are corruptive because they are too far removed from the truth, in the sense that a play is an imitation of an action in life, which is likewise an imitation of an idea or mental construct (for example, the idea of justice, or even of triangularity, which can be expressed onstage in an object such as a three-legged stool). Thus, a play is an imitation of an imitation, twice removed, and therefore a kind of lie or deception. In the *Poetics* (330 BC), by contrast, Aristotle argues that tragedy is an imitation of an action in a way that is embellished and *perfected*.

GLOSSARY OF DRAMATIC TERMS

Modernism: a departure from artistic tradition that took place at the end of the nineteenth century and continued through the first half of the twentieth. Reflecting the social, technological, and philosophical changes that distinguished the modern world from earlier ages, modernism featured radical experimentation in drama as well as literature and the other arts. Bertolt Brecht, Luigi Pirandello, and Samuel Beckett are examples of modernist playwrights; Antonin Artaud's dramatic theories are modernist as well.

Monologue: a long speech or narrative spoken by one character. A monologue can be addressed to another character onstage, spoken to oneself, or shared with the audience as a means of elucidating a character's internal thoughts or desires that cannot be expressed in formal dialogue. A soliloquy is a form of monologue, and an aside, if lengthy, can be characterized as a monologue.

Morality plays: a secular form of medieval drama that was popular between 1400 and 1550, predominantly in England and France. Didactic in tone and allegorical in structure, morality plays dealt with the individual's moral life, the battle between figures representing good and evil, and the journey to salvation. *Everyman* (late 15th century) is an example of a morality play, and Christopher Marlowe's *Doctor Faustus* (1592) shows the influence of the morality tradition on later drama. See "Allegory."

Motivation: the thought or desire that drives a character to actively pursue a want or need, which in acting theory is called the "objective." A character generally has an overall objective or long-term goal in a drama but may change his or her objective, and hence motivation, from scene to scene when confronted with various obstacles.

Naturalism: a literary and theatrical movement that thrived in the late nineteenth century in reaction against earlier styles and as an attempt to reproduce life as exactly as possible: truthfully, objectively, and with scientific accuracy. In naturalism, which is often associated with philosophical determinism, the physiological disposition of a character is the focus of the drama and heredity or physical environment dictates his or her fate. In literature, naturalism is considered an extreme form of realism, one that concentrates on exhibiting causes and effects (especially among the lower classes) and upon depressing, unadorned social situations. The concept of naturalism can also be applied to the way in which a play is staged: for example, a naturalist set may incorporate a real working fireplace or a faucet with running water.

Neoclassicism: a seventeenth-century movement (especially in France and England), prompted by a renewed interest in the writings of Aristotle and other classical theorists, that lasted well into the eighteenth century.

Pastoral drama: a form of drama developed and popularized during the Italian Renaissance that sought to imitate the idyllic pastoral (rural) settings of Greek mythology. Perhaps influenced by the Greek satyr plays, pastoral dramas incorporate mythic elements in their depictions of the travails of young lovers, typically shepherds. Giovanni Battista Guarini's *The Faithful Shepherd* (1590) and Shakespeare's *As You Like It* (1599) are probably the best-known pastoral dramas.

Pathetic fallacy: the representation of nature as being in sympathy with, or affected by, the emotions and actions of human beings. The onset of Lear's stormy madness, in Shakespeare's *King Lear* (1606), is reflected in the real storm thundering over his head.

Pathos: a quality of a play's action that stimulates the audience to feel pity for a character. Pathos in this sense is always an aspect of tragedy, and may be present in comedy as well. In another sense, pathos refers to a lack of recognition, awareness, or self-understanding on the part of a character who falls short of the tragic: e.g., Prince Arthur's pleading to Hubert not to blind him in Act IV of Shakespeare's *King John* (1596).

Peripeteia (peripety): a Greek word meaning a "reversal of circumstances"; applied to the point in the plot where the action undergoes a lasting reversal, or change in direction—i.e., where, it is clear, the hero's fortunes are or will be changed. See "Crisis" or "Turning point."

Plot: the interlocking arrangement of incidents in a play that propels a drama forward from conflict to resolution; this is an arrangement designed to show not only sequence but also cause and effect. Plots may be simple or complex, and any single play may have more than one plot (and plays from experimental, avant-garde, or postmodern traditions may calculatedly eschew plot altogether).

Point of attack: the point in the story at which the playwright has chosen to begin the action of his or her play; it can be late or early. If the point of attack is late, the play's action has a long past that is not depicted onstage.

Postmodernism: a movement that emerged in the 1960s in reaction against many of the cultural and aesthetic assumptions of modernism. While modernist dramatists often sought clear, cohesive artistic construction in their works, for example, postmodern artists sought to embrace inconsistencies in style and to collapse literary boundaries. Pastiche is consequently a predominant element of postmodern art. Postmodernism questions master narratives like Christianity and Marxism, thinkers like Jean-Paul Sartre and Albert Camus and, later, Samuel Beckett and Jacques Derrida. It is skeptical as to such privileged discourses that use language—an unstable medium—and thus it gave rise to Deconstruction and Poststructuralist theory.

Problem play: a late-nineteenth-century and early-twentieth-century form of drama that addressed social issues, such as class, workers' rights, women's rights, etc. The early dramas of Henrik Ibsen and George Bernard Shaw are examples of problem plays, sometimes called social-problem plays or examples of the "play of ideas."

Prologue: literally, a "speech before," or monologue by an actor introducing the action of the play; in some plays, the opening scene in which information is revealed about events that occurred prior to the play's start.

Props or properties: articles or objects that appear onstage during a play. The Christmas tree in *A Doll House* (1879) and Laura's collection of glass animals in *The Glass Menagerie* (1944) are examples.

Proscenium arch: the picture frame formed by the side and top walls of the modern stage, which provide the opening through which the audience sees the stage. See "Fourth wall."

Protagonist: the hero or central character in a play, who is the main focus of the audience's attention. Derived from the ancient Greek term *protagonistes*, meaning "first contestant" or "leading actor." In traditional drama, the protagonist often engages in conflicts with an antagonist.

Realism: a literary and theatrical style that seeks to depict life as it really is without artifice, or without violation of conventional appearances and probability. The origins of realism can be traced to late-nineteenth-century Europe, when playwrights and theater practitioners sought to move away from traditional, often melodramatic, plays and productions so as to create drama that portrayed real people confronted with plausible situations. The most common setting for realistic drama, as well as its most common subject, is middle-class life; among the playwrights associated with the rise of realism are Henrik Ibsen and George Bernard Shaw.

Repertory: a set of plays; a repertory acting company will perform a series of plays, previously prepared for performance, in rotation, alternating productions in a given theatrical space during a specific period of time.

Resolution: the concluding event, or series of events, that resolves the fundamental conflict that had sustained the play's main action. A resolution can also be a *dénouement*.

Restoration drama: the theatrical period (1660–1700) marked by the return of Charles II to the throne of England after the Commonwealth period. Restoration drama was written for and represented the new aristocracy, which repudiated the moral strictures of Puritanism. Restoration plays, particularly the comedies, often feature bawdy and licentious humor and situations *The Country Wife* (1675), by William Wycherley, and *The Way of the World* (1700), by William Congreve, are perhaps the best-known Restoration comedies. See "Comedy of manners."

Revenge tragedy: a form of sensational tragedy revolving around stories of murder and revenge for the death of a relative, with much intrigue, madness, and mayhem thrown into the mix. The genre flourished in England during the reigns of Elizabeth I (r. 1558–1603) and James I (r. 1603–25). Thomas Kyd's *The Spanish Tragedy* (1587), Shakespeare's *Hamlet* (1601), and Webster's *The Duchess of Malfi* (1614) are among the best-known revenge tragedies.

Reversal: the point at which the action of a drama turns in an unexpected direction for the protagonist. Oedipus's and Othello's "recognitions," for example, are also reversals. They learn what they did not expect to learn. See "Anagnorisis."

GLOSSARY OF DRAMATIC TERMS

Rising action: the portion of a play's structure, in its first half, in which events complicate the situation that existed at the beginning of a play, thereby intensifying the conflict, or introducing new conflict, and leading to the drama's crisis or turning point.

Romance play: a term used primarily to describe Shakespeare's later plays that mix the comic with the tragic. A romance play's action moves between pastoral and court or city settings and often incorporates magical elements. The reuniting of long-separated family members is also a common motif. Shakespeare's romance plays include *Cymbeline* (1609), *Pericles* (1608), *The Tempest* (1611), and *The Winter's Tale* (1610).

Romanticism: a literary and artistic movement that began in England and Germany in the late eighteenth century, continued into the early nineteenth, and emphasized imagination and emotion over the neo-classical ideals of intellect and reason. Largely influenced by the philosopher Jean-Jacques Rousseau (1712–78), Romantic literature generally reflects a belief in the innate goodness of man in his natural state. The early dramas of the Germans Goethe (*Götz von Berlichingen*, 1773) and Schiller (*The Robbers*, 1781) are examples.

Root action: the process by which the root conflict of the play is resolved. A statement of the root action tells us not only who the competing forces or agents are, but also how the conflict is resolved. If the root conflict of *Oedipus Tyrannos* (430 BC) is Oedipus versus the gods, then the root action might be the following: Oedipus wrests the secret to the lifting of the plague from the gods, only to find in such a victory his own destruction. The statement of the root action distils the play into one sentence that isolates the "power source" of the dramatic event.

Root conflict: the basic conflict of the play that underlies and motivates the main action. The root conflict identifies the main competing forces in the drama, and these forces almost always center in characters. The protagonist (usually the central character) is named first and the antagonist second. The root conflict of Hamlet might be described, then, as Hamlet versus Claudius.

Round characters: a round character is depicted with such psychological depth and detail that he seems like a "real" person. The complex round character contrasts with the simplified flat character, who serves a specific or minor dramatic function in a text, and who may be a stock figure or stereotype. If the round character changes or evolves over the course of a play or appears to have the capacity for such change, the character is also "dynamic" as opposed to "static." See "Flat characters."

Scene: the traditional segmentation of a play's structure to indicate a change in time or location, to jump from one subplot to another, to introduce new characters, or to rearrange the actors on the stage. Traditionally plays are composed of acts, which are then broken down into scenes. In the French tradition as practiced by Molière and Racine, a new scene begins whenever a character enters or exits the stage. In Elizabethan England, the absence of the stage curtain meant that the end of a scene was indicated by a rhyming couplet, as in these lines from Shakespeare's *Julius Caesar* (1599): "'Tis three o'clock, and, Romans, yet ere night. / We shall try fortune in a second fight."

Scène-à-faire: literally, "scene that must be done" (French) or the "obligatory scene"; any scene of a play that the audience has been led to expect as inevitable and that comprises the end of a well-made play.

Sentimental comedy (comédie larmoyante or "weeping comedy"): a genre of comedy popularized in eighteenth-century England that departed from the bawdy and titillating themes of Restoration comedy (1660–1710) and emphasized instead the simple and innate goodness of humankind. Interest in the theories of Jean-Jacques Rousseau (1712–78) and other philosophers fueled the assumption that people could be saved from vice if instructed to follow their natural instincts. Like domestic tragedy, sentimental comedy (which often was not truly comic) centered on and appealed to the middle class, inviting sentimental reflections from its audience on bravery, youth, motherhood, etc. See "Laughing comedy."

Set: the design, decoration, and scenery of the stage during a play, usually meant to represent the location or locations in the drama. Plays may have a single set or several sets.

Setting: the time and location in which a play takes place. A play can have multiple settings and incorporate more than one time period, as well.

Slapstick: originally, a wooden sword worn by the *commedia dell'arte* character Harlequin that figured prominently in his comedic routine; the sword was a two-piece stick that made a tremendous noise when it struck another character As a subgenre, slapstick is a form of physical comedy often characterized by farcical situations, sudden falls, crude jokes, slaps in the face, and generally reckless behavior.

Soliloquy: a monologue uttered by a character alone onstage that provides insight into his or her thoughts. This theatrical convention is common in plays from the Renaissance through the eighteenth century and is generally associated with Shakespeare's works. The device was discarded by modern dramatists, such as August Strindberg, who were concerned with creating realistic depictions onstage.

Spectacle: generally, the elements in a play's production that appeal to the *visual* theatricality of the piece, such as costumes, scenery, props, or stage tricks. Described in Aristotle's *Poetics* (330 BC) as the sixth element of tragedy (after plot, character, thought, diction, and song).

Stage directions: in the text of a play, directions or actions indicated by the playwright that describe the physical movements or emotional responses of the characters onstage. Stage directions may also note the setting, as well as the physical appearance of the characters and their relationships with one another.

Stichomythia: dialogue in Greek drama, in which the characters alternately speak single lines of verse, one line to each, with great speed and emphasis. Similar to, but more formalized than, repartee.

Stock Character: a recognizable character type that can be found in many plays. Comedies have traditionally relied on such stock characters as the braggart soldier, the miserly father, the beautiful ingénue, or the trickster servant. The *commedia dell'arte*, for example, relied entirely on the peculiarities of stock characters to provide inspiration for creating scenarios. See "*Commedia dell'arte.*"

Subplot: a secondary plot that usually shares a relationship with the main plot, either thematically, in terms of the action itself, or both. The subplot often deals with the secondary characters in the play. Sometimes called "parallel plot," "double plot," or "underplot."

Subtext: Konstantin Stanislavsky's term for unspoken text; for an actor, the internal motivations or responses never explicitly stated in the dialogue, but understood either by the audience or the characters themselves. The dramatist creates subtext to underscore the emotional or intellectual truth of a character's life that is unspoken but implied.

Surrealism: a style of drama promulgated by André Breton and intended to express the automatic workings of the unconscious. Representative surrealist plays are *The Magnetic Fields* (1919), by Breton and Philippe Soupault, and Roger Vitrac's *Mysteries of Love* (1927).

Suspension of disbelief: Samuel Taylor Coleridge first used the term in 1817. Basically it means that you accept something as real or representing the real when it obviously is not real. In drama this is a crucial condition. On entering the theater, audience members let their imaginations take them into another world and they ignore their literal surroundings. For example, they accept that the few actors playing soldiers in Shakespeare's *Henry V* (1599) represent the thousands that took part in the battle.

Symbolism: a style of drama that used language and silence to create an evocative, supernatural world in which mood supplanted plot as the primary theatrical element. In such plays as *Interior* (1894), *The Blind* (1890), and *The Intruder* (1891), the Belgian Maurice Maeterlinck was one of the first writers to embody the symbolist vision onstage.

Theater of the Absurd: a type of drama that conveys a sense of life as devoid of order, meaning, and purpose. The term was coined in 1961 by the critic Martin Esslin, who described and analyzed a group of mid twentieth-century plays in his book *The Theater of the Absurd*, including the work of Samuel Beckett and Eugène Ionesco. Absurdist plays transcend the tradition of realism and frequently combine elements from theatrical movements such as expressionism, surrealism, and symbolism to create a tone or atmosphere that conveys an irrational, godless world through which characters are left to stumble aimlessly. Alfred Jarry's *Ubu Roi* (1896) is a precursor to the Theater of the Absurd. See "Avant-garde."

Theatricalism: a broad term for a number of non-realistic styles; it is usually applied when great reliance is placed in production on a non-realistic stage design and an equally non-realistic use of lighting and sound.

Theme: the idea, concept, or argument that a playwright wishes to express in a play. Aristotle listed "thought," or theme—taken to refer to intellectual content or meaning—as one of the six elements essential to the drama

Tragedy: a form of drama that arose in ancient Greek culture; a play dealing with a serious subject in an elevated style and ending in catastrophe and death. Though the mode and structure of tragedy have varied over the centuries to reflect the cultural beliefs and conventions of each age, the central dramatic conflict remains constant: the human being struggles to overcome some antagonistic force and is ultimately defeated. In classical Greek tragedy, the protagonist is a man of political or social stature and the gods play a role in the reversal of his fortune from good to bad. In modern drama, tragedies often reflect the struggle of middle-class citizens to overcome societal restraints or their own private domestic conflicts.

Tragic flaw: a weakness or limitation of character that exacerbates the tragic hero's internal conflict or division, resulting ultimately in his downfall. Othello's jealous and too trusting nature is one example, as he struggles to choose between his devotion to the loving Desdemona and his confidence in his subordinate Iago. See "Hubris" and "Tragedy."

Tragicomedy: the term used to describe a drama that incorporates both tragic and comic elements. This hybrid form was popularized in the sixteenth and seventeenth centuries in such works as Giovanni Battista Guarini's pastoral play *The Faithful Shepherd* (1590) and the dramatic collaborations of Francis Beaumont (1584–1616) and John Fletcher (1579–1625). Plays written in this mode often featured tragic conflicts that resolve happily through unexpected—sometimes improbable—plot twists. The term *tragicomedy* has also been applied to modern and contemporary plays that do not fit the traditional categories of tragedy and comedy, such as Samuel Beckett's *Waiting for Godot* (1953), subtitled "a tragicomedy in two acts."

Turning point: the point where a decisive change in the action occurs and the ending of the play becomes predictable or foreseeable, if not inevitable. See "Crisis" or "Peripeteia."

Unities: the principles of dramatic structure, derived from Aristotle's *Poetics* (330 BC), that require a plot's action to be singular (no subplots), to complete itself within a twenty-four-hour period, and to take place in one location. Aristotle mentioned only the unities of action and time, but French neoclassical theorists of the sixteenth and seventeenth centuries added place and made the unities a so-called rule of drama.

Vaudeville: an entertainment popular in the United States in the first third of the twentieth century. It consisted of singing, dancing, and comedy in individual sketches with no plot or connecting thread.

Well-made play: also called *pièce bien-faite* (French), a play that relies heavily on the orchestration of highly complicated plots rather than characterization or themes. The genre dominated French theater for much of the nineteenth century; its playwrights (Scribe, Sardou) sought to integrate conventions such as overheard conversations, mistaken identities, and sudden appearances and disappearances to create suspense and intrigue. The well-made play concludes with a *scène à faire*, or the final confrontation of characters that resolves the dramatic action.

STUDY GUIDES

The following five study guides are designed to enhance students' reading of plays in general and the plays in this book, in particular. The first guide consists of the Parts of Drama (adapted from Aristotle's Poetics *[330 BC]), and is a mini-guide to play analysis in itself. The second, third, and fourth guides contrast, respectively, the arts of theater and film; the genres of tragedy, comedy, and farce; and the styles of realism and naturalism. The second guide should be especially useful as the student considers the plays discussed in 4, "Drama and Film":* Electra, The Balcony, Equus, The Elephant Man, The Crucible, Miss Julie, *and* The Cherry Orchard. *The third and fourth guides will be helpful as the student considers the following tragedies, comedies, or farces treated in this book:* The Hairy Ape, Loot, Major Barbara, A Streetcar Named Desire, Romeo and Juliet, Antigone, Death of a Salesman, Golden Guts, Of Mice and Men, The Front Page, Riders to the Sea, *and* Ubu Roi. *The fifth guide concerns the practice of theater criticism—in effect, the analysis of a play on the stage as opposed to the page. This guide should be consulted if the student is asked to write a critical review of a production, in contrast to an analytical essay about a play.*

1 The Parts of Drama (after Aristotle)

I Plot: The overall structure of the play, or the story and method through which its dramatic action is organized.
  A. BEGINNING
     1. Exposition
     2. Inciting incident
     3. Major dramatic question

  B. MIDDLE
     1. Complication
     2. Turning point

C. END
   1. Reversal and recognition (understanding, awareness, or comprehension on the part of the main character of what has occurred during the play and why)
   2. Climax
   3. Resolution or dénouement

II Character: The primary material from which plots are created.
   A. LEVELS OF CHARACTERIZATION (the playwright's primary means of differentiating one character from another)
      1. Physical
      2. Social
      3. Psychological (the most essential)
      4. Moral: Moral choices or decisions differentiate characters more fully than any other type, since such decisions cause characters to examine their motives, in the process of which their true natures are revealed both to themselves and to the reader or spectator.

   B. METHODS FOR REVELATION OF CHARACTER
      1. Descriptions in the stage directions
      2. Preface or other explanatory material that is not part of the dialogue
      3. What the character says
      4. What others say about the character
      5. What the character does (the most important)

   C. RANGE OF CHARACTER
      4. Typified ——————— Individualized
      5. Sympathetic ——————— Unsympathetic

III Thought: Present in all plays, even the most light-hearted farce; a playwright cannot avoid expressing some ideas, since events and characterization always imply some view of human behavior.
   A. THEMES, IDEAS, ARGUMENTS, AND OVERALL MEANING OF THE ACTION:
   Meaning in drama is usually *implied*, rather than stated directly. It is suggested by the relationships among the characters; the ideas associated with unsympathetic and sympathetic characters; the conflicts and their resolution; and such devices as spectacle, music, and song. Sometimes the author's intention is clearly stated in the script, as when "mouthpiece" or *raisonneur* characters advocate a certain line of action, point of view, or specific social reform.

STUDY GUIDES

B. DEVICES TO PROJECT IDEAS, APART FROM THE IMPLICATIONS OF ACTION AND DIALOGUE
  1. Chorus (a form of direct statement)
  2. Soliloquies and asides (forms of direct statement)
  3. Allegory
  4. Symbol

IV **Diction:** Language, the playwright's primary means of expression.
  A. PURPOSES OF LANGUAGE
    1. To impart information
    2. To characterize
    3. To direct attention to important plot elements
    4. To reveal the themes and ideas of the play
    5. To establish tone or mood and level of probability (that is, logical or internal consistency)
    6. To establish tempo and rhythm

  B. LANGUAGE OR DICTION IS SELECTED, ARRANGED, AND HEIGHTENED by the playwright, even in the most realistic or naturalistic of dramas.

  C. LANGUAGE OR DICTION SHOULD BE APPROPRIATE TO THE CHARACTERS, the situation, the level of probability, and the type of play.

V **Music:** All the musical, lyrical, or aural elements of a play-in-production.
  A. TYPES
    1. Sound of the actors' voices
    2. Incidental songs and background music
    3. Song and instrumental accompaniment (e.g., as in musical comedy and opera)
    4. Sound effects

  B. FUNCTIONS
    1. Establishes mood
    2. Characterizes
    3. Suggests ideas
    4. Compresses characterization or exposition (by presenting information, feelings, or motivations in a song)
    5. Lends variety
    6. Is pleasurable in itself

VI Spectacle: All the visual elements of a play-in-production; they should be appropriate and distinctive.
- A. MOVEMENT AND THE SPATIAL RELATIONS OF CHARACTERS
- B. DESIGN OF THE LIGHTING, SETTINGS, AND COSTUMES (including properties)

2 Table of Contrasts: Theater and Film

Characteristics of Theater
1. A three-dimensional, ephemeral performance of events.
2. Continuous, "big" acting aimed at a live audience; does not employ amateur actors.
3. Immediate relationship between the actors and the audience, both of whom are physically present in the same space at the same time.
4. Except in rare cases, has no narrator.
5. Relatively active audience that must choose for itself where to look or what to see; what the audience sees is unmediated by a camera.
6. A verbal art primarily, but it also has a visual component (through costumes, sets, lights, choreography, and action itself).
7. A collaborative art, with the actor finally in control on the stage.
8. A total work of art or *Gesamtkunstwerk*, but not quite to the extent that film is.
9. Irreducible: to have theater, you must have living actors performing before a real audience in a more or less demarcated-space.
10. A group experience, as it occurs in a theatrical auditorium of one kind or another.
11. The most popular art form of the nineteenth century and before.
12. Its essence consists of human beings in conflict with each other or themselves.
13. The conjunction belonging to the theater is "therefore" rather than "then"; in other words, the theater gives primacy to causality more than it does to succession.
14. Deals with the relationship between people.
15. There is only one "shot": the full picture of the stage.
16. Intermissions are common, and scene changes (as well as costume, make-up, and lighting changes) can be slow and laborious. Space is therefore less manipulable and time is less flexible.
17. The dramatic text is an independent artwork that can be read *or* performed.

STUDY GUIDES

18. Usually dramatizes the *consequences* of action; characters are often victims of their pasts.

Characteristics of Film
1. A two-dimensional, permanent visual record of a performance.
2. Discontinuous, "smaller" acting aimed at the camera lens; can employ amateur actors.
3. No immediate or physical interrelationship between the actors and the audience.
4. Has a narrator: the camera.
5. Relatively passive audience for whom the camera chooses what will be seen.
6. A visual art primarily, but also a dramatic art that enacts stories (with words once the sound era begins) and a narrative art that tells those stories through the mediation of the camera.
7. A collaborative art, with the director ultimately in control.
8. A total work of art, or *Gesamtkunstwerk*.
9. Reducible to DVD, video, television, etc.
10. Can be a solitary experience, especially if you are watching a film alone at home.
11. The most popular art form of the twentieth century and beyond.
12. Can dispense with overt conflicts, climaxes, and even plots; indeed, can be almost completely non-theatrical or -dramatic.
13. The particle belonging to the cinema is "then" rather than "therefore"; in other words, the cinema gives primacy to succession more than it does to causality.
14. Deals with the relationship of people not only to other people, but also to things and places.
15. The camera can provide the viewer with multiple visual perspectives, through different shots.
16. Intermissions are rare, and scenes changes (as well as costume, make-up, and lighting changes) are accomplished swiftly and easily through cuts or editing. Space is therefore manipulable and time is flexible.
17. The film script is not an independent artwork and cannot be read by itself fruitfully, nor can its words be "performed" as a play's words could be; a screenplay is a preparatory sketch for a future art work, a fully realized cinematic experience.
18. Usually concentrates on action *per se*, even when this action is "interior" or psychological; characters are often makers of their own destinies in the present.

3 Table of Contrasts: Tragedy, Comedy, and Farce

Tragedy tends to exalt man as an individual, by exploring his place in a world inhabited by fateful forces, and by showing how important he can be in the face of insuperable odds. Comedy tends to see man as a social animal, and to belittle his dignity by making him one of the crowd. Tragedy tends to punish man with a punishment out of all proportion to his sin, but only for making us feel that he is being crucified for sins that are ours too. Comedy gently mocks man for his ultimate unimportance, but only after we have shared a little of his humiliation. Tragedy encourages us to be passionate; comedy usually seeks to bring the intellect into play. Life, it can therefore be said, is a comedy to the man who thinks, and a tragedy to the man who feels.

The simple logic of traditional comedy and the coherence of tragic feeling have on the whole been rejected by 20th- and 21st-century art. Tragedy depends on a confidence in the extraordinary capabilities and resilience of man; comedy depends on a confidence in the reason and resilience of the social order. But the frequent appearance of tragicomedy in the 20th and 21st centuries suggests that our moral and social values are uncertain and shifting. Moreover, artists frequently believe that it is too difficult to depict the suffering and cataclysm of these centuries with unrelieved seriousness, and that it would be somewhat irresponsible to impose a wholly comic vision on such a world. Such absolute and disparate forms often do not seem relevant to artists, who regard tragicomedy as the more realistic and relevant form.

Oppositions between Tragedy and Comedy

Tragedy	*Comedy*
Individual	Society
Metaphysical	Social
Death	Endurance
Error	Folly
Suffering	Joy
Pain	Pleasure
Sacrificial	Procreative
Isolation	(Re)union
Terror	Euphoria
Unhappiness	Happiness
Irremediable	Remediable
Decay	Growth
Destruction	Continuation
Defeat	Survival

STUDY GUIDES

Extremes	Moderation
Inflexible	Flexible
Exceptionality	Commonality
Cathartic & enervating (tears)	Life-giving & renewing (laughter)

Characteristics of Farce
1. In farce, there is an emphasis on plot.
2. Farce is physical or "low" comedy.
3. Farce is comedy of situation as opposed to character.
4. Farcical characters are almost never aware that they are funny, unlike some characters in "high" comedy.
5. In farce, action replaces thought; where real-life characters think, farcical characters use instinct, as they are in the thick of things and do not have time to think.
6. In farce, single-minded characters pursue an endeavor fervently; they have short-range goals and want immediate gratification.
7. The stakes are high in farce; characters often find themselves in life-and-death situations (frequently over trifles), but there are rarely consequences. That is, no one gets hurt and everything turns out all right.
8. Action leads to objects in farce, and objects are always defeating the characters.
9. The pace in a theatrical production of farce should be very fast, for one must not give audience members time to question the reality or probability of what they are seeing onstage.
10. In farce, characters are dehumanized and humans are presented as unthinking machines. Farcical plays themselves, with their fast-paced and intricately connected plots, are like well-oiled machines.
11. In farce, unlikely or even impossible situations are made to seem totally probable.

4. Table of Contrasts: Realism and Naturalism

Realism
1. Realistic plays treat middle-class life and feature educated, articulate characters.
2. Drama is a conflict of wills in which human beings make conscious decisions and face the consequences of their actions. Realism tends to oversimplify motivation, having characters act out of a

single motive or only out of conscious (as opposed to unconscious) motives.
3. Realism adapts the well-made play to the "problem play" or play of ideas.
4. In realistic drama, heredity and environment are important in the development of character, but so too is the character's conscious will to oppose and transcend them.
5. Realism's viewpoint is ameliorative and humanistic; realism nourishes the hope that human beings possess the reason and will to improve their condition.
6. In a realistic play, humans are depicted as dignified, special beings seeking to control their own fates, apart from any belief in God or a higher spiritual being

Naturalism
1. Naturalistic plays treat lower-class life and feature uneducated, inarticulate characters.
2. Naturalistic characters are often driven by irrational impulses; a whole set of causal principles operates beneath the surface of character, complicating motivation and action. Naturalism substitutes the Freudian id for conscious will, with the subconscious or unconscious mind acting as a motivating force.
3. Naturalism's form tends toward the episodic, the fragmented, or the desultory—a form thought to be more "realistic" or slice-of-life-like than well-made dramatic form.
4. In naturalistic drama, heredity and environment overwhelm character.
5. Naturalism's viewpoint is pessimistic and fatalistic; naturalism would improve the lot of the oppressed but seems to have as its ultimate ideal a humanity redeemed from this earth.
6. In a naturalistic play, human beings are depicted as animals and objects for scientific study or control.

5. Types of Theater or Production Criticism

1. *Descriptive criticism* provides information about a play or production.
2. *Appreciative or denunciatory criticism* is gushing in its praise or sweeping in its condemnation; it may tell a great deal about a critic's responses but little about the production itself.

3. *Evaluative criticism:*
    a. Its primary aim is to judge effectiveness.
    b. The critic may analyze the structure, characterization, and ideas of a script; may explain the playwright's purported intentions and the director's interpretation of them, and may then go on to assess how effectively the script has been realized on the stage.
    c. The evaluation usually gives some attention to all the elements involved in a production and how each has contributed to the overall effect; the critic is concerned with both the good and bad points of the production and with a final verdict on the effectiveness of what has been presented.
    d. Three basic problems of evaluative criticism:
        1. Understanding: what were the playwright, director, and other theater practitioners attempting to do from an artistic point of view? What was their goal?
        2. Effectiveness: how well did these theater practitioners do what they set out to do? How well was the director's concept realized through the acting, scenery, costumes, and lighting?
        3. Ultimate worth: was this particular play worth producing? Was it served well by this production?
    e. Questions to be answered by the informed and perceptive, "evaluative" critic:
        1. Who was responsible for, or involved in, the production? What are the names of the producer, director, designers, and major actors?
        2. Where and when did the performance take place? Will there be additional performances?
        3. Which play was performed? Is it a significant work? Who is the dramatist? What information about the dramatist or the script is important to an understanding of the production?
        4. How effectively was the script produced—i.e., directed, acted, and designed?
        5. Should others see this production? Why or why not?
        6. Does the play reflect (or refract) some historical (or current) event?

TOPICS FOR WRITING AND DISCUSSION

The following questions treat all the plays discussed in this book and are intended as essay assignments or group-discussion topics. As much as possible, they encourage the student to compare and contrast plays, playwrights, and periods. The questions are also designed, in some cases, to go beyond the section headings listed in the Model Essays. In addition to subjects like Style and Genre, Character and Role, and Form and Structure, the questions below deal with such issues as language and symbol, image and allusion, and context and reception.

1. "In modern drama characters often speak different languages, and words become barriers rather than bridges to understanding." Discuss two of the following plays in light of this statement: *The Birthday Party*, *A Streetcar Named Desire*, *The Hairy Ape*, *Major Barbara*, and *Of Mice and Men*.
2. Choose three of the followings plays (but not two plays by the same author) and discuss the extent to which each is primarily realistic or naturalistic, or a combination of the two styles: *The Glass Menagerie*, *Riders to the Sea*, *Mother Courage and Her Children*, *Candida*, *Curse of the Starving Class*, *Miss Julie*, *Slag*, and *Of Mice and Men*.
3. Discuss *Antigone*, *Hamlet*, and *Death of a Salesman* as exemplars of three of the Four Great Ages of Drama: ancient Greek, Elizabethan-Jacobean, Spanish Golden Age/French neoclassicism, and modern Euro-American. Why are these ages great, and what makes these plays exemplars of such greatness?
4. *The Homecoming* and *Loot* have been described as flip sides of the same dramatic coin, or opposite treatments of a similar subject: the one serious, the other comic. Discuss, being sure to consider the extent to which each of these plays can be considered vile or immoral art, as opposed to the humanistic, ameliorative kind we are accustomed to.
5. Discuss the idea of Yank and Stanley as ape-like figures in *The*

TOPICS FOR WRITING AND DISCUSSION

Hairy Ape and *A Streetcar Named Desire*, respectively, being sure to account for the sociological significance of the ape-figure in these American plays.

6. The Spanish playwright Federico García Lorca once declared, "If in certain scenes of a play the audience doesn't know what to do, whether to laugh or cry, that will spell success to me." Discuss the blending of the comic and the serious or tragic (a blending sometimes called the "grotesque") in two of the following plays: *The Hostage, The Trial of the Innocents* or *Arsenic, Tonight!, The Hairy Ape,* and *Loot* or *Entertaining Mr. Sloane*.

7. Discuss the extent to which each of the following two plays can be considered "dream plays"—or nightmare visions: *The Homecoming* and *Miss Julie*.

8. Discuss the extent to which *Golden Guts* is a comedy of humours.

9. Discuss the extent to which both *Riders to the Sea* and *Henry IV, Part Two* are concerned with ritualistic sacrifice.

10. Discuss *Our Town* and *Under Milk Wood* as antitheses of the following statement: "If one considers main characters as 'ideas' or ethical/moral agents, many a dramatic plot can be converted into a sort of dialectic in which one 'idea' conflicts with or opposes another."

11. Discuss the pivotal roles played by Stella in *A Streetcar Named Desire* and Linda in *Death of a Salesman,* despite the underwritten nature of their characters and their apparent exclusion from the major dramatic *agon* (in *Streetcar,* Stanley versus Blanche; in *Salesman,* Willy versus Biff). As you write, consider the veracity of the following remark: "When women characters on the American stage are depicted by men, they invariably are seen from the outside, in their relationship to males, but not from their own perspective."

12. It has been said that "the fundamental subject of almost all serious plays of the nineteenth and twentieth centuries is the attempt to resurrect fundamental ethical certainties *without* resurrecting the fundamental spiritual certainty of a judgmental God." Keeping this statement in mind, discuss the role of God and/or Christian symbolism in two of the following plays: *Riders to the Sea, Major Barbara, The Crucible,* and *Our Town.*

13. The following statement comes from Arthur Miller's essay "Tragedy and the Common Man": "Where pathos rules, where pathos is finally derived, a character has fought a battle he could not possibly have won. The pathetic is achieved when the protagonist is, by virtue of his witlessness, his insensitivity, or the very air

TOPICS FOR WRITING AND DISCUSSION

he gives off, incapable of grappling with a much superior force." Discuss how this statement applies, or does not apply, to two of the following characters: Maurya, from *Riders to the Sea*; Willy Loman, from *Death of a Salesman*; George Milton, from *Of Mice and Men*; Stanley from *The Birthday Party* or Teddy from *The Homecoming*; Blanche, from *A Streetcar Named Desire*; and Yank, from *The Hairy Ape*.

14. Consider *Edmond*, on the one hand, and *Curse of the Starving Class*, on the other, in light of the following statement: "David Mamet's rise to the forefront of American drama has been seen as the triumph of a minimalist, the most obvious component of whose signature style is his dialogue. Only Sam Shepard has a comparably emphatic signature style, but his depends less on the shape and sound of words than on an offbeat, sometimes surreal use of scenic elements."
15. Compare and contrast *Doctor Faustus Lights the Lights* with Marlowe's *Dr. Faustus* and Goethe's two-part *Faust*.
16. Compare and contrast the settings—and the thematic significance of those settings—for *Electra* and *Miss Julie*.
17. Consider the settings—or, better, the reason for the location of those settings—of *The Caucasian Chalk Circle* and *The Good Person of Setzuan*.
18. Compare and contrast the characters and actions of Tom Wingfield, from *The Glass Menagerie*, and Biff Loman, from *Death of a Salesman*.
19. Discuss Brecht's poetry *of* the theater (as opposed to the use of poetry *in* the theater, or the quoting of actual poems by dramatic characters): his use of a poetry of theatrical elements and effects rather than words in plays such as *The Caucasian Chalk Circle* and *Life of Galileo*.
20. Discuss the relationship between myth and realism in the following two plays: *Riders to the Sea* and *The Passion of Antígona Pérez*.
21. Discuss the role of expressionistic, even dream-like, elements—in scene design, dramatic structure, and/or characterization—in two of the following plays: *Death of a Salesman, Edmond, A Streetcar Named Desire,* and *The Hairy Ape*.
22. Discuss the significance of the titles of three of the following plays: *Under Milk Wood, The Good Person of Setzuan* (a.k.a. *The Good Woman of Setzuan*), *Riders to the Sea, Life of Galileo, Of Mice and Men, Curse of the Starving Class, The Cherry Orchard, Slag,* and *Candida*.
23. Discuss the role of the narrator in both *The Glass Menagerie* and

TOPICS FOR WRITING AND DISCUSSION

Our Town, each play's use of a dual time-frame (to distinguish present action from past action), and the genre of each play. As you write, keep in mind Harold Pinter's statement that "the past is what you remember, imagine you remember, convince yourself you remember, or pretend you remember."

24. "Embedded in every major play written by an American playwright is a critique of American society." Discuss two of the following plays in light of this statement: *The Glass Menagerie, Death of a Salesman, Our Town, Edmond, A Streetcar Named Desire, The Hairy Ape, Curse of the Starving Class,* and *The Crucible*.

25. Discuss the extent to which *Candida* is a social-problem play. That is, what is the social problem in this drama, and to what extent is it resolved? By contrast, then discuss why *A Yorkshire Tragedy* is *not* a social-problem play, although it may on its surface appear to be one.

26. Chose two of the following plays and compare and contrast them as (satirical) farces: *The Front Page, Golden Guts, Loot,* and *Ubu Roi*.

27. Discuss the role of escape or illusion—of the illusion-making capacity of the human mind—as a (relatively) minor element in *The Glass Menagerie* and *Old Times* and a major factor in *Death of a Salesman*. As you write, keep in mind Larry Slade's argument in O'Neill's *The Iceman Cometh* that pipe-dreaming "gives life to the whole misbegotten mad lot of us."

28. Discuss the dramatic relevance of the idea of Jewishness to the play *Death of a Salesman*.

29. Answer one of the following questions: Between *The Passion of Antígona Pérez* and Sophocles' *Antigone*, which play do you prefer, and why? Between *Under Milk Wood* and *Our Town*, which work do you prefer, and why? Between *Fanshen* and *The Good Person of Setzuan*, which play do you prefer and why?

30. Choose two of the following character pairings and comment on the nature of each relationship: Hamlet/Horatio, from *Hamlet*; Pierre-Auguste/Barbulesque, from *Golden Guts*; George/Lennie, from *Of Mice and Men*; Stanley/Mitch, from *A Streetcar Named Desire*; and Hildy/Walter Burns, from *The Front Page*.

31. Consider the action of *Romeo and Juliet* in light of the following statement: "The meaning and significance of *Romeo and Juliet* may be better understood if we see the play as part of the greater movement toward a more relative and flexible view of human nature and human conduct—a movement begun during the Renaissance and championing the Hellenic view of life against the Hebraic one,

TOPICS FOR WRITING AND DISCUSSION

which prevailed during the Middle Ages and tended to regard human character and behavior in absolute terms of wrong and right."

32. S. K. Langer once observed that "the tension between past and future is what gives to acts, situations, and even such constituent elements as gestures and attitudes the peculiar intensity known as dramatic quality." Discuss this statement in relation to two of the following plays: *Death of a Salesman*, *The Glass Menagerie*, *Hamlet*, *Old Times*, *Riders to the Sea*, *Of Mice and Men*, *A Streetcar Named Desire*, *The Homecoming*, and *Curse of the Starving Class*.

33. Compare and contrast what can be called the music-hall tradition—the use of song, comedy, politics, and drama—in *The Hostage* and *Mother Courage and Her Children*.

34. Contrast a play like *Old Times*, which exemplifies the theater of the word that understands the unsaid, with a play like *Major Barbara*, which exemplifies the theater of the word that understands *the said*.

35. Discuss the avant-garde or non-representational techniques of one of the following plays: *The Birthday Party*, *Our Town*, or *The Invasion*. That is, how does the play revolt (or speciously revolt) against conventional dramatic form and representational or illusionistic theater? Then consider the extent to which conventional dramatic form and representational or illusionistic theater have been completely banished from two of the following avant-garde dramas: Cixous's *Portrait of Dora*, Kantor's *The Dead Class*, Müller's *Explosion of a Memory/Description of a Picture*, and Clarke & Mee's *Vienna: Lusthaus*.

36. Consider the extent to which global terror today—in 2022—is a greater, or lesser, threat than the social and political terror dramatized some decades ago in Gambaro's *Stripped*, Abdoh's *The Hip-Hop Waltz of Eurydice*, and Churchill's *Far Away*.

37. Compare and contrast *Ubu Roi* and its Shakespearean sources: *Macbeth* and some parts of *Hamlet* and *King Lear*.

38. Films have been made of the following plays: *Romeo and Juliet*, *Of Mice and Men*, *Death of a Salesman*, *The Front Page*, *The Homecoming*, *Edmond*, *Electra*, *The Balcony*, *Equus*, *The Elephant Man*, *The Crucible*, *Miss Julie*, *The Cherry Orchard*, *Our Town*, *Loot*, *Entertaining Mr. Sloane*, *Hamlet*, *Major Barbara*, *Curse of the Starving Class*, *The Glass Menagerie*, *The Birthday Party*, *A Streetcar Named Desire*, *Antigone*, and *Life of Galileo*, as well as *Henry IV, Part One*, *Henry IV, Part Two*, *Richard II*, *Henry V*, and *The Merry Wives of Windsor* (the bases for the film *Chimes at Midnight*). Choose at least two of these plays and discuss how

TOPICS FOR WRITING AND DISCUSSION

well—or how badly—each one has made the transition to cinema. If you have not seen any of the film adaptations of the dramas listed above, choose two of them nonetheless and, keeping in mind the distinctions made between theater and cinema in the Study Guides (as well as some of the definitions in the Glossary of Dramatic Terms), discuss from a theoretical perspective the feasibility of adapting each play to the screen.

39. Discuss the use of language in *Riders to the Sea* in light of the following statement by its author, J. M. Synge:

> In countries where the imagination of the people, and the language they use, is rich and living, it is possible for a writer to be rich and copious in his words, and at the same time to give the reality, which is the root of all poetry, in a comprehensive and natural form. In the modern literature of towns, however, richness is found only in sonnets, or prose poems, or in one or two elaborate books that are far away from the profound and common interests of life. One has, on one side, Mallarmé and Huysmans producing this literature; and on the other, Ibsen and Zola dealing with the reality of life in joyless and pallid words. On the stage one must have reality, and one must have joy; and that is why the intellectual modern drama has failed, and people have grown sick of the false joy of the musical comedy, that has been given them in place of the rich joy found only in what is superb and wild in reality. In a good play every speech should be as fully flavoured as a nut or apple, and such speeches cannot be written by anyone who works among people who have shut their lips on poetry. In Ireland, for a few years more, we have a popular imagination that is fiery and magnificent, and tender; so that those of us who wish to write start with a chance that is not given to writers in places where the springtime of the local life has been forgotten, and the harvest is a memory only, and the straw has been turned into bricks.

40. Discuss how the following statement applies to *Hamlet*:

> A certain degree of trust in others is indispensable in any human relations. It was relatively easier, however, to have and maintain this trust as long as there was little or no separation in men's minds between formal and substantial relations, as long as the name and the thing, the word and the deed, the mask and the face, were held to be indissolubly bound in a single unity. No one suspected in the Middle Ages, for instance, that a host or a guest would act

otherwise than as the names host and guest implied. Even by the Renaissance this situation had changed. The schism between names and things had doubtless always been present to some degree, but it was becoming characteristic of larger and larger areas of thought and behavior.

Bibliographical Resources

Altenbernd, Lynn, & Leslie Lisle Lewis. *A Handbook for the Study of Drama.* New York: Macmillan, 1966.

American Drama Criticism: Interpretations, 1890–1977 (plus Supplements to 1992). Hamden, Conn.: Shoe String Press, 1979–1992.

Arranged alphabetically by playwright and sub-categorized by the title of the work, these volumes list journal articles and reviews that appear in academic journals, general magazines, and theater publications.

American Playwrights Since 1945: A Guide to Scholarship, Criticism, and Performance. Westport, Conn.: Greenwood Press, 1989.

Informative and economically written, this book is a useful tool for theater and literary practitioners. This guide to the state of research on forty major American playwrights and the history of their productions is among the first of its kind. It is actually many books: a bibliography, a stage history, an assessment of scholarly works about each playwright, and an invaluable guide to the types of research studies—biographical, bibliographical and critical—that remain to be done on each playwright. The essays were written by leading experts in American drama and theater and focus on playwrights whose works have in some way shaped and influenced the American stage. Each essay follows a standard format and provides information on the playwright's reputation and achievements; primary bibliography; production history of where, when, how often, and how well his or her works were performed; a rigorous identification and evaluation of secondary materials in bibliographies, biographies, influence studies, and general works; analyses of plays; and, most significantly, a detailed analysis of future research opportunities.

Australasian Drama Studies.

Australasia's academic journal for research in drama, theater, and performance. *ADS* publishes articles, interviews, and production casebooks on world theater by Australasian and international scholars. The journal also publishes reviews of scholarly books and published play texts. https://www.adsa.edu.au/ADSjournal

Ball, David. *Backwards & Forwards: A Technical Manual for Reading Plays.* Carbondale: Southern Illinois University Press, 1983.

Barry, Jackson. *Dramatic Structure: The Shaping of Experience.* Berkeley: University of California Press, 1970.

Beckerman, Bernard. *Dynamics of Drama: Theory and Method of Analysis*. New York: Alfred A. Knopf, 1970.
Bradby, David, et al. *Studying Drama: A Handbook*. London: Croon Helm, 1983.
British Playwrights, 1880–1956: A Research and Production Sourcebook. Westport, Conn.: Greenwood Press, 1996.
British Playwrights, 1956–1995: A Research and Production Sourcebook. Westport, Conn.: Greenwood Press, 1996.
Brustein, Robert. *The Theater of Revolt: Studies in Modern Drama from Ibsen to Genet*. Boston: Little, Brown, 1964.
Burgoyne, Suzanne, & Patricia Downey. *Thinking through Script Analysis*. Boston: Focus Publishing/R. Pullins Co., 2012.
Cambridge Companion to English Renaissance Drama. Cambridge, UK: Cambridge University Press, 1990.
Cambridge Companion to Medieval English Theater. Cambridge, UK: Cambridge University Press, 1994.
Cambridge Companion to Shakespeare On Stage. Cambridge, UK: Cambridge University Press, 2002.
Cambridge Guide to American Theater. 2nd ed. New York: Cambridge University Press, 2007.
Cambridge Guide to Theater. 2nd ed. Cambridge, UK: Cambridge University Press, 1995.
  Alphabetical listing of theater culture and history, attempting to present a comprehensive view of the history and present practice of theater in all parts of the world, thus pointing to the dynamic interaction of performance traditions from all cultures in present-day theater.
Cambridge History of American Theater. 3 vols. New York: Cambridge University Press, 2006.
Cambridge History of British Theater. New York: Cambridge University Press, 2004.
  Three-volume set covering the history of theatrical performance in Britain. v. 1: Origins to 1660; v. 2: 1660–1895; v. 3: since 1895.
Castagno, Paul C. *New Playwriting Strategies: Language and Media in the 21st Century*. 2nd ed. New York: Routledge, 2012.
Columbia Encyclopedia of Modern Drama. 2 vols. New York: Columbia University Press, 2007.
  Covers 1860 to the present. Entries emphasize the cultural context of dramatic works and their authors and their relationship to significant social, political, artistic, and philosophical movements. Includes articles on emerging authors and the conventional and experimental theater worldwide.

Comparative Drama.
  Comparative Drama is a scholarly journal devoted to studies international in spirit and interdisciplinary in scope; it is published semi-annually (spring

and winter) at Western Michigan University and is a member of the Council of Editors of Learned Journals. https://scholarworks.wmich.edu/compdr/

Concise Oxford Companion to the Theater. 2nd ed. New York: Oxford University Press, 1993.
This concise version of the acclaimed *Oxford Companion to the Theater* covers all aspects of theater worldwide and throughout the ages. It contains entries on a vast range of theatrical styles, dramatists, performers, and directors, as well as information on theaters, festivals, and such technical topics as lighting, sound, and method acting.

Contemporary Dramatists. 6th ed. London: St. James Press, 1999.
Provides biographical and bibliographic information, as well as brief critical essays, on 433 English-language dramatists, all of whom were alive at the time of its publication. Most are from North America and the British Isles.

The Continuum Companion to Twentieth-Century Theater. London: Continuum, 2002.

Dictionary of the Theater: Terms, Concepts, and Analysis. Toronto: University of Toronto Press, 1998.
While covering much of the basic historical and literary terminology of the discipline, this dictionary emphasizes the specialized theoretical vocabulary that is now regularly employed in theoretical writing about the theater.

Dowdy, Joanne K., & Sarah Kaplan, eds. *Teaching Drama in the Classroom: A Toolbox for Teachers.* Rotterdam, Neth.: Sense Publishers, 2011.

Drama Research: An International Journal of Drama in Education.
An international, refereed e-journal that provides a forum for practitioners and researchers across the spectrum of drama in educational settings. It publishes research-based articles from established and new writers to promote knowledge, understanding, and dialogue about drama in learning contexts.
https://www.nationaldrama.org.uk/journal/#

Dramatic Index for 1909–1949. Boston: Boston Book Co., 1909–1952.
The *Dramatic Index* serves as an index to books, journal articles, illustrations, play texts and reviews. Covers general and specialized English-language periodicals. Articles are entered under subject only, with reviews of plays found under the title of the play. An important but often overlooked resource.

Esslin, Martin. *The Theater of the Absurd.* Harmondsworth, UK: Penguin, 1961.

———. *An Anatomy of Drama.* New York: Hill and Wang, 1976.

European Drama Criticism, 1900–1975. 2nd ed. Hamden, Conn.: Shoe String Press, 1977.
A comprehensive listing of criticism which has appeared in books and

periodicals in English and foreign languages, from 1900 to 1975. Arrangement is alphabetical by playwright, with plays alphabetized under the playwright. Cross-references are included.

Fisher, Mark. *How to Write about Theater*. London: Bloomsbury, 2015.

Fliotsos, Anne L. *Interpreting the Play Script: Contemplation and Analysis*. New York: Palgrave Macmillan, 2011.

Griffiths, Richard. *Reading Drama*. London: Hodder and Stoughton, 2001.

Gross, Roger. *Understanding Playscripts: Theory and Method*. Bowling Green, Ohio: Bowling Green University Press, 1974.

Grote, David. *Script Analysis: Reading and Understanding the Playscript for Production*. Belmont, Calif.: Wadsworth, 1985.

A Guide to Critical Reviews. New York: Scarecrow Press, 1966–1971.
Contents: pt. 1. American drama from O'Neill to Albee; pt. 2. The musical from Rodgers and Hart to Lerner and Loewe; pt. 3. British and continental drama from Ibsen to Pinter; pt. 4. The screenplay, from *The Jazz Singer* to *Dr. Strangelove* (2 vols.).
2ND EDITION, 1973–1976:
Contents: pt. 1. American drama, 1909–1969; pt. 2. The musical, 1909–1974; pt. 3. Foreign drama, 1909–1977.
3RD EDITION, 1984–1991:
Contents: pt. 1. American drama, 1909–1982; pt. 2. The musical, 1909–1989.

Harrison, Martin. *The Language of Theater*. 1993. Chicago: Shelfmark, 2003. Defines approximately 1,200 contemporary and historical theatrical terms. Bibliography included.

Hayman, Ronald. *How to Read a Play*. New York: Grove Press, 1977.

Hornbrook, ed. *On the Subject of Drama*. London: Routledge, 1998.

How to Locate Reviews of Plays and Films: A Bibliography of Criticism from the Beginnings to the Present. Metuchen, NJ: Scarecrow Press, 1976.
Lists resources for finding theatrical reviews, including indexing services, theater periodicals, reference guides, etc. Somewhat dated, but still useful for historical research.

Hudson, Suzanne. *Writing about Theater and Drama*. 2000. Belmont, Calif.: Wadsworth, 2005.

Ingham, Rosemary. *From Page to Stage: How Theater Designers Make Connections Between Scripts and Images*. Portsmouth, N.H.: Heinemann, 1998.

International Bibliography of Theater. New York: Publishing Center for Cultural Resources, CUNY, 1982–1999.
A comprehensive annual bibliography covering theater on an international basis. Contains an extensive subject index.

International Dictionary of Theater. 3 vols. Chicago: St. James Press, 1992–1996.

BIBLIOGRAPHICAL RESOURCES

In three volumes, Vol. 1: *Plays*, Vol. 2: *Playwrights*, and Vol. 3: *Actors, Directors, and Designers*. Entries for plays provide a synopsis of the play, date of first publication and production, and a selected list of critical material. Entries for playwrights provide a discussion of the playwright's work, a list of works, and a short list of general criticism. Entries for actors, directors and designers provide basic biographical information, a list of their roles, and a short list of other biographical sources.

An International Dictionary of Theater Language. Westport, Conn.: Greenwood, 1985.

15,000 terms described, spanning theater history from ancient times to the present day. Extensive bibliography and numerous cross references make this a valuable research tool.

Journal for Contemporary Drama in English.

The *Journal of Contemporary Drama in English* focuses on issues in contemporary Anglophone dramatic literature and theater performance. It renegotiates the understanding of contemporary aesthetics of drama and theater by treating dramatic texts of the last fifty years. This peer-reviewed journal publishes essays that engage in close readings of plays and also touch upon historical, political, formal, theoretical, and methodological aspects of contemporary drama, theater, and performance. *JCDE* appears twice a year: the first issue is based on the annual international conferences held by CDE; the second issue invites individual essays on contemporary theater and drama in English. The journal also contains a review section.
https://www.degruyter.com/journal/key/JCDE/html

Journal of American Drama and Theater.

The *Journal of American Drama and Theater* publishes thoughtful and innovative work by leading scholars on theater, drama, and performance in the Americas – past and present. Provocative articles provide valuable insight and information on the heritage of American theater, as well as its continuing contribution to world literature and the performing arts.
https://jadtjournal.org/

Journal of Dramatic Theory and Criticism.

The *Journal of Dramatic Theory and Criticism* publishes full-length articles that contribute to the varied conversations in dramatic theory and criticism, explore the relationship between theory and theater practice, and/or examine the body of work by an individual author or a recent theoretical or critical trend. *JDTC* is published semiannually at the University of Kansas: the fall issue is published in December; the spring issue, in June.
https://journals.ku.edu/jdtc

Kiely, Damon. *Script Analysis for Directors: How to Read a Play*. New York: Focal Press, 2016.

Knopf, Robert. *Script Analysis for Theater: Tools for Interpretation, Collaboration, and Production.* New York: Bloomsbury, 2017.

Leonard, John, & Mary Luckhurst. *The Drama Handbook: A Guide to Reading Plays.* New York: Oxford University Press, 2002.

Letwin, David, et al. *The Architecture of Drama: Plot, Character, Theme, Genre, and Style.* Lanham, Md. : Scarecrow, 2008.

Levitt, Paul M. *A Structural Approach to the Analysis of Drama.* The Hague, Neth.: Mouton, 1971.

Longman, Stanley V. *Page and Stage: An Approach to Script Analysis.* Boston: Allyn & Bacon, 2004.

McGraw-Hill Encyclopedia of World Drama: An International Reference Work in Five Volumes. 2nd ed. 5 vols. New York: McGraw-Hill, 1984.

The purpose of the book is to present, in the clearest possible format, factual information and critical evaluations of numerous dramatists' work and stature. Most entries contain a biographical sketch, a brief critique of the dramatist's work, a selection of synopses of his or her plays, a bibliography of editions and usually a list of critical and biographical works. Emphasis is on English and Western European playwrights. Includes some general essays on drama of the world as well as many photographs taken during actual productions.

Meisel, Martin. *How Plays Work: Reading and Performance.* New York: Oxford University Press, 2007.

Millett, Fred B. *Reading Drama: A Method of Analysis with Selections for Study.* 1950. Freeport, NY: Books-for-Libraries Press, 1970.

Modern Drama.

Modern Drama was founded is the most prominent journal in English to focus on dramatic literature. The terms "modern" and "drama" are the subject of continuing and fruitful debate, but the journal has been distinguished by the excellence of its close readings of both canonical and lesser-known dramatic texts from a range of methodological perspectives. The journal features articles written from a variety of geo-political points of view that enhance our understanding, both formal and historical, of the dramatic literature of the past two centuries; there is also an extensive book review section.

https://moderndrama.utpjournals.press/

Modern Drama Scholarship and Criticism, 1966–1980: An International Bibliography. Toronto: University of Toronto Press, 1986.

A classified, selective list of publications on world drama since Ibsen, this volume is intended mainly for students of modern dramatic literature. Play and playwright, rather than performance and performer, hold center stage.

Modern Drama Scholarship and Criticism, 1981–1990: An International Bibliography. Toronto: University of Toronto Press, 1997.

Updates and continues the previous volume, with additions and corrections to it. Emphasizes contemporary theory and performance theory more than its predecessor. Continues as an annual bibliography published in the journal *Modern Drama*.

Muneroni, Stefano. *Play Analysis: The Dramaturgical Turn*. Dubuque, Ia.: Kendall Hunt, 2014.

Murray, Edward. *Varieties of Dramatic Structure: A Study of Theory and Practice*. Lanham, Md.: University Press of America, 1990.

NTC's Dictionary of Theater and Drama Terms. Lincolnwood, Ill.: National Textbook Co., 1992.

New York Theater Critics' Reviews. New York: Critics' Theater Reviews, Inc., 1870–2000.

This is a complete guide and record of the New York stage, reprinted from the *New York Sun*, *New York Times*, *New York Herald Tribune*, *New York Post*, *New York Daily News*, *New York World Telegram*, *Wall Street Journal*, *Time*, *Women's Wear Daily*, *Christian Science Monitor*, and *Newsweek*. The first 21 volumes cover the years 1870–2000. Since then volumes have been published biannually

O'Toole, John. *The Process of Drama: Negotiating Art and Meaning*. London: Routledge, 1992.

Oxford Companion to the Theater. 4th edition. Ed. Phyllis Hartnoll. New York: Oxford University Press, 1983.

This handbook provides information on every aspect of the theater up to the end of 1982. Coverage is international in scope. Some articles deal with contemporary theater in foreign countries, dramatic criticism, musical comedy, scenery, opera, Shakespearean Festivals, and blacks in the American theater. All articles are signed. Separate sections in the back include a select list of theater books, and notes on the illustrations.

The Oxford Companion to Theater and Performance. Ed. Dennis Kennedy. Oxford, UK: Oxford University Press, 2010.

Oxford Encyclopedia of Theater and Performance. 2 vols. Ed. Dennis Kennedy. New York: Oxford University Press, 2003.

Provides information about theater and performance internationally, through history and in the present. The 4,300 entries are complemented by over 100 illustrations. Coverage ranges from ancient Greek theater to 21st century developments in London, Paris, New York, and around the globe. Pays special attention to non-Western styles through articles on theater and performance throughout Asia and Africa, often written by practitioners or critics from those areas. Dance, opera, performance art, radio, film, and television are covered at length. Also embraces para-theatrical, non-dramatic, and popular performance, including ritual, carnivals, parades, the circus, and public executions. Biographical entries cover the lives and work of major figures from the past and present: actors, playwrights, directors, designers, and critics. Entries on cities and regions place performance in its local social and political context.

BIBLIOGRAPHICAL RESOURCES

Oxford Companion to American Theater. Ed. Gerald Bordman & Thomas S. Hirshak. New York: Oxford University Press, 2011.
A guide to the American stage from its beginnings to the present, the volume includes playwrights, plays, actors, directors, producers, songwriters, famous playhouses, dramatic movements, etc. The book covers classic works (such as *Death of a Salesman*) as well as many commercially successful plays (such as *Getting Gertie's Garter*), plus entries on foreign figures that have influenced dramatic development in the U.S. (from Shakespeare to Beckett and Pinter). New entries include relatively recent plays such as *Angels in America* and *Six Degrees of Separation*, performers such as Eric Bogosian and Bill Irwin, playwrights like David Henry Hwang and Wendy Wasserstein, and relevant developments and issues including theatrical producing by Disney and the rise in solo performance.

Patterson, Michael. *Oxford Dictionary of Plays*. New York: Oxford University Press, 2015.
The *Oxford Dictionary of Plays* provides essential information on the 1,000 best-known, best-loved, and most important plays in world theater. Each entry includes details of title, author, date of composition, date of first performance, genre, setting, and the composition of the cast, and more. A synopsis of the plot and a brief commentary, perhaps on the context of the play, or the reasons for its enduring popularity, follow. Around 80 of the most significant plays—from *The Oresteia* to *Waiting for Godot*—are dealt with in more detail. Genres covered include: burlesque, comedy, farce, historical drama, Kabuki, masque, melodrama, morality play, mystery play, Noh, romantic comedy, tragicomedy, satire, and tragedy.

Pfister, Manfred. *The Theory and Analysis of Drama*. 1988. New York: Cambridge University Press, 2000.

Pickering, Kenneth. *Key Concepts in Drama and Performance*. 2nd ed. Basingstoke, UK: Palgrave Macmillan, 2010.

Play Index. Bronx, New York: H. W. Wilson Co.
Index to more than 30,000 plays written from antiquity to the present and published from 1949 to the present; includes mysteries, pageants, plays in verse, puppet performances, radio and television plays, and classic drama.

Price, W. T. *Analysis of Play Construction and Dramatic Principle*. Memphis, Tenn.: General Books, 2012.

Prior, Moody E. *The Language of Tragedy*. 1947. Bloomington: Indiana University Press, 1966.

Pritner, Cal, & Scott Walters. *Introduction to Play Analysis*. 2nd ed. New York: McGraw-Hill, 2017.

Ratcliff, Gerald Lee. *Playscript Interpretation and Production*. New York: Rosen Publishing, 1985.

Reaske, Christopher R. *How to Analyze Drama*. 1966. New York: Monarch, 1984.

Research in Drama Education.
> *RIDE* publishes international research on drama and theater that applies performance practices to cultural engagement and educational innovation. https://www.tandfonline.com/toc/crde20/current

Renaissance Drama.
> *Renaissance Drama* explores the rich variety of theatrical and performance traditions and practices in early modern Europe and intersecting cultures. The sole scholarly journal devoted to the full expanse of Renaissance theater and performance, this journal publishes articles that extend the scope of our understanding of early modern playing, theater history, and dramatic texts and interpretation, encouraging innovative theoretical and methodological approaches to these traditions, examining familiar works, and revisiting well-known texts from fresh perspectives. *Renaissance Drama* welcomes articles on the full range of early modern theatrical traditions, the discourses and institutions shaped by performance, and manifestations of performance and performativity both on and beyond the stage. Occasionally, issues of the journal may be devoted to special topics of particular interest. https://www.journals.uchicago.edu/toc/rd/current

Rodriguez, Domingo. *Conceptual Thinking: A New Method of Play Analysis.* New York: World Audience, 2008.

Rush, David. *A Student Guide to Play Analysis.* Carbondale: Southern Illinois University Press, 2005.

Sanger, Keith. *The Language of Drama.* 2001. London: Routledge, 2015.

Scanlon, David. *Reading Drama.* Mountain View, Calif.: Mayfield, 1988.

Scholes, Robert, & Carl H. Klaus. *Elements of Drama.* 1971. New York: Oxford University Press, 1980.

Scolnicov, Hanna, & Peter Holland. *Reading Plays: Interpretation and Reception.* New York: Cambridge University Press, 1991.

Shepherd, Simon, & Mick Wallis. *Understanding Drama: An Introduction.* London: Arnold, 1998.

Skenè: Journal of Theater and Drama Studies.
> *Skenè: JTDS* hosts a lively debate on drama texts and theater practices from antiquity to the present. The journal welcomes contributions dealing with the forms, modes, and genres of play texts and the impact of dramaturgy and performance on their codification. *Skenè* endeavors to stimulate a lively discussion on critical approaches within an interdisciplinary context spanning textual, linguistic, rhetorical, semiotic, and translation studies, as well as literary and philosophical hermeneutics, reception studies, the sociology of theater, and performance studies.
> https://skenejournal.skeneproject.it/index.php/JTDS

Smiley, Sam, & Norman A. Bert. *Playwriting: The Structure of Action.* 2nd ed. New Haven, Conn.: Yale University Press, 2005.

Styan, J. L. *The Dramatic Experience: A Guide to the Reading of Plays.* New York: Cambridge University Press, 1975.

BIBLIOGRAPHICAL RESOURCES

Taylor, Giles, & Philip Wilson. *Dramatic Adventures in Rhetoric*. London: Oberon Books, 2015.

Tennyson, G. B. *An Introduction to Drama*. New York: Holt, Rinehart, and Winston, 1967.

Thomas, James. *Script Analysis for Actors, Directors, and Designers*. 6th ed. New York: Focal Press, 2020.

Thompson, Alan R. *The Anatomy of Drama*. 1946. Berkeley: University of California Press, 1990.

20th Century Theater. 2 vols. New York: Facts on File, 1983.

> This work is designed to offer an overview of theater activity in North America and the British Isles since 1900, and to provide a "date-finder" for those who want information about a particular theater event, production, personality or playhouse. Arrangement is chronological, beginning with 1900 and ending with 1979. Within each year, arrangement is by month and covers theater productions, American and British play premieres, revivals and repertoires, and births, deaths, and débuts. An author, title, subject index at the end of the volume helps to provide access to specific items. There is, in addition, an excellent bibliography of books about the theater.

Varma, Prem. *Theater Words: A Dictionary*. New Delhi: Kay Pee Publishers, 1989.

Vaughn, Maura. *The Anatomy of a Choice: An Actor's Guide to Text Analysis*. Lanham, Md.: University Press of America, 2010.

Vena, Gary. *How to Read and Write about Drama*. New York: Arco, 1988.

Vogler, Christopher. *The Writer's Journey: Mythic Structure for Writers*. 3rd ed. Studio City, Calif.: Michael Wiese Productions, 2007.

Waxberg, Charles S. *The Actor's Script: Script Analysis for Performers*. Portsmouth, N.H.: Heinemann, 1998.

Whitman, Robert F. *The Play-Reader's Handbook*. Indianapolis: Bobbs-Merrill, 1966.

Who's Who in Contemporary World Theater. Ed. Daniel Meyer-Dinkgrafe. New York: Routledge, 2000.

> Contains 1,400 brief biographical entries on theater artists—actors, directors, designers, dramatists—from 68 countries. Excludes those primarily working in dance and opera.

World Encyclopedia of Contemporary Theater, 6 vols. Ed. Don Rubin et al. New York: Routledge, 1994–2000.

> Beginning with 1945, surveys the range of national theatrical activity on a country-by-country basis from a specifically national standpoint. Each article covers a nation's theatrical history, artistic trends, structure in its theater community, artistic profile, dance theater, youth theater, puppet theater, theater space and architecture, theatrical training, and theater criticism, scholarship and publishing. Bibliographies included.
> v. 1., Europe; v. 2., Americas; v. 3, Africa; v. 4, Arab World;
> v. 5, Asia; v. 6., Bibliography/Cumulative index.

BIBLIOGRAPHICAL RESOURCES

World Shakespeare Bibliography. Ed. James L. Harner. Baltimore, Md.: Johns Hopkins University Press, 1968–2003.

Published for the Folger Shakespeare Library. Electronic coverage as of June 3, 2003. When complete, it will provide annotated entries for all important books, articles, book reviews, dissertations, theatrical productions, reviews of productions, audio-visual materials, electronic media, and other scholarly and popular materials related to Shakespeare and published or produced since 1900.

Online Resources

https://elon.libguides.com/theater/playscriptBottom of Form
　　This guide suggests resources for research related to acting, drama & theater studies, and theatrical design & technology.

https://libguides.bc.edu/theaterstudies/plays
　　A guide to finding plays in print sources and online sources.

https://writingcenter.tamu.edu/Students/Writing-Speaking-Guides/Alphabetical-List-of-Guides/Academic-Writing/Analysis/Analyzing-Plays
　　A guide to analyzing plays.

https://www.lonestar.edu/departments/libraries/UniversityParkLibrary%5CAssignmentGde_EDUC2301_drama.pdf
　　A guide to the literary analysis of drama.

https://literarydevices.net/drama/
　　A glossary of dramatic terms.

https://writingcenter.unc.edu/tips-and-tools/drama/
　　A guide to writing about drama.

http://www.analysisofdrama.net/

http://www.analysisofdrama.net/what-to-look-for-when-watching-a-play.html
　　A guide to the analysis of dramatic structure, as well as to the act of watching a play.

https://libguides.dickinson.edu/criticism/drama
　　An introduction to dramatic criticism, including databases.

https://www2.southeastern.edu/Academics/Faculty/cfrederic/playanalysis.htm
　　A discussion of the elements of play analysis.

https://guides.nyu.edu/actorspage/play-analysis
　　A guide to play analysis for actors.

https://www.clevelandplayhouse.com/files/assets/ch04scriptanalysis.pdf
　　A guide to script analysis.

235

ONLINE RESOURCES

theaterhistory.com
theaterlinks.com
 Guides to the history of drama and theater.

http://www.teacheroz.com/literature.htm
 A guide to the study of drama and literature.

Professional Associations

1. Society for Theater Research (UK): http://www.str.org.uk/
   The Society for Theater Research serves all those interested in the history and technique of British and British-related theater: academic and independent scholars, researchers, performers, other theater workers—and, of course, theatergoers.

2. American Society for Theater Research: https://www.astr.org/
   The American Society for Theater Research (ASTR) is a U.S.-based professional organization that fosters scholarship on worldwide theater and performance, both historical and contemporary.

3. The Theater Research Society (Finland): http://teats.fi/esittely/introduction/
   The Theater Research Society welcomes scholars from various fields of the performing arts: from drama and repertory theater to dance theater and opera, from performance studies to the study of circus, and from research on Finnish theater to the study of foreign theatrical traditions.

4. Association for Theater in Higher Education (ATHE, USA): http://www.athe.org/
   An advocate for the field of theater and performance in higher education, the Association for Theater in Higher Education serves as an intellectual and artistic center for producing new knowledge about theater and performance-related disciplines, cultivating vital alliances with other scholarly and creative disciplines, and linking with professional and community-based theaters.

5. Standing Conference of University Drama Departments (SCUDD, UK): http://www.scudd.org.uk/
   SCUDD represents the interests of drama, theater, and performance in the higher-education sector of the UK. It acts as a mediating body with organizations such as funding and arts councils, and is consulted by such organizations when matters of future policy are discussed and decided. SCUDD is concerned, above all, to promote the multi-disciplined areas of drama, theater, and performance.

6. Theater and Performance Research Association (TaPRA, UK): http://tapra.org/
   The Theater and Performance Research Association was formed by a group of senior academics in theater and performance eager to promote the growth of research in the field by fostering a co-operative and collaborative ethos—one that would benefit postgraduate students and early career researchers, as well as provide a platform for everyone interested in sharing the variegated discoveries of the discipline.

7. Literary Managers and Dramaturgs of the Americas: http://lmda.org/
   Literary Managers and Dramaturgs of the Americas (LMDA) was founded as a volunteer membership organization for the professions of literary management and dramaturgy. LMDA believes that theater is a vital art form that has the power to nourish, educate, and transform individuals and their communities, and that dramaturgy itself is central to the process of theater-making.

8. Drama Australia: https://dramaaustralia.org.au/
   Drama Australia is the national body that represents and advocates on behalf of all state and territory drama education associations in Australia. Drama Australia represents drama teachers, academics, applied theater workers, and theater-in-education practitioners at national arts and curriculum forums, as well as in national and international associations such as IDEA (International Drama/Theater and Education Association).

Index

Abdoh, Reza, 161, 171–173, 221
Abel, Lionel, 197
Absurdism, 14, 27, 34–40, 94, 100, 172, 183–186, 195, 205
Adamov, Arthur, 14, 34–40, 94, 180
Adaptation, 89–113
The Adding Machine, 169
Adler, Jacob H., 65
Aeschylus, 9, 160
After the Fall, 104
Akara, 182
Alcestis, 152
Alienation Effect: see "Verfremdungseffekt"
Alighieri, Dante, 16, 29–30
Allegory, 185, 198
Allen, Joan, 105
"All of That" (Pinter), 45–47
Altman, Robert, 97
American Buffalo, 21, 25
The American Clock, 104
American Repertory Theater (Cambridge, Mass.), 152
Anderson, Sherwood, 129
Angelico, Fra, 59
Angry Young Man, 186
Anouilh, Jean, 127
Antigone, 92, 113, 124, 188, 208, 217, 220–221
Antonioni, Michelangelo, 93
Apollonianism, 186
Appia, Adolphe, 179
Arden of Faversham, 51
Aristotelianism, 191–192
Aristotle, 185, 187, 191–192, 195, 197, 199, 204, 206–208
Arlen, Harold, 63
Arms and the Man, 195
Arrabal, Fernando, 181–183
The Arrest, 15
Arrivi, Francesco, 123
Arsenic, Tonight!, 26–29, 218

Art and Revolution, 194
Artaud, Antonin, 35, 171–173, 180, 182, 198
Association for Real Art: see "Oberiuty"
As You Like It, 199
Avant-gardism, 26–27, 119, 149–154, 161–166, 171–173, 186, 199, 205, 221

Badlands, 100
Baker, Howard, 171
The Balcony, 89, 94–96, 208, 221
The Bald Soprano, 182–183
Bancroft, Anne, 101
Barrie, J. M., 127
Bates, Alan, 111
Bathrick, David, 120
Batista, Fulgencio, 123
Batman, 111
Baty, Gaston, 181
Beaumont, John, 206
Beckett, Samuel, 17, 94, 100, 180, 182–183, 190, 198, 200, 205–206
The Beggar, 193
The Beggar's Opera, 187
Behan, Brendan, 40, 48–49
La Belle Époque, 119
Benedek, Laszlo, 96
Benét, Stephen Vincent, 133
Bentley, Eric, 62, 102, 107
Bergman, Ingmar, 90, 97, 99
Bergren, Eric, 101
Bernstein, Leonard, 105
Betti, Ugo, 26, 195
Beyle, Marie-Henri: see "Stendhal"
The Big Break, 95
The Birthday Party, 40, 43–48, 171, 217, 219, 221
The Birth of Tragedy, 186
Birth Rate, 151
Blin, Roger, 35, 39

239

INDEX

The Blind, 205
Blood Wedding, 158
Boccioni, Umberto, 15, 194
Bock, D. Heyward, 116
Bond, Edward, 171
Boorman, John, 98
Borderie, Raymond, 104
The Bouncing Knight, 77
Branagh, Kenneth, 105
Brecht, Bertolt, 40–43, 113, 120–122, 126, 158, 174–175, 191–192, 198
Breton, André, 205
Broadway (New York), 33, 97, 131
Brod, Max, 35
Broken Glass, 104
Brook, Peter, 149, 182
Brooks, Mel, 101
Büchner, Georg, 22, 141, 166, 169, 171
Buffalo Bill and the Indians, 97
Burke, Edmund, 24
Burlesque, 187
Burns, Robert, 139, 157
Burrows, Saffron, 106
Burton, Richard, 98
Burton, Tim, 111
Busse, Fred, 132

Cabell, James Branch, 77
Cacoyannis, Michael, 89, 92–94, 109–112
Cage, John, 151
Calderwood, James L., 76
Caldwell, Erskine, 141, 156
Calverley, Walter, 51–56
Camus, Albert, 200
Candida, 65–67, 217, 219–220
Cangiullo, Francesco, 15, 194
Capitalism, 67, 121, 143
Capone, Al, 132
Cartlidge, Katrin, 111
Castronovo, David, 146
Catholicism, 19, 51, 125, 146, 164, 196
The Caucasian Chalk Circle, 40–43, 219
CBS (radio), 164
Celticism, 128
Champion, Gower, 99
Chaplin, Charles, 95
Chapman, George, 116
Charles II (King of England), 201
Chekhov, Anton, 9, 89, 109–112, 196

The Cherry Orchard, 89, 109–112, 208, 219, 221
Chiarelli, Luigi, 195
"A Child's Christmas in Wales" (Thomas), 127
Chimes at Midnight, 76, 221
Christianity, 4, 16, 24, 32, 41, 51, 56–62, 65, 76, 106, 200, 218
A Christmas Carol, 127
Churchill, Caryl, 161, 171–173, 221
Citizen Kane, 90
Civil War (U.S.), 145
Cixous, Hélène, 140, 149–154, 221
Clair, René, 39
Clarke, Martha, 140, 149–154, 221
Classicism, 33, 92–93, 97, 109, 114, 121, 124, 131, 194–195, 199, 202, 206
Closet drama, 188
Cocteau, Jean, 95, 97, 160
Cold War, 128
Coleridge, Samuel Taylor, 205
Columbia Broadcasting System: see "CBS"
Comedy, 5, 12, 17, 19, 22, 26–30, 32, 52, 57, 63–64, 66, 72–73, 75–77, 79, 81–82, 84, 91, 95, 102, 116, 128, 146, 173, 188–189, 191–193, 195–197, 199, 201–204, 206–208, 210, 213–214, 217–218, 221–222
Comedy of humours, 113, 116–120, 195, 218
Comedy of manners, 189, 201
Commedia: see *Divine Comedy*
Commedia dell'arte, 76, 189, 203–204
Commonwealth (England), 201
Communism, 15, 102, 105, 122–123, 125, 176–178
Communist Party (China), 176
Comte, Auguste, 141, 165
Congreve, William, 19, 189, 201
Conservatism, 24, 149
Cooper, Helen, 108
Copernicus, Nicolaus, 164
Coriolanus, 41
The Country Wife, 201
Coveney, Michael, 120
Craig, Edward Gordon, 179, 181
Creative Evolution, 58
Cristofer, Michael, 98
The Critic, 187

INDEX

Criticism (Theater), 2, 78, 91, 96, 102, 134, 190, 208, 215–216
Crommelynck, Fernand, 76, 113, 116–120
Cronyn, Hume, 79
The Crucible, 89, 102–105, 208, 218, 220–221
Curse of the Starving Class, 40, 49–50, 65, 68–72, 157, 217, 219–221
Cymbeline, 202

Dadaism, 119, 134, 151, 182, 186, 190
The Dance of Death, 113, 190
Dancing at Lughnasa, 170
Dante: see "Alighieri, Dante"
Danton's Death, 171
Darwin, Charles, 114, 141, 165
Darwinism, 58, 115
Day-Lewis, Daniel, 105
The Dead Class, 140, 149–154, 221
The Death of Character, 149
The Death of Falstaff, 77
Death of a Salesman, 1, 96–97, 104, 140–144, 156, 208, 217–221
Deconstruction, 163, 200
Dee, Ruby, 95
Deighton, Len, 174–175
Delhomme, Benoit, 108
Democratic Party (U.S.), 103
Depression, Great, 141, 144
Derrida, Jacques, 200
Determinism, 32, 163, 198
De Vore, Christopher, 101
Diabolism, 103
Díaz, Porfirio, 123
Dickens, Charles, 127
Diderot, Denis, 191
Dionysianism, 23, 186
The Divine Comedy, 29–30
Doctor Faustus, 51, 56, 198, 219
Doctor Faustus Lights the Lights, 130, 133–135, 219
Docudrama, 51–57
Documentary, 40, 126, 144, 163–164
A Doll House, 107, 115, 194, 200
Donen, Stanley, 91
Don Juan's Wife, 28
Drama vs. film: see "Theater vs. film"
Drame bourgeois, 191
Dream play, 113–116, 218
A Dream Play, 113–114

The Duchess of Malfi, 201
Dunnigan, Ann, 110

Ecce homo, 24
Edmond, 14, 21–25, 219–221
The Effect of Gamma Rays on Man-in-the-Moon Marigolds, 99
Einstein, Albert, 165
Electra, 1, 89, 92–94, 109, 208, 219, 221
The Elephant Man, 89, 100–102, 208, 221
Eliot, T. S., 117
Elizabeth I (Queen of England), 74, 201
Elizabethanism, 5, 53, 76, 190, 203, 217
Emerson, Ralph Waldo, 32
The Emperor Jones, 169
Enck, John, 116–117
Endgame, 183
Enough Is as Good as a Feast, 51
Entertaining Mr. Sloane, 14, 17–20, 218, 221
Epic Theater, 161, 174, 191–193
Equus, 89, 96–100, 208, 221
"Essay on the Theatre" (Goldsmith), 196
Esslin, Martin, 205
Estrangement Effect: see "*Verfremdungseffekt*"
Euripides, 9, 89, 92–94, 152, 160, 190
Everyman, 198
Every Man Out of His Humour, 117
Existentialism, 4, 16
Exorcist II, 98
Explosion of a Memory/Description of a Picture, 140, 149–154, 221
Expressionism, 14, 21–23, 25, 27, 29, 113, 119, 128, 166, 169, 171, 186, 193, 196, 205, 219

Fabbri, Diego, 26, 195
The Faithful Shepherd, 199, 206
Falk, Peter, 95
Falstaff, 76
Falstaff's Wedding: A Comedy, 77
The Famous Victories of Henry the Fifth, 75
Fanshen, 113, 120–122, 161, 173–178, 220
Far Away, 161, 171–173, 221

241

INDEX

Farce, 5, 14, 17, 20, 26, 29, 95, 97, 116, 193, 204, 208–209, 213–214, 220
Fascism, 15
The Father, 115
Faust, 188, 219
Fellini, Federico, 99
Feminism, 4, 76, 137
Fenton, George, 105
Ferguson, Otis, 91
Fergusson, Francis, 41, 109, 144
"Fern Hill" (Thomas), 127
Fertis, Yannis, 93
Figgis, Mike, 89, 105–109
Film vs. drama: see "Theater vs. film"
Film vs. theater: see "Theater vs. film"
Fiorentino, Giovanni, 76
First World War: see "World War I"
Firth, Peter, 98
Five Kings, 76
Five Lectures on Psycho-Analysis, 153
Fletcher, John, 206
Fosse, Bob, 99
Francis, Freddie, 100
Frazer, J. G., 73
Freud, Sigmund, 107, 114–115, 141, 151, 153
Freudianism, 4, 77, 108, 215
Friel, Brian, 170
From Morn to Midnight, 22, 24, 193
The Front Page, 130–133, 208, 220–221
Fuchs, Elinor, 149
Futurism, 14–17, 27, 32, 151, 166, 186, 194

Galilei, Galileo, 41–42, 164
Gambaro, Griselda, 161, 171–173, 221
Gangster film, 105, 131
Garriga, Olga Viscal, 123
The Gas Heart, 190
The Gates of Hell, 31
Gay, John, 187
Genet, Jean, 89, 94–96, 182, 197
Genius and Culture, 15
The Gentleman Caller: see *The Glass Menagerie*
Gesamtkunstwerk (Total artwork), 194, 211–212
Ghelderode, Michel de, 181
Ghosts, 188
Gide, André, 39
Gilbert-Lecomte, Roger, 35

Gilroy, Frank D., 99
Gimpel, René, 118
A Girl in Black, 109
The Glass Menagerie, 161, 142, 169–171, 188, 200, 217, 219–221
Glengarry Glen Ross, 21
Goethe, Johann Wolfgang von, 188, 202, 219
Golden Age, Spanish, 217
Golden Age of Cinema, 92, 112
The Golden Bough, 73
Golden Guts, 113, 116–120, 208, 218, 220
Goldsmith, Oliver, 196
The Good Hope, 158
The Good Person of Setzuan, 40–43, 219–220
The Good Soldier Schweik, 41–42
The Good Woman of Setzuan: see *The Good Person of Setzuan*
Götz von Berlichingen, 202
Gough, Michael, 111
Grabbe, Christian Dietrich, 166
The Graduate, 96
Grand guignol, 181
Grant, Lee, 96
The Grapes of Wrath, 157
The Grass Is Greener, 91
Great Ages of Drama, Four, 217
Great War: see "World War I"
Green Grow the Lilacs, 141, 156
Gregory, Andre, 110
Griffith, D. W., 99
Grosbard, Ulu, 99
Grossvogel, David, 182
Grotesque, Theater of the, 14, 26–29, 195, 218
Guarini, Giovanni Battista, 199, 206

Hahn-Hahn, Ida, 133
The Hairy Ape, 14–17, 29–34, 142, 208, 217–220
Hall, Peter, 99, 155
Hamlet, 1, 7–11, 65, 77–82, 185, 187–189, 194, 201–202, 217, 220–222
Handel, George Frideric, 93
Harburg, E. Y., 63
Hare, David, 113, 120–122, 130, 137–139, 161, 173–178
Hasenclever, Walter, 127, 193
Hearst, William Randolph, 132

INDEX

Hébert, Félix-Frédéric, 178
Hebraism, 220
Hecht, Ben, 130–133
Hedda Gabler, 107, 116, 188
Heifitz, Josef, 112
Heijermans, Hermann, 158
Hellenism, 220
Henry V, 72–75, 77, 93, 105, 205, 221
Henry IV, Part One, 72–78, 195, 221
Henry IV, Part Two, 72–78, 195, 218, 221
Herald-Examiner (Chicago), 132
He Who Says No, 120
He Who Says Yes, 120
Heywood, Thomas, 51
The Hip-Hop Waltz of Eurydice, 161, 171–173, 221
History play, 72–78, 195
Hollywood, 90, 94, 131, 170
Holm, Ian, 79
Holocaust: see "World War II"
Holtei, Karl von, 133
Home Before Dark, 91
The Homecoming, 20, 65, 87–88, 99, 140, 154–156, 161, 166–169, 217–219, 221
The Hostage, 40, 48–49, 218, 221
Howard, Andrew, 111
Howey, Walter Crawford, 132–133
Humanism, 19, 21, 32, 215, 217
An Humourous Day's Mirth, 116
Humours comedy: see "Comedy of humours"
Hurt, John, 102
Huysmans, Joris-Karl, 222
Hytner, Nicholas, 89, 102–105

Ibsen, Henrik, 9, 42, 47, 107, 115–116, 188, 191, 194, 200–201, 222
Ibsenism, 108, 141
The Iceman Cometh, 142, 220
I Had More Respect for Hydrogen, 28
Illusionism, 161, 220–221
Imperialism, 121
The Importance of Being Earnest, 19
Impressionism, 169, 171, 196
Incident at Vichy, 104
Indians, 97
Industrial Workers of the World: see "International Workers of the World"
Interior, 205

International Workers of the World, 31
The Interpretation of Dreams, 114
Intimate Theater (Stockholm), 114
The Intruder, 205
The Invasion, 14, 34–40, 221
Ionesco, Eugène, 94, 180–183, 205
Iphigenia, 109
I.R.A.: see "Irish Republican Army"
Irish Republican Army, 48–49
Isolationism, 144–149
Israel, Robert, 153
"It's Only a Paper Moon" (Arlen), 63–64
I.W.W.: see "International Workers of the World"

Jackson, Zachariah, 77
Jacobeanism, 217
James I (King of England), 201
Jameson, Joyce, 95
Jarry, Alfred, 161, 178–184, 205
Jens, Arnette, 95
Johnson, Hilding, 132
Johnson, Samuel, 77
Jones, James Earl, 111
Jonson, Ben, 113, 116, 195
Joyce, James, 129
Judaism, 30, 220
Judith, 27–28
Julius Caesar, 203

Kafka, Franz, 35
Kaiser, Georg, 22, 24, 169, 193
Kane, Sarah, 171
Kanin, Michael, 99
Kantor, Tadeusz, 140, 149–154, 221
Kaprow, Allan, 151
Kazan, Elia, 105
Kendal, Mrs. Madge, 101
Kennedy, Maria Doyle, 106
Kenrick, William, 77
Kharms, Daniil, 171
King John, 199
King Lear, 8–9, 185, 199, 221
Kirkman, Francis, 77
Kleist, Heinrich von, 169
The Knight of the Moon, or Sir John Falstaff, 76
Kopit, Arthur, 96–97
Kuomintang (China), 177
Kurosawa, Akira, 99, 170
Kyd, Thomas, 201

INDEX

The Lady with the Dog, 112
Lahr, John, 18
Land/Scape/Theater, 149
Langer, S. K., 221
The Large and the Small Maneuver, 34
Lassally, Walter, 93
Lavinia Among the Damned, 28
Lawrence, D. H., 99
Lawson, John Howard, 148, 157
Leaving Las Vegas, 105
Léger, Jack-Alain, 77
Lehrstücke (Learning plays), 120
LeRoy, Melvyn, 91
Lester, Richard, 97
Liberty, 27
The Life and Humours of Falstaff, 77
Life of Galileo, 40–43, 120, 219, 221
Lights, 15
Lindbergh, Charles, 145–146
A Little Night Music, 99
Liturgical drama, 196
Llareggub, a Piece for Radio Perhaps: see *Under Milk Wood*
The Loneliness of the Long Distance Runner, 93
Long Day's Journey into Night, 99, 157
Long Wharf Theatre (New Haven, Conn.), 106
Look Back in Anger, 186
Loot, 14, 17, 19–21, 208, 217–218, 220–221
Lorca, Federico García, 158, 218
Louisiana Purchase, 145
Lumet, Sidney, 89, 96–100
Lynch, David, 89, 100–102

MacArthur, Charles, 130–133
Macbeth, 8, 11, 178, 193, 221
Macbett, 180
Machiavelli, Niccolò, 165
Machiavellianism, 78
Machinal, 169
Machine Age, 16
Maddow, Ben, 94–95
The Madness of King George, 105
Maeterlinck, Maurice, 205
The Magnetic Fields, 205
Major Barbara, 40, 57–63, 208, 217–218, 221
Malick, Terrence, 100
Mallarmé, Stéphane, 222
Malle, Louis, 110

Mamet, David, 14, 21–25, 219
A Man's a Man, 121
Marinetti, F. T., 15–17, 194
Marlowe, Christopher, 51, 56, 133, 198, 219
Marowitz, Charles, 171, 182
Marqués, René, 123
Marx Brothers, 95
Marx, Karl, 141, 165
Marxism, 4, 16, 200
The Mask and the Face, 195
Masters, Edgar Lee, 129
Mastroianni, Marcello, 91
McCarthyism, 103
McDonagh, Martin, 171
McNally, Terrence, 97
The Measures Taken, 120
Medievalism, 16–17, 57, 66, 75, 183, 185, 196, 198
Medium Cool, 96
Mee, Charles, 140, 149–154, 221
Melodrama, 20, 77, 132, 197, 201
Melville, Herman, 77
Memory play, 161, 169
The Merchant of Venice, 189
Merrick, John, 100–102
The Merry Wives of Windsor, 74, 76, 221
Messaline, 182
Metatheater, 197
Middle Ages, 22, 190, 221–222
A Midsummer Night's Dream, 114
Mifune, Toshiro, 91
Miller, Arthur, 89, 96–97, 102–105, 140–144, 156, 191
Minimalism, 21, 219
Misalliance, 57
The Miser, 117
The Miseries of Enforced Marriage, 52
Miss Julie, 1, 89, 105–109, 113–116, 208, 217–219, 221
Mr. Hulot's Holiday, 90
Mnouchkine, Ariane, 151
Modernism, 5, 14, 16–17, 40, 89, 113, 127, 130, 140, 161, 198, 200
Molière, 117, 203
Monet, Claude, 196
Monroe, Marilyn, 89–90
Monroe Doctrine, 145
Montagu, Ashley, 101
Montaigne, Michel de, 165
Morality play, 25, 56, 75, 185, 198

INDEX

Moral Tales, 100
Morning's at Seven, 156
Mother Courage and Her Children,
    40–43, 120, 217, 221
Mrs. Warren's Profession, 62
Mullan, Peter, 106
Müller, Heiner, 140, 149–154, 221
Musical comedy, 210, 222
Music hall, 221
My Own Private Idaho, 76
The Mysteries of Love, 171, 205
Mystery play, 25, 66
Mysticism, 58, 62
Myth, 133, 141, 180, 219

Nationalist Party (Puerto Rico), 123
National Theatre (London), 96
Naturalism, 21, 25, 27, 29, 32, 51,
    113–116, 140–141, 158, 166, 169,
    171, 179, 195, 198–199, 208, 210,
    214–215, 217
Neoclassicism, 114, 191, 196, 199,
    202, 207, 217
Neorealism (Italian), 92
New American Cinema, 96
New Deal, 144
Newman, Paul, 91, 98–99
New Republic, 102
"The New Theology" (Shaw), 58
New York Theater Workshop, 172
Nichols, Mike, 96
Nietzsche, Friedrich, 24, 114–115, 141,
    165, 186
Nights of Cabiria, 99
Nihilism, 27
Nixon, 105
Nominalism, 75
No Peace for the Ancient Faun, 28
"Notes on the Theater of Cruelty"
    (Marowitz), 171
Nye, Robert, 77

O'Banion, Dion, 132
Oberiuty (Soviet), 171
O'Connor, Tommy, 131
Odets, Clifford, 148, 157
Oedipalism, 19
Oedipus Tyrannos, 8, 73, 185, 188, 197,
    201–202
Off-Broadway (New York), 94, 109
Of Mice and Men, 130, 139–141, 143,
    156–158, 208, 217, 219–221

Old Times, 40, 43–48, 170, 220–221
Olivier, Laurence, 93
O'Neill, Eugene, 14–17, 29–34, 99,
    142, 157, 169, 191
On the Waterfront, 105
Open Theater (New York), 149
Orton, Joe, 14, 17–21
Osborn, Paul, 156
Osborne, John, 186
Othello, 8, 10, 191, 206
Our Theatres in the Nineties, 58
Our Town, 113, 127–130, 140, 142,
    144–149, 161–166, 218, 220–221

Papas, Irene, 93
Parker, Lottie Blair, 99
Parody, 19, 56, 178, 187
The Parody, 34–35, 37
The Passion of Antígona Pérez, 113,
    122–127, 219–220
Pastoralism, 199, 202
Pathos, 33, 142, 199, 218
Paul, Leslie, 186
Paul, Saint (the Apostle), 75
The Pawnbroker, 96
Peaslee, Richard, 153
Il pecorone, 76
Pericles, 202
Pièce à clef (Play-with-a-key), 130–131
Pièce bien-faite: see "Well-made play"
Pietro, Guido di: see "Angelico, Fra"
Ping-Pong, 37
Pinter, Harold, 17, 20, 40, 43–48, 65,
    87–88, 94, 99, 140, 154–156, 161,
    166–171, 220
Pirandellianism, 28
Pirandello, Luigi, 26–27, 162, 170,
    195, 197–198
Plato, 197
Play of ideas, 200, 215
Poetics, 185, 187, 197, 204, 206, 208
Pomerance, Bernard, 89, 100–102
Poquelin, Jean-Baptiste: see "Molière"
Porter, Thomas E., 144
Portrait of Dora, 140, 149–154, 221
Post-colonialism, 4
Postmodernism, 5, 140, 149,
    199–200
Poststructuralism, 200
Prévert, Jacques, 39
The Price, 104
Prince, Harold, 99

245

INDEX

Princeton University (New Jersey), 129
Problem play, 51, 166, 200, 215, 220
Proletarianism, 27, 32–33
Protestantism, 51, 147
Proust, Marcel, 118–119
Provincetown Playhouse (New York), 33
Pulitzer Prize, 99
Puritanism, 201

Quite Early One Morning: see *Under Milk Wood*

Racine, Jean, 203
Radio drama, 113
Rampling, Charlotte, 111
Raphael (Raffaello Sanzio da Urbino), 59, 62
Rashomon, 99, 170
Rationalism, 183–184
Realism, 11–12, 26–27, 29–30, 42, 46–47, 51, 54, 59, 93, 98–100, 109, 114, 126, 141, 154, 161, 166, 169–171, 179, 193–194, 198, 200–201, 204–205, 208, 210, 213–215, 217, 219
The Red and the Black, 74
Redgrave, Michael, 79
Renaissance (Europe), 16, 75, 92, 121, 199, 204, 220, 223
Representationalism, 12, 149–150, 154, 170, 179–180, 221
Republic, 197
Resistance (Italian), 27
Restoration (England), 19, 77, 189, 201, 203
Rice, Elmer, 148, 169
Richard II, 75, 195, 221
Richard III, 195
Richardson, Tony, 93
Riders to the Sea, 141, 158–160, 194, 208, 217–219, 221–222
Riggs, Lynn, 141, 156
Rise and Fall of the City of Mahagonny, 41
Ritualism, 76, 90, 172, 218
The Ritz, 97
The Rivals, 196
The Robbers, 202
Rodin, Auguste René, 30
Rohmer, Éric, 100
Romance play, 202

Romanticism, 22, 25, 127, 141, 169, 202
Romeo and Juliet, 65, 83–84, 208, 220–221
Roosevelt, Franklin D., 144
Rose, Billy, 63
Rousseau, Jean-Jacques, 158, 202–203
Royal Dramatic Theater (Stockholm), 106
Różewicz, Tadeusz, 151
The Ruffian on the Stair, 17, 20
Ryder, Winona, 105

Saint Joan, 57
Salem witch trials, 102
Salvation Army, 22
Sánchez, Luis Rafael, 113, 122–127
Sand, George, 133
Sardou, Victorien, 207
Sartre, Jean-Paul, 103, 200
Satire, 19–21, 48, 95, 178, 187–189, 220
Satyr play, 199
Savage Eye, 95
Schaustücke (Showpieces), 120
Schiller, Friedrich, 202
Schnitzler, Arthur, 196
The School for Scandal, 196
Scofield, Paul, 105
Scribe, Eugène, 207
The Sea at Dauphin, 158
Second World War: see "World War II"
Seneca, Lucius Annaeus, 188
Señora Carrar's Rifles, 158
Sentimentalism, 128, 134, 139, 161, 173, 194, 196, 203
Serreau, Geneviève, 35
Serreau, Jean-Marie, 35
The Shadow Box, 98
Shaffer, Peter, 89, 96–100
Shakespeare, William, 6, 8, 11, 65, 72–84, 89, 94, 116, 187, 192, 195, 199, 201–205
Shakespeareanism, 178, 221
Shakespeare's Genius Justified, 77
Shavianism, 28
Shaw, George Bernard, 40, 57–63, 65–67, 194, 200–201
Shepard, Sam, 40, 49–50, 65, 68–72, 157, 219
Sheridan, Richard Brinsley, 187, 196

INDEX

Sherrell, Richard, 37
Short, Charles, 77
Shyer, Laurence, 152
Simmons, Jean, 90
The Simpleton: see *Il pecorone*
Six Characters in Search of an Author, 170
Sjöberg, Alf, 106, 108
The Skin of Our Teeth, 128
Slag, 130, 137–139, 217, 219
Smiles of a Summer Night, 99
Smith, J. Percy, 57
Snuggs, Henry, 117
Socialism, 137–138, 152
Social-problem play: see "Problem play"
Social realism, 93
Sokel, Walter, 120–121
Some Like It Hot, 89, 94, 99
The Son, 193
Sophocles, 93, 113, 124–125, 127, 160, 188
Sorge, Reinhard, 193
Soupault, Philippe, 205
The Spanish Tragedy, 201
Spoon River Anthology, 129
Sprinchorn, Evert, 107
Stanislavsky, Konstantin, 112, 204
Starrett, Vincent, 131–132
Station drama, 17, 22
The Stationers' Register (London), 52–53
Stein, Gertrude, 130, 133–135, 149–150, 154, 166
Steinbeck, John, 130, 139–141, 143, 156–158
Stella, 109
Stendhal, 73
Stephens, George D., 144
Sternberg, Josef von, 131
Stone, Oliver, 105
Stormy Monday, 105
A Streetcar Named Desire, 40, 63–65, 84–87, 115, 130, 135–137, 142, 208, 217–221
Strick, Joseph, 89, 94–96
Strindberg, August, 89, 105–109, 113–116, 190–191, 204
Strindbergianism, 29, 113, 141
Stripped, 161, 171–173, 221
Studio des Champs-Elysées (Paris), 34
The Subject Was Roses, 99

Sugar, 99
Le surmâle, 182
Surrealism, 27, 150, 153, 166, 171–172, 182, 186, 205, 219
Sweet Charity, 99
Sydow, Max von, 90
Symbolism, 27, 85, 95, 97, 150, 166, 179, 186, 205, 218
Synge, John Millington, 141, 158–160, 194, 222
Szondi, Peter, 121

A Taste of Honey, 93
Tati, Jacques, 90
Teale, Owen, 111
The Tempest, 6, 202
Terron, Carlo, 14, 26–29, 195
Terror drama, 168, 171–173, 221
Theater of the Absurd: see "Absurdism"
Theater of Cruelty, 171–172
Theater vs. film, 7, 89–112, 155, 170, 208, 211–212, 221–222
Theatre Arts, 91
Théâtre des Noctambules (Paris), 35
Theatricalism, 161, 205
"The Thinker" (Rodin), 30
Thomas, Dylan, 113, 127–130
Tidblad, Inga, 106
Tieck, Ludwig, 166
The Times (London), 101
Tobacco Road, 141, 156
To Damascus, 113
"To a Mouse" (Burns), 139, 157
Tourneur, Cyril, 190
The Town that Was Mad: see *Under Milk Wood*
Tragedy, 5, 12, 26, 29–30, 33, 37, 51–56, 60, 77, 82, 84, 86, 91, 93, 104, 107, 113, 119, 121, 130, 146, 157–158, 160, 170, 173, 176, 178, 183, 185, 187–189, 191, 195–197, 199, 201–204, 206, 208, 213–214, 218
"Tragedy and the Common Man" (Miller), 218
Tragicomedy, 14, 29–34, 52, 206, 213
Transfiguration, 59
Transfiguration of Christ, 59
Treadwell, Sophie, 169
Treaty of Versailles, 145–146
Treves, Frederick, 101

INDEX

The Trial of the Innocents, 14, 26–29, 218
The Tribune (Chicago), 132
The Trojan Women, 109
Trujillo, Rafael, 123
Trump, Donald, 103
Tudor, House of (England), 74
The Tutor, 41
Two Lamentable Tragedies, 56
Two Most Unnaturall and Bloodie Murthers, 52–54, 56
Tzara, Tristan, 190
Tzavellas, George, 93

Übermensch, 24
Ubu the King: see *Ubu Roi*
Ubu Roi, 161, 178–184, 205, 208, 220–221
Ulysses, 128
Uncle Vanya, 110
Under Milk Wood, 113, 127–130, 218–220
Underworld, 131

Valentin, Karl, 41
van Sant, Gus, 76
Vanya on 42nd Street, 110
Vaudeville, 89, 187, 207
Vauthier, Jean, 182
Verdi, Giuseppe, 76
The Verdict, 21
Verfremdungseffekt, 192
Verism, 21–22
Verse drama, 4, 187
Vian, Boris, 182–183
Victorianism, 67, 100
Vienna: Lusthaus, 140, 149–154, 221
A View from the Bridge, 104
"A View of the Party" (Pinter), 44–46
Vian, Boris, 182–183
Vilar, Jean, 34, 39
The Virgin Spring, 90
Vitrac, Roger, 171, 205
Vvedensky, Aleksandr, 171

Wager, William, 51
Wagner, Richard, 194
Waiting for Godot, 190, 206
Walcott, Derek, 158

Walken, Christopher, 106
Wandlingsdrama: see "Station drama"
War of the Roses (England), 74
The War of the Worlds, 164
Way Down East, 99
The Way of the World, 201
Webster, John, 190, 201
Webster's New World Dictionary, 137–138
The Wedding on the Eiffel Tower, 160
Weingarten, Romain, 182
Welles, Orson, 76, 90, 164
Well-made play, 107, 203, 207, 215
Wells, H. G., 164
Wexler, Haskell, 96
What the Butler Saw, 17, 19
Wilde, Oscar, 19
Wilder, Billy, 89, 94, 99, 131
Wilder, Thornton, 113, 127–130, 140, 142, 144–149, 161–166
Wilhelmianism, 22
Wilkins, George, 52
Williams, Tennessee, 40, 63–65, 84–87, 115, 130, 135–137, 142, 161, 169–171, 188, 191
Wilson, Dover, 77
Wilson, Robert, 149–150, 152
Winesburg, Ohio, 129–130
Winters, Shelley, 95
The Winter's Tale, 202
The Witches of Salem, 104
The Wits, or Sport upon Sport, 77
A Woman Killed with Kindness, 51
Wooster Group (New York), 149
World War I, 16, 62, 119, 128, 145, 190, 193, 195
World War II, 26, 70, 92, 122, 128, 146, 152, 173
Woyzeck, 22–23, 141
Wycherley, William, 19, 189, 201

Yale University (New Haven, Conn.), 129
A Yorkshire Tragedy, 40, 51–57, 220

Zindel, Paul, 99
Zola, Émile, 114, 141, 222
Zorba the Greek, 109